FOREIGN
AFFAIRS
Agenda 1996

FOREIGN
AFFAIRS

Agenda 1996

Critical Issues
in Foreign Policy

Foreign Affairs
New York

Contents

[VI]

Social Capital and the Global Economy

Francis Fukuyama

A REDRAWN MAP OF THE WORLD

CONVENTIONAL MAPS of the global economy divide the major players into three groups: the United States and its partners in the North American Free Trade Agreement, the European Union (EU), and East Asia, led by Japan but with the four dragons (South Korea, Taiwan, Hong Kong, and Singapore) and the People's Republic of China catching up rapidly. This three-pronged geography is said to correspond to major divisions in the approach to political economy: at one pole lie Japan and the newly industrialized Asian economies, which have relied heavily on state-centered industrial policies to guide their development, while at the other extreme lies the United States, with its commitment to free-market liberalism. Europe, with its extensive social welfare policies, lies somewhere in between.

This familiar map, while not wrong, is today not the most useful way of understanding global economic geography. The most striking difference among capitalist countries is their industrial structure. Germany, Japan, and the United States were quick to adopt the corporate form of organization as they industrialized in the late nineteenth and early twentieth centuries, and today their economies are hosts to giant, professionally managed corporations like Siemens, Toyota, Ford, and Motorola. By contrast, the private sectors of France, Italy, and capitalist Chinese societies like Hong Kong, Taiwan, and the marketized parts of the People's Re-

FRANCIS FUKUYAMA is a Senior Social Scientist at the RAND Corporation. This article is adapted from his new book, *Trust: The Social Virtues and the Creation of Prosperity*, published by The Free Press.

[1]

public of China (PRC) are dominated by smaller, family-owned and -managed businesses. These societies have had much greater difficulties institutionalizing large-scale private corporations; their relatively small companies, while dynamic, tend to fall apart after a generation or two, whereupon the state is tempted to step in to make possible large-scale industry.

The reasons for these differences in industrial structure have less to do with level of development than with a key cultural characteristic, what the sociologist James Coleman has labeled social capital—that is, the component of human capital that allows members of a given society to trust one another and cooperate in the formation of new groups and associations. In this redrawn map of the world, Germany, Japan, and the United States are societies with healthy endowments of social capital and thus have more in common with each other than any of them do with low-trust countries like Taiwan, Hong Kong, Italy, or France. The competitiveness literature of the past decade has it wrong when it describes the United States and Japan as polar opposites with respect to individualism and group orientation. In fact, the strong historical propensity of Americans to form voluntary associations is quite similar to that of the Japanese, and it is no accident that these two societies pioneered the development first of the corporate form of business organization and later the smaller, decentralized network.

Virtually all economic activity, from running a laundry to building the latest-generation microprocessor, is carried out not by individuals but by organizations that require a high degree of social cooperation. As economists argue, the ability to form organizations depends on institutions like property rights, contracts, and a system of commercial law. But it also depends on a prior sense of moral community, that is, an unwritten set of ethical rules or norms that serve as the basis of social trust. Trust can dramatically reduce what economists call transaction costs—costs of negotiation, enforcement, and the like—and makes possible certain efficient forms of economic organization that otherwise would be encumbered by extensive rules, contracts, litigation, and bureaucracy. Moral communities, as they are lived and experienced by their members, tend to be the product not of rational choice in the economists' sense of the term, but of nonrational habit.

A number of forms of social capital enable people to trust one another and build economic organizations. The most obvious and natural one is the family, with the consequence that the vast majority of businesses, historically and at present, are family businesses. Family structure affects the nature of family businesses: the large extended families of southern China or central Italy have become the basis for rather large-scale and dynamic enterprises. Beyond the family, there are kinship ties like the lineages of China and Korea that expand the radius of trust.

Families, however, are a mixed blessing with regard to economic development. The most important form of sociability from an economic standpoint is the ability of strangers (that is, non-kin) to trust one another and work together in new and flexible forms of organization. This type of spontaneous sociability is frequently weakened by cultures that emphasize family relationships to the exclusion of all others. In many cultures, there is something of a tradeoff between the strength of family ties and the strength of non-kinship bonds. Moreover, if familism is not accompanied by the strong emphasis on education and work in Confucian or Jewish cultures, for example, then it can lead to a stifling morass of nepotism and inbred stagnation.

THE SIGNIFICANCE OF SOCIAL CAPITAL

TRUST VARIES from one society to another. Japan is typically portrayed as a highly group-oriented society, while the United States is seen as the epitome of individualism. In fact, both societies are quite similar to one another insofar as they have both historically been relatively high-trust societies. American society has always been characterized by a dense network of voluntary associations—private schools, hospitals, choral societies, literary clubs, Bible study groups, and private business organizations both large and small. Indeed, Alexis de Tocqueville saw this art of association as a key virtue of American democracy, one that served to moderate the political system's inherent tendency toward individualism by schooling people in social cooperation and public-spiritedness. These countries were among the first, both chronologically and within the time frame of their own development, to form large-scale, hierarchical, professionally managed corporations in which ownership was dispersed and separated from management.

The significance of social capital to an economy becomes clear when contrasting a high-trust society like Japan with a low-trust society like China. The industrial structure of capitalist Chinese societies, including

Hong Kong, Taiwan, and the market sector of the PRC, is characterized by small scale. In *Fortune*'s list of the 150 largest Pacific Rim firms, only one—a state-owned petroleum company—is Chinese. Taiwan has a GDP 5 percent as large as Japan's, but its 10 largest companies are only 2 percent as large (by revenues) as Japan's 10 largest. There is a strong cultural resistance in Chinese society to bringing in unrelated professional managers; as a consequence, there are relatively few large, hierarchical, professionally managed corporations of a Japanese variety. While some of these businesses, like the empires of Li Kashing or the late Y. K. Pao in Hong Kong, have grown to be enormous, they remain family-managed at the top and pervaded by kinship ties in their management structures.

The reason for the relatively small scale of Chinese businesses is the centrality of the family in Chinese culture. In sharp contrast to Japan, family relations trump all other social obligations. While the level of trust within families and, to a lesser extent, extended kinship groups like lineages, is high, it comes at the expense of trust between people who are unrelated. Hence the extraordinary difficulty that Chinese firms have in institutionalizing themselves once the founding family passes from the scene. Japanese families, by contrast, are smaller and have exerted a much weaker social pull than their Chinese counterparts. Loyalty to groups not based on kinship has eclipsed family relations since at least Tokugawa times, a practice still reflected in the Japanese manager's willingness to abandon spouse and children in favor of work colleagues evenings and weekends.

The contrast between Japan and China is replicated in other parts of the world. Germany is a high-trust society that since medieval times has been crisscrossed by innumerable intermediate associations. Italy, by contrast, has relatively few large private corporations, all of them clustered in the northern industrial triangle. Italy's GDP is two-thirds that of Germany, but its ten largest private companies are only one-third as large as Germany's top ten. The dynamic part of the Italian economy over the past two generations has been the innumerable small-scale family firms that have cropped up in what has come to be known as la terza Italia, or the third Italy, encompassing the central regions of Tuscany, Emilia-Romagna, and the Marche. In certain regions of Italy, the family remains the principal form of social capital; trust among non-kin, as in Chinese societies, is relatively weak and impedes the formation of large, professionally managed corporations. France has never been family-oriented like central or southern Italy but was subject to ambitious centralizing governments that undermined its civil society and created a deficit of intermediate organizations between the family and the state. The French private sector consequently has always been weaker than its German and American counterparts and for many years has been organized around conservative family businesses.

A society may also have neither strong families nor strong associations outside of kinship—in other words, it may be deficient in social capital across-the-board. Edward Banfield, in his classic analysis of a peasant village in southern Italy, described a culture whose families were nuclear, small, and weak. Family businesses remained marginal, and entrepreneurs failed to build factories because they believed it was the obligation of the state to do so for them. The African-American poor in contemporary American inner cities, where single-parent families predominate and larger social groups are weak, are another case. With the destruction of the mir and other traditional communal organizations after the Bolshevik revolution, the Russian countryside lost any significant associational life outside of the collectivized state farms, and the Russian peasant family was at the same time troubled and weak. One of the reasons that decollectivization of agriculture in China has been so much easier to implement than in Russia is the enduring strength of the Chinese peasant household, which became the backbone of a revitalized countryside after the economic reforms of 1978. It would appear that in many contemporary African cities, older political structures and family ties have broken down with rapid urbanization but have not been replaced by strong voluntary associations outside of kinship. Needless to say, this kind of atomized society does not provide fertile ground for economic activity, supporting neither large organizations nor family businesses.

One notable thread that runs through such societies is that of delinquent community: the strongest community structures tend to be criminal organizations. It is as if there is a natural, universal human impulse toward sociability, which, if blocked from expressing itself through social structures like the family or voluntary organizations, appears in forms like criminal gangs. Indeed, mafias have appeared as a major form of social organization precisely in places like southern Italy, the American inner city, Russia, and many sub-Saharan African cities, which lack social capital.

This map is not immutable. There are indications that the American art of association has been in serious decline over the past couple of generations and that Americans are becoming as individualistic as they have always believed themselves to be. Social capital, just like economic capital, will be depleted if not periodically renewed.

CORPORATE TRUSTS

IT IS NOT clear that the inability of low-trust societies to create large-scale organizations constitutes a particular constraint on rates of aggregate economic growth, at least in the early phases of industrialization. What small companies give up in terms of financial clout, technological resources, and staying power, they gain in flexibility, lack of bureaucracy, and speed of decision-making. Throughout the 1980s, Italy's economy and those of other familistic Latin Catholic societies in the EU grew faster than Germany's. Those who, like Max Weber, argued that Chinese familism would impede economic modernization were simply wrong. Indeed, it is likely that small Chinese and Italian family businesses will prosper more than large Japanese or German corporations in sectors serving fast-changing, highly segmented consumer markets. If the only objective of these societies is the maximization of aggregate wealth, then they have no particular need to move beyond relatively small-scale family businesses.

The primary impact of spontaneous sociability would appear to be not on growth rates but on industrial structure—that is, the number and importance of large versus small corporations in a national economy and the ways in which they interact. Culture inhibits the growth of large companies in some societies, permits it in others, and stimulates the emergence of new forms of economic enterprise, such as the Japanese network organization, in still others. Industrial structure, in turn, determines the sectors of the global economy in which a country participates. The purpose of large corporations is to exploit economies of scale in sectors that are capital-intensive, involve complex manufacturing processes, or require extensive distribution networks. Small companies, on the other hand, tend to be better at organizing more labor-intensive activities and cluster in sectors demanding flexibility, innovativeness, and speed in decision-making. A society hosting giant corporations will gravitate toward automobiles, semiconductors, aerospace, and the like, while those inclined toward small businesses will tend to concentrate in industries like apparel, machine tools, and furniture.

In the absence of a wide radius of trust and an inclination for spontaneous association, a society has two options for building large-scale economic organizations. The first has been exploited from time immemorial: use of the state as a promoter of economic development, often directly in the form of state-owned and state-managed enterprises. Taiwan, for example, has always had a large state sector, which at one time accounted for almost 30 percent of GDP. While declining in importance over time, the state sector was critical to Taiwan's ability to develop industries requiring large scale, like petrochemicals, aerospace, and defense. The Italian and French states have had to step in repeatedly to shore up failing large private companies and the employment they created. The state was particularly critical to France's drive to be a player in certain high-tech fields where scale was important. In low-trust societies like Taiwan, France, and Italy, the absence of private, large-scale firms leads to a saddle-shaped distribution of enterprises, with numerous dynamic small firms at one end of the scale and a small number of large, state-supported companies at the other.

Large organizations in a low-trust society may also be built through foreign direct investment or joint ventures with large foreign partners. This route has been taken by many of the fast-developing states of Southeast Asia: a list of the largest companies in countries like Singapore, Malaysia, or Thailand will often include, besides state-owned companies, local subsidiaries of major multinationals. This pattern also holds true in much of Latin America and seems to be developing in parts of the former communist world as well.

One might argue that because the failure to generate large-scale economic organizations in the private sector can be overcome either by the intervention of the state or through foreign investment, the whole issue of spontaneous sociability is, in the long run, not important. In some sense that is true: France, despite the weakness of its private sector, has still managed to achieve front-rank status as a technologically advanced power through its state-owned and subsidized companies. There are, however, important caveats to this line of argument. State-run companies are almost always less efficient than their private counterparts: managements are constantly tempted to base decisions on political rather than market criteria, and strategic state investment may be misdirected because of simple miscalculation. In some cultures state-run companies can be better managed than in others, and mechanisms exist to shield them from political pressures. But though parastatals in Singapore and Taiwan may have been run better than those of Brazil or Mexico, they still have tended to be less efficient and dynamic than their private-sector counterparts.

Foreign direct investment causes problems of a different sort. The technology and management skills brought in by foreign multinationals ultimately diffuse into the local economy. But that can take many years. In the meantime, countries whose leading companies are subsidiaries of foreign corporations face problems starting competitive businesses owned and managed by locals. Many of the fast modernizers in Asia like Japan, Korea, and Taiwan permitted inflows of foreign capital but constrained direct investment by foreign multinationals in order to give native businesses a chance to ramp up to global standards.

THE CONFUCIAN COMPLICATION

GIVEN THE sharp contrasts between the economic cultures of China and Japan noted above, there is no single Asian model of economic development and no unified Confucian challenge to the West. There are, of course, aspects of culture common to virtually all East Asian societies. Among these is respect for education, which has been shared equally by Japanese, Chinese, Koreans, and the other cultures touched by Confucianism in a significant way. Similarly, all East Asian cultures share a strong work ethic. All these societies have come to terms with the legitimacy of worldly labor; aristocratic or religious values disdaining commerce, money-making, and the dignity of everyday work have largely disappeared. Finally, in most Asian societies, the state has played a rather large and active role in shaping the direction of economic development. That is far from a universal characteristic of Asian development, however. There is wide variation in the degree of state intervention throughout East Asia, from the hyperactivity of the Korean state in the Park Chung Hee period to the almost totally laissez-faire administration of the British colonial government in Hong Kong.

In terms of sociability, however, there are major differences between Japan, China, and Korea, differences that have resulted in distinct industrial structures, management practices, and forms of organization. Many Americans and Europeans tend to see Asia as more homogeneous than it actually is, with Taiwan, Singapore, the PRC, and other states in Southeast Asia rising fast and following the same development trajectory as Japan, only on a later schedule. This view has been reinforced by promoters of the concept of a Confucian challenge from East Asia.

The reality is that Asian countries have been segmented into different sectors of the global economy and are likely to stay there for some time. Japan and Korea, with their large corporations, have moved into areas like automobiles, consumer electronics, and semiconductors that are directly competitive with large North American and European industries. Those sectors are not, however, a natural strength of most Chinese societies, which do better in sectors where flexibility rather than scale is important. There are in fact two rival economic cultures arising in Asia, one Japanese and the other Chinese. Each of these cultures is unified in a literal sense by large network organizations based, characteristically, on generalized social trust in the Japanese case and on family and kinship in the Chinese. These networks obviously interact with each other at many points, but their internal wiring diagrams proceed along very distinct paths.

The difficulties experienced by Chinese societies in establishing large, private, professionally managed corporations are likely to have long-run economic consequences. In sharp contrast to the first half of the twentieth century, when most people believed industrial modernity required gigantic enterprises, the fashion today has swung in the opposite direction, toward the belief that small is beautiful. The latter view, however, drawn largely from the fast-changing computer industry, may well be overdrawn: the future may belong to neither large nor small companies per se, but rather to those societies that can innovate and create the appropriate organizations to meet the needs of 21st century businesses. Japan, Germany, and the United States all have vigorous small companies in addition to their giant corporations. They are more likely to adapt to new organizational requirements than a society like China, in which kinship ties and a deficit of trust continue to act as a constraint. Unforeseen technological developments may restore the prestige of large enterprises, which would create special problems for China.

Moreover, many countries believe that the acquisition of industries in certain key strategic sectors is a good thing in itself, either because they believe that they know better than the market where the best long-run returns will be or else because they are seeking noneconomic ends like international prestige or national security. France and Korea are prime examples, and China is likely to follow suit. The lack of a spontaneous tendency toward large organizations may create particular pitfalls for China because of the problematic character of the Chinese state. The Chinese economy is currently bifurcated into an old, inefficient, and declining state sector (that boasts, among other things, the world's least efficient automobile manufacturing operation) and a new market sector composed mostly of small family businesses or joint ventures with foreign partners. What does not exist in China today is a modern, efficient, private large-company sector. China's astounding rate of aggregate growth in recent years (some 13 percent per year in 1992 and 1993) has been fueled largely by the capitalist small business sector and by foreign investment. These rates of growth have been made possible by the introduction of market incentives into a hugely inefficient command economy. At the moment, China is too poor to worry about the sectoral distribution of its industries; everyone is grateful enough that they are growing at such a rapid rate. There are many basic problems that have yet to be worked out, such as the establishment of a stable system of property rights and commercial law.

But China will face major problems if it catches up to the current per capita income of Taiwan or Hong Kong in the next generation or two. China watchers are familiar with a litany of potential problems that may brake the country's future growth, such as inflationary pressures, absent infrastructure, and bottlenecks from too-rapid development; vast disparities in per capita income between the coastal provinces and the hinterland; and a large number of environmental time bombs that will explode in another generation or two. In addition to facing these problems, however, China will need to develop large, modern, professionally managed corporations. While Taiwan or Singapore might be willing to leave certain high-prestige forms of manufacturing to others while they grow faster along more market-directed lines, the same is unlikely to be true for mainland China. China as a great power is not going to want to be left out of the high end of industrial modernity. China's very size dictates that it eventually develop a balanced economy, including both capital- and labor-intensive sectors; it cannot expect to reach a high level of overall development as a niche player like the small states of East Asia.

The shift from family business to modern corporations is going to be more problematic for the PRC than it was for Japan or the United States, and the state will have to play a larger role. China needs, at a minimum, political stability born of a basic legitimacy of its political institutions and a competent state structure prone neither to excessive corruption nor outside political influence. China's communist political structure, however, lacks legitimacy and, increasingly, competence. It is not at all clear to most observers whether China's political institutions will survive the enormous socioeconomic pressures its headlong industrialization has created, or whether there will even be a unitary state by the 21st century. An unstable China, or a China ruled by a nervous and capricious government, will not be a propitious environment for wise economic policymaking. Nor will an economic environment in which a strong state is constantly required to step in to guide development be favorable to the growth of Chinese democracy.

The contrast between Japanese and Chinese economic culture has important implications for Japan as well. With the latter become an economic superpower in recent years, there has been talk among certain Japanese of a Japanese model for the other nations of Asia, if not other parts of the world. And indeed, the Japanese have a great deal to teach other nations of Asia (not to mention competitors in North America and Europe), which have already benefited greatly from Japanese technology and management skills in the recent past. In terms of industrial structure, however, there is a wide gap between Japan and other Asian cultures and some reason for thinking that it will be difficult for Sinitic societies to adopt Japanese practices. The *keiretsu* system, for example, would seem to be very difficult to export to a Chinese society. Chinese firms and entrepreneurs are too individualistic to cooperate in that fashion and in any case have their own kinship networks to fall back on.

THE POVERTY OF ECONOMIC DISCOURSE

THERE IS a cautionary tale embedded in the analysis of the ways in which different societies came by their relative endowments of social capital. A common condition applies to many familistic societies experiencing a low degree of trust between non-kin. China, France, southern Italy, and other low-trust societies all went through a period of strong political centralization, when an absolute emperor, monarch, or state deliberately set out to eliminate competitors for power. In such societies, the social capital that existed in the period before absolutist centralization was depleted. Intermediate social structures like the French guilds were first placed in the service of the state and then, after the Revolution, abolished altogether.

By contrast, those societies experiencing a high degree of social trust, such as Japan, Germany, and the United States, never experienced a pro-

Francis Fukuyama

longed period of centralized state power. With political power more dispersed—as in the Japanese and German feudal periods, or as a deliberate result of constitutional structure in the United States—a rich profusion of social organizations could flourish without interference and become the basis for economic cooperation. In Germany, for example, the guilds were never abolished but rather modernized in such a way that they eventually became the basis for that country's much-admired apprenticeship system of industrial training.

The foregoing suggests that societies that rely on a powerful and all-encompassing state to promote economic development run a double risk. Not only will state-supported companies be less efficient and risk breaking national budgets in the short run, but the very intervention of the state may weaken the society's underlying propensity for spontaneous sociability in the long run. France, which enjoyed a dense web of civil associations at the end of the Middle Ages, saw them systematically undercut more than 500 years ago by a modernizing monarchy. To this day, despite countless efforts to decentralize political life and energize the private sector, the French continue to have great difficulties associating with one another spontaneously, outside the framework of centralized, bureaucratic, rule-bound authority.

Awareness of the importance of social capital illuminates the poverty of contemporary economic discourse. For the past decade, the central debate over the global economy has taken place between the neomercantilists and orthodox neoclassical economists. The former group, represented by writers like James Fallows, Clyde Prestowitz, and Chalmers Johnson, have argued that neoclassical economists have ignored the central role of the state in promoting Asian economic development, a role they claim invalidates standard models of market-oriented development. The neoclassicists, for their part, argue that Asian development happened despite state intervention, and they point to failures on the part of Japan's Ministry of International Trade and Industry and other planning ministries.

What both sides in this debate miss is the role of culture. For all their awareness of the peculiarities of Asian development, the neomercantilists are as universalistic in their policy prescriptions as the neoclassical economists. They argue that America's unwillingness to implement an Asian industrial policy is harming its global competitive position. It is clear, however, that both the need for an industrial policy and the ability to implement one effectively are dependent on cultural factors like social capital. Japan, Germany, and the United States have robust private sectors able to generate large-scale organizations spontaneously; China, Italy, and France do not, so it is perfectly natural there that the state should step in to promote this kind of organization. The ability to manage state-owned corporations or to distribute subsidies effectively is also very much dependent on culture. Asia is distinctive because many of the states there have succeeded in shielding their public authorities from pressure to maintain employment or direct subsidies toward politically influential sectors, something that has eluded public bureaucrats in much of Europe and Latin America. One therefore cannot argue for or against industrial policy on abstract grounds; its chances for success depend on the specific cultural, political, and historical environment in which it is implemented.

We are at the end of a prolonged period in which modern states have been key promoters of economic growth and social transformation. No one would deny that in the past, state intervention in the modernization process has been effective. National governments have abolished entire social classes; engaged in land reform; introduced modern legislation guaranteeing equality of rights for ever larger circles of the population; built cities and encouraged urbanization; educated populations; and provided the infrastructure for modern, complex, information-intensive societies.

This institution-building, however, has reached a dead end with the establishment of liberal democratic political institutions and capitalist economic structures throughout the developed world. While institutional differences between different parts of the developed world remain, their scope has narrowed considerably over the past couple of generations as the socialist alternative collapsed and nations became ever more interdependent through trade and investment. The essential meaning of the end of history is not that turbulence has ceased or that the world has become completely uniform, but rather that there are no serious systematic institutional alternatives to liberal democracy and market-based capitalism for the world's most advanced countries. Put another way, social engineering, while at one time the key to progressive government, has today reached a dead end. The most important factors affecting the real quality of life in such societies lie safely beyond what national governments can affect in positive ways. For while state power can effectively undermine civil society by uprooting neighborhoods, abolishing communities, and creating perverse incentives that destabilize two-parent families, it is much less able to promote strong bonds of special solidarity or the moral fabric that underlies community.

Institutional convergence has not, however, meant an end of significant differences between modern societies. In the post–Cold War world, the most important distinctions between nations are no longer institutional but cultural: it is the character of their civil societies, the social and moral habits that underlie institutions, that differentiate them. In this respect, Samuel Huntington has been quite right to assert that culture will be the key axis of international differentiation—though not necessarily an axis of conflict.

The traditional argument between left and right over the appropriate role of the state, reflected in the debate between the neomercantilists and neoclassical economists, misses the key issue concerning civil society. The left is wrong to think that the state can embody or promote meaningful social solidarity. Libertarian conservatives, for their part, are wrong to think that strong social structures will spontaneously regenerate once the state is subtracted from the equation. The character of civil society and its intermediate associations, rooted as it is in nonrational factors like culture, religion, tradition, and other premodern sources, will be key to the success of modern societies in a global economy.☯

Democratization and War

Edward D. Mansfield and Jack Snyder

DANGERS OF TRANSITION

THE IDEA that democracies never fight wars against each other has become an axiom for many scholars. It is, as one scholar puts it, "as close as anything we have to an empirical law in international relations." This "law" is invoked by American statesmen to justify a foreign policy that encourages democratization abroad. In his 1994 State of the Union address, President Clinton asserted that no two democracies had ever gone to war with each other, thus explaining why promoting democracy abroad was a pillar of his foreign policy.

It is probably true that a world in which more countries were mature, stable democracies would be safer and preferable for the United States. But countries do not become mature democracies overnight. They usually go through a rocky transition, where mass politics mixes with authoritarian elite politics in a volatile way. Statistical evidence covering the past two centuries shows that in this transitional phase of democratization, countries become more aggressive and war-prone, not less, and they do fight wars with democratic states. In fact, formerly authoritarian states where democratic participation is on the rise are more likely to fight wars than are stable democracies or autocracies. States that make the biggest leap, from total autocracy to extensive mass democracy—like contemporary Russia—are about twice as likely to fight wars in the

EDWARD D. MANSFIELD is Associate Professor of Political Science at Columbia University and author of *Power, Trade, and War*. JACK SNYDER, Professor of Political Science and Director of the Institute of War and Peace Studies at Columbia University, is the author of *Myths of Empire*. A longer version of this article will appear in the Summer 1995 issue of *International Security*.

decade after democratization as are states that remain autocracies.

This historical pattern of democratization, belligerent nationalism, and war is already emerging in some of today's new or partial democracies, especially some formerly communist states. Two pairs of states— Serbia and Croatia, and Armenia and Azerbaijan—have found themselves at war while experimenting with varying degrees of electoral democracy. The electorate of Russia's partial democracy cast nearly a quarter of its votes for the party of radical nationalist Vladimir Zhirinovsky. Even mainstream Russian politicians have adopted an imperial tone in their dealings with neighboring former Soviet republics, and military force has been used ruthlessly in Chechnya.

The following evidence should raise questions about the Clinton administration's policy of promoting peace by promoting democratization. The expectation that the spread of democracy will probably contribute to peace in the long run, once new democracies mature, provides little comfort to those who might face a heightened risk of war in the short run. Pushing nuclear-armed great powers like Russia or China toward democratization is like spinning a roulette wheel: many of the outcomes are undesirable. Of course, in most cases the initial steps on the road to democratization will not be produced by any conscious policy of the United States. The roulette wheel is already spinning for Russia and perhaps will be soon for China. Washington and the international community need to think not so much about encouraging or discouraging democratization as about helping to smooth the transition in ways that minimize its risks.

THE EVIDENCE

OUR STATISTICAL analysis relies on the classifications of regimes and wars from 1811 to 1980 used by most scholars studying the peace among democracies. Starting with these standard data, we classify each state as a democracy, an autocracy, or a mixed regime—that is, a state with features of both democracies and autocracies. This classification is based on several criteria, including the constitutional constraints on the chief executive, the competitiveness of domestic politics, the openness of the process for selecting the chief executive, and the strength of the rules governing participation in politics. Democratizing states are those that made any regime change in a democratic direction—that is, from autocracy to democracy, from a mixed regime to democracy, or from autocracy to a mixed regime. We analyze wars between states as well as wars between a state and a non-state group, such as liberation movements in colonies, but we do not include civil wars.[1]

Because we view democratization as a gradual process, rather than a sudden change, we test whether a transition toward democracy occurring over one, five, and ten years is associated with the subsequent onset of war. To assess the strength of the relationship between democratization and war, we construct a series of contingency tables. Based on those tables, we compare the probability that a democratizing state subsequently goes to war with the probabilities of war for states in transition toward autocracy and for states undergoing no regime change. The results of all of these tests show that *democratizing states were more likely to fight wars than were states that had undergone no change in regime.* This relationship is weakest one year into democratization and strongest at ten years. During any given ten-year period, a state experiencing no regime change had about one chance in six of fighting a war in the following decade. In the decade following democratization, a state's chance of fighting a war was about one in four. When we analyze the components of our measure of democratization separately, the results are similar. On average, an increase in the openness of the selection process for the chief executive doubled the likelihood of war. Increasing the competitiveness of political participation or increasing the constraints on a country's chief executive (both aspects of democratization) also made war more likely. On average, these changes increased the likelihood of war by about 90 percent and 35 percent respectively.

The statistical results are even more dramatic when we analyze cases in which the process of democratization culminated in very high levels of mass participation in politics. States changing from a mixed regime to democracy were on average about 50 percent more likely to become engaged in war (and about two-thirds more likely to go to war with another nation-state) than states that remained mixed regimes.

The effect was greater still for those states making the largest leap,

---

[1] On the definition of war and the data on war used in this analysis, see Melvin Small and J. David Singer, *Resort to Arms: International and Civil Wars, 1816–1980*, Beverly Hills: Sage, 1982.

from full autocracy to high levels of democracy. Such states were on average about two-thirds more likely to become involved in any type of war (and about twice as likely to become involved in an interstate war) than states that remained autocracies. Though this evidence shows that democratization is dangerous, its reversal offers no easy solutions. On average, changes toward autocracy also yielded an increase in the probability of war, though a smaller one than changes toward democracy, compared to states experiencing no regime change.

NATIONALISM AND DEMOCRATIZATION

THE CONNECTION between democratization and nationalism is striking in both the historical record and today's headlines. We did not measure nationalism directly in our statistical tests. Nonetheless, historical and contemporary evidence strongly suggests that rising nationalism often goes hand in hand with rising democracy. It is no accident that the end of the Cold War brought both a wave of democratization and a revival of nationalist sentiment in the former communist states.

In eighteenth-century Britain and France, when nationalism first emerged as an explicit political doctrine, it meant self-rule by the people. It was the rallying cry of commoners and rising commercial classes against rule by aristocratic elites, who were charged with the sin of ruling in their own interests, rather than those of the nation. Indeed, dynastic rulers and imperial courts had hardly been interested in promoting nationalism as a banner of solidarity in their realms. They typically ruled over a linguistically and culturally diverse conglomeration of subjects and claimed to govern by divine right, not in the interest of the nation. Often, these rulers were more closely tied by kinship, language, or culture to elites in other states than to their own subjects. The position of the communist ruling class was strikingly similar: a transnational elite that ruled over an amalgamation of peoples and claimed legitimacy from the communist party's role as the vanguard of history, not from the consent of the governed. Popular forces challenging either traditional dynastic rulers or communist elites naturally tended to combine demands for national self-determination and democratic rule.

This concoction of nationalism and incipient democratization has been an intoxicating brew, leading in case after case to ill-conceived wars of expansion. The earliest instance remains one of the most dramatic. In the French Revolution, the radical Brissotin parliamentary faction polarized politics by harping on the king's slow response to the threat of war with other dynastic states. In the ensuing wars of the French Revolution, citizens flocked to join the revolutionary armies to defend popular self-rule and the French nation. Even after the revolution turned profoundly antidemocratic, Napoleon was able to harness this popular nationalism to the task of conquering Europe, substituting the popularity of empire for the substance of democratic rule.

After this experience, Europe's ruling elites decided to band together in 1815 in the Concert of Europe to contain the twin evils of nationalism and democratization. In this scheme, Europe's crowned heads tried to unite in squelching demands for constitutions, electoral and social democracy, and national self-determination. For a time nationalism and democratization were both held back, and Europe enjoyed a period of relative peace.

But in the long run, the strategy failed in the face of the economic changes strengthening popular forces in Western and Central Europe. British and French politicians soon saw that they would have to rule by co-opting nationalist and democratic demands, rather than suppressing them. Once the specter of revolution returned to Europe in 1848, this reversal of political tactics was complete, and it led quickly to the Crimean War. British Foreign Secretary Palmerston and French Emperor Napoleon III both tried to manage the clamor for a broader political arena by giving democrats what they wanted in foreign affairs—a "liberal" war to free imprisoned nations from autocratic rule and, incidentally, to expand commerce.

But this was just the dress rehearsal for history's most potent combination of mass politics and rising nationalism, which occurred in Germany around the turn of the twentieth century. Chancellor Otto von Bismarck, counting on the conservative votes of a docile peasantry, granted universal suffrage in the newly unified Reich after 1870, but in foreign and military affairs, he kept the elected Reichstag subordinate to the cabinet appointed by the kaiser. Like the sorcerer's apprentice, however, Bismarck underestimated the forces he was unleashing. With the rise of an industrial society, Bismarck's successors could not control this truncated democracy, where over 90 percent of the population voted. Everyone was highly politicized, yet nobody could achieve their aims through the limited powers of the Reichstag. As a result, people organized direct pressure groups outside of electoral party politics. Some of these clamored for economic benefits, but many of them found it tactically useful to cloak their narrow interests in a broader vision of the nation's interests. This mass nationalist sentiment exerted constant pressure on German diplomacy in the Wilhelmine years before 1914 and pushed its vacillating elites toward war.

Democratization and nationalism also became linked in Japan on the eve of the Manchurian invasion in 1931. During the 1920s Japan expanded its suffrage and experimented with two-party electoral competition, though a council of military elder statesmen still made the ultimate decisions about who would govern. These semi-elected governments of the 1920s supported free trade, favored naval arms control, and usually tried to rein in the Japanese army's schemes to undermine the Open Door policy in China. During the 1920s, Young Turks in the army developed a populist, nationalist doctrine featuring a centrally planned economy within an autarkic, industrialized, expanded empire, while scapegoating Japan's alleged internal and external enemies, including leftist workers, rich capitalists, liberals, democrats, Americans, and Russians. After the economic crash of the late 1920s, this nationalist formula became persuasive, and the Japanese military had little trouble gaining popular support for imperial expansion and the emasculation of democracy. As in so many previous cases, nationalism proved to be a way for militarist elite groups to appear populist in a democratizing society while obstructing the advance to full democracy.

The interconnection among nationalism, democratization, and war is even clearer in new states. In today's "Weimar Russia," voters disgruntled by economic distress backed belligerent nationalists like Zhirinovsky, put ostensible liberals like President Boris Yeltsin and Foreign Minister Andrei Kozyrev on the defensive on ethnic and foreign policy issues, and contributed to the climate that led to war in Chechnya. In "Wilhelmine Serbia," the political and military elites of the old regime, facing inexorable pressure for democratization, cynically but successfully created a new basis for legitimacy through nationalist propaganda and military action, and they recently won elections that were only partially manipulated. Until its recent decree suspending the activities of the main opposition party, Armenia had moved quite far toward full democracy while at the same time supporting an invasion of its ethnic foes in Azerbaijan. The Azeris have been less successful in sustaining momentum toward democracy. However, in Azerbaijan's one relatively free and fair presidential election, the winner, Abulfaz Ali Elchibey, attacked the incumbent for being insufficiently nationalist and populist. Elchibey's platform emphasized Turkic identity and the strengthening of the Azeri nation-state to try to mount a counteroffensive against the Armenians. In other ethnically divided societies, where holding an election is like taking a census, democratization has often become an opportunity to exercise the tyranny of the majority.

THE SORCERER'S APPRENTICE

ALTHOUGH democratization in many cases leads to war, that does not mean that the average voter wants war. Public opinion in democratizing states often starts off highly averse to the costs and risks of war. In that sense, the public opinion polls taken in Russia in early 1994 were typical. Respondents said, for example, that Russian policy should make sure the rights of Russians in neighboring states were not infringed, but not at the cost of military intervention. Public opinion often becomes more belligerent, however, as a result of propaganda and military action presented as faits accomplis by elites. This mass opinion, once aroused, may no longer be controllable.

For example, Napoleon III successfully exploited the domestic prestige from France's share of the victory in the Crimean War to consolidate his rule, despite the popular reluctance and war-weariness that had accompanied the war. Having learned this lesson well, Napoleon tried this tactic again in 1859. On the eve of his military intervention in the Italian struggle with Austria, he admitted to his ministers that "on the domestic front, the war will at first awaken great fears; traders and speculators of every stripe will shriek, but national sentiment will [banish] this domestic fright; the nation will be put to the test once more in a struggle that will stir many a heart, recall the memory of heroic times, and bring together under the mantle of glory the parties that are steadily drifting away from one another day after day."[2] Napoleon was trying not just to follow opinion but to make public opinion bellicose, in order to stir a national feeling that would enhance the state's ability to govern a split and

---

[2] Alain Plessis, *The Rise and Fall of the Second Empire, 1852-1871*, Cambridge: Cambridge University Press, 1985, pp. 146-47.

stalemated political arena.

Much the same has happened in contemporary Serbia. Despite the memories of Ustashe atrocities in World War II, intermarriage rates between Croats and Serbs living in Croatia were as high as one in three during the 1980s. Opinion has been bellicized by propaganda campaigns in state-controlled media that, for example, carried purely invented reports of rapes of Serbian women in Kosovo, and even more so by the fait accompli of launching the war itself.

In short, democratizing states are war-prone not because war is popular with the mass public, but because domestic pressures create incentives for elites to drum up nationalist sentiment.

THE CAUSES OF DEMOCRATIC WARS

DEMOCRATIZATION typically creates a syndrome of weak central authority, unstable domestic coalitions, and high-energy mass politics. It brings new social groups and classes onto the political stage. Political leaders, finding no way to reconcile incompatible interests, resort to shortsighted bargains or reckless gambles in order to maintain their governing coalitions. Elites need to gain mass allies to defend their weakened positions. Both the newly ambitious elites and the embattled old ruling groups often use appeals to nationalism to stay astride their unmanageable political coalitions.

Needing public support, they rouse the masses with nationalist propaganda but find that their mass allies, once mobilized by passionate appeals, are difficult to control. So are the powerful remnants of the old order—the military, for example—which promote militarism because it strengthens them institutionally. This is particularly true because democratization weakens the central government's ability to keep policy coherent and consistent. Governing a society that is democratizing is like driving a car while throwing away the steering wheel, stepping on the gas, and fighting over which passenger will be in the driver's seat. The result, often, is war.

Political stalemate and imperialist coalitions. Democratization creates a wider spectrum of politically significant groups with diverse and incompatible interests. In the period when the great powers were first democratizing, kings, aristocrats, peasants, and artisans shared the historical stage with industrialists, an urban working class, and a middle-class intelligentsia. Similarly, in the post-communist world, former party appa-ratchiks, atavistic heavy industrialists, and downwardly mobile military officers share the stage with populist demagogues, free-market entrepre-neurs, disgruntled workers, and newly mobilized ethnic groups. In prin-ciple, mature democratic institutions can integrate even the widest spec-trum of interests through competition for the favor of the average voter. But where political parties and representative institutions are still in their infancy, the diversity of interests may make political coalitions difficult to maintain. Often the solution is a belligerent nationalist coalition.

In Britain during the period leading up to the Crimean War, neither the Whigs nor Tories could form a lasting governing coalition because so many groups refused to enter stable political alliances. None of the old elites would coalesce with the parliamentary bloc of radicals elected by urban middle-class and Irish voters. Moreover, protectionist Tories would not unite with free-trading Whigs and Peelite Tories. The social and po-litical mid-Victorian equipoise between traditional and modern Britain created a temporary political stalemate. Lord Palmerston's pseudo-liberal imperialism turned out to be the only successful formula for creating a durable ruling coalition during this transitional period of democratization.

The stalemate in Wilhelmine-era electoral politics was even more se-rious. In principle, coalitions of the left and right might have formed a two-party system to vie for the favor of the average voter, thus moderating policy. In fact, both left and right were too internally divided to mount effective coalitions with internally consistent policies. Progressive dreamed of a bloc extending "from Bassermann to Bebel," from the liberal-democ-ratic middle classes through the Marxist working classes, but the differ-ences between labor and capital chronically barred this development. Conservatives had more success in forging a "marriage of iron and rye," but fundamental differences between military-feudal Junkers and Ruhr in-dustrialists over issues ranging from the distribution of tax burdens to mil-itary strategy made their policies incoherent. Germany wound up with plans for a big army and a costly navy, and nobody willing to pay for it.

In more recent times, incipient democratization has likewise caused political impasses by widening the political spectrum to include too many irreconcilable political forces. In the final days of Yugoslavia, efforts by moderates like former Prime Minister Ante Marković to pro-mote a federalist, democratic, economic reformist platform were hin-dered not only by ethnic divisions but also by the cleavage between market-oriented business interests on the one hand and party bosses and military officers on the other. Similarly, in Russia, the difficulty of reconciling liberal, neo-communist, and nationalist political platforms and the social interests behind them has led to parliamentary stalemate, attempts to break the stalemate by presidential decree, tanks in the streets, and the resort to freelancing by breakaway regions, the military, and spontaneous privatizers of state property. One interpretation of Yeltsin's decision to use force in Chechnya is that he felt it necessary to show that he could act decisively to prevent the unraveling of central authority, with respect not only to ethnic separatists but also to other ungovernable groups in a democratizing society. Chechnya, it was hoped, would allow Yeltsin to demonstrate his ability to coerce Russian society while at the same time exploiting a potentially popular nationalist issue.

Inflexible interests and short time horizons. Groups threatened by social change and democratization, including still-powerful elites, are often compelled to take an inflexible view of their interests, especially when their assets cannot be readily adapted to changing political and economic conditions. In extreme cases, there may be only one solution that will maintain the social position of the group. For Prussian landowners, it was agricultural protection in a nondemocratic state; for the Japanese military, it was organizational autonomy in an autarkic empire; for the Serbian military and party elites, it was a Serbian nationalist state. Since military bureaucracies and imperial interest groups occupied key positions in many authoritarian great powers, whether monarchal or communist, most interests threatened by democratization have been bound up with military programs and the state's international mission. Compromises that may lead down the slippery slope to social extinction or irrelevance have little appeal to such groups. This adds to the difficulty of finding an exit from the domestic political impasse and may make powerful domestic groups impervious to the international risks of their strategies.

Competing for popular support. The trouble intensifies when elites in a democratizing society try to recruit mass allies to their cause. Threatened elite groups have an overwhelming incentive to mobilize mass backers on the elites' terms, using whatever special resources they might retain. These resources have included monopolies of information (the Wilhelmine navy's unique "expertise" in making strategic assessments), propaganda assets (the Japanese army's public relations blitz justifying the invasion of Manchuria), patronage (Lord Palmerston's gifts of foreign service postings to the sons of cooperative journalists), wealth (the Krupp steel company's bankrolling of mass nationalist and militarist leagues), organizational skills and networks (the Japanese army's exploitation of rural reservist organizations to build a social base), and the ability to use the control of traditional political institutions to shape the political agenda and structure the terms of political bargains (the Wilhelmine ruling elite's agreement to eliminate anti-Catholic legislation in exchange for Catholic support in the Reichstag on the naval budget).

This elite mobilization of mass groups takes place in a highly competitive setting. Elite groups mobilize mass support to neutralize mass threats (for instance, creating patriotic leagues to counter workers' movements) and counter other elite groups' successful efforts at mass mobilization (such as the German Navy League, a political counterweight to the Junker-backed Agrarian League). The elites' resources allow them to influence the direction of mass political participation, but the imperative to compete for mass favor makes it difficult for a single elite group to control the outcome of this process. For example, mass groups that gain access to politics through elite-supported nationalist organizations often try to outbid their erstwhile sponsors. By 1911, German popular nationalist lobbies were in a position to claim that if Germany's foreign foes were really as threatening as the ruling elites had portrayed them, then the government had sold out German interests in reaching a compromise with France over the Moroccan dispute. In this way, elite mobilization of the masses adds to the ungovernability and political impasse of democratizing states.

Ideology takes on particular significance in the competition for mass support. New entrants to the political process, lacking established habits and good information, may be uncertain where their political interests lie. Ideology can yield big payoffs, particularly when there is no efficient free marketplace of ideas to counter false claims with reliable facts. Elites try out all sorts of ideological appeals depending on the social position they are defending, the nature of the mass group they want to recruit, and the kinds of appeals that seem politically plausible. A nearly universal element of these ideological appeals, however, is nationalism, which has the advantage of positing a community of interest uniting elites and masses. This distracts attention from class cleavages that divide elites from the masses they are trying to recruit.

The weakening of central authority. The political impasse and recklessness of democratizing states is deepened by the weakening of the state's authority. The autocrat can no longer dictate to elite interest groups or mass groups. Meanwhile, democratic institutions lack the strength to integrate these contending interests and views. Parties are weak and lack mass loyalty. Elections are rigged or intermittent. Institutions of public political participation are distrusted because they are subject to manipulation by elites and arbitrary constraints imposed by the state, which fears the outcome of unfettered competition.

Among the great powers, the problem was not excessive authoritarian power at the center, but the opposite. The Aberdeen coalition that brought Britain into the Crimean War was a makeshift cabinet headed by a weak leader with no substantial constituency. Likewise, on the eve of the Franco-Prussian War, Napoleon III's regime was in the process of caving in to its liberal opponents, who dominated the parliament elected in 1869. As Europe's armies prepared to hurtle from their starting gates in July 1914, Austrian leaders, perplexed by the contradictions between the German chancellor's policy and that of the German military, asked, "Who rules in Berlin?" Similarly, the 1931 Manchurian incident was a fait accompli by the local Japanese military; Tokyo was not even informed. The return to imperial thinking in Moscow today is the result of Yeltsin's weakness, not his strength. As the well-informed Moscow analyst Sergei Karaganov recently argued, the breakdown of the Leninist state "has created an environment where elite interests influence [foreign] policy directly."[3]

In each of these cases, the weak central leadership resorts to the same strategies as do the more parochial elite interests, using nationalist ideological appeals and special-interest payoffs to maintain their short-run viability, despite the long-run risks that these strategies may unleash.

Prestige strategies. One of the simplest but riskiest strategies for a hard-pressed regime in a democratizing country is to shore up its prestige at home by seeking victories abroad. During the Chechen intervention, newspaper commentators in Moscow and the West were reminded of Russian Interior Minister Viacheslav Plehve's fateful remark in 1904, on the eve of the disastrous Russo-Japanese War, that what the tsar needed was "a short, victorious war" to boost his prestige. Though this strategy often backfires, it is a perennial temptation as a means for coping with the political strains of democratization. German Chancellor Johannes

---

[3] Karaganov, "Russia's Elites," in Robert Blackwill and Sergei Karaganov, *Damage Limitation*, Washington: Brassey's, 1994, p. 42.

Miquel, who revitalized the imperialist-protectionist "coalition of iron and rye" at the turn of the century, told his colleagues that "successes in foreign policy would make a good impression in the Reichstag debates, and political divisions would thus be moderated."[4] The targets of such strategies often share this analysis. Richard Cobden, for example, argued that military victories abroad would confer enough prestige on the military-feudal landed elite to allow them to raise food tariffs and snuff out democracy: "Let John Bull have a great military triumph, and we shall have to take off our hats as we pass the Horse Guards for the rest of our lives."[5]

Prestige strategies make the country vulnerable to slights to its reputation. Napoleon III, for example, was easily goaded into a fateful declaration of war in 1870 by Bismarck's insulting editorial work on a leaked telegram from the kaiser. For those who want to avoid such diplomatic provocations, the lesson is to make sure that compromises forced on the leaders of democratizing states do not take away the fig leaves needed to sustain their domestic prestige.

MANAGING THE DANGERS

THOUGH MATURE democratic states have virtually never fought wars against each other, promoting democracy may not promote peace because states are especially war-prone during the transition toward democracy. This does not mean, however, that democratization should be squelched in the interests of peace. Many states are now democratizing or on the verge of it, and stemming that turbulent tide, even if it were desirable, may not be possible. Our statistical tests show that movements toward autocracy, including reversals of democratization, are only somewhat less likely to result in war than democratization itself. Consequently, the task is to draw on an understanding of the process of democratization to keep its unwanted side effects to a minimum.

Of course, democratization does not always lead to extreme forms of aggressive nationalism, just as it does not always lead to war. But it makes those outcomes more likely. Cases where states democratized without

---

[4] J. C. G. Rohl, *Germany without Bismarck*, Berkeley: University of California Press, 1967, p. 250.

[5] Letter to John Bright, October 1, 1854, quoted in John Morley, *The Life of Richard Cobden*, abridged ed., London: Thomas Nelson, pp. 311-12.

triggering a nationalist mobilization are particularly interesting, since they may hold clues about how to prevent such unwanted side effects. Among the great powers, the obvious successes were the democratization of Germany and Japan after 1945, due to occupation by liberal democracies and the favorable international setting provided by the Marshall Plan, the Bretton Woods economic system, and the democratic military alliance against the Soviet threat. More recently, numerous Latin American states have democratized without nationalism or war. The recent border skirmishes between Peru and Ecuador, however, coincide with democratizing trends in both states and a nationalist turn in Ecuadorian political discourse. Moreover, all three previous wars between that pair over the past two centuries occurred in periods of partial democratization.

In such cases, however, the cure is probably more democracy, not less. In "Wilhelmine Argentina," the Falkland Islands/Malvinas War came when the military junta needed a nationalist victory to stave off pressure for the return of democracy; the arrival of full democracy has produced more pacific policies. Among the East European states, nationalist politics has been unsuccessful in the most fully democratic ones—Poland, the Czech Republic, and Hungary—as protest votes have gone to former communists. Nationalism has figured more prominently in the politics of the less democratic formerly communist states that are nonetheless partially democratizing. States like Turkmenistan that remain outright autocracies have no nationalist mobilization—indeed no political mobilization of any kind. In those recent cases, in contrast to some of our statistical results, the rule seems to be: go fully democratic, or don't go at all.

In any given case, other factors may override the relative bellicosity of democratizing states. These might include the power of the democratizing state, the strength of the potential deterrent coalition of states constraining it, the attractiveness of more peaceful options available to the democratizing state, and the nature of the groups making up its ruling coalition. What is needed is to identify the conditions that lead to relatively peaceful democratization and try to create those circumstances.

One of the major findings of scholarship on democratization in Latin America is that the process goes most smoothly when elites threatened by the transition—especially the military—are given a golden parachute. Above all, they need a guarantee that they will not wind up in jail if they relinquish power. The history of the democratizing great powers broadens this insight. Democratization was least likely to lead to war when the old elites saw a reasonably bright future for themselves in the new social order. British aristocrats, for example, had more of their wealth invested in commerce and industry than in agriculture, so they had many interests in common with the rising middle classes. They could face democratization with relative equanimity. In contrast, Prussia's capital-starved, small-scale Junker landholders had no choice but to rely on agricultural protection and military careers.

In today's context, finding benign, productive employment for the erstwhile communist nomenklatura, military officer corps, nuclear scientists, and smokestack industrialists ought to rank high on the list of priorities. Policies aimed at giving them a stake in the privatization process and subsidizing the conversion of their skills to new, peaceful tasks in a market economy seem like a step in the right direction. According to some interpretations, Russian Defense Minister Pavel Grachev was eager to use force to solve the Chechen confrontation in order to show that Russian military power was still useful and that increased investment in the Russian army would pay big dividends. Instead of pursuing this reckless path, the Russian military elite needs to be convinced that its prestige, housing, pensions, and technical competence will improve if and only if it transforms itself into a Western-style military, subordinate to civilian authority and resorting to force only in accordance with prevailing international norms. Not only do old elites need to be kept happy, they also need to be kept weak. Pacts should not prop up the remnants of the authoritarian system, but rather create a niche for them in the new system.

Another top priority must be creating a free, competitive, and responsible marketplace of ideas in the newly democratizing states. Most of the war-prone democratizing great powers had pluralistic public debates, but the debates were skewed to favor groups with money, privileged access to the media, and proprietary control over information ranging from archives to intelligence about the military balance. Pluralism is not enough. Without a level playing field, pluralism simply creates the incentive and opportunity for privileged groups to propound self-serving myths, which historically have often taken a nationalist turn. One of the rays of hope in the Chechen affair was the alacrity with which Russian journalists exposed the costs of the fighting and the lies of the government and the military. Though elites should get a golden parachute regarding their pecuniary interests, they should be given no quarter on the battlefield of ideas. Mythmaking should be held up to the utmost

Edward D. Mansfield and Jack Snyder

scrutiny by aggressive journalists who maintain their credibility by scrupulously distinguishing fact from opinion and tirelessly verifying their sources. Promoting this kind of journalistic infrastructure is probably the most highly leveraged investment the West can make in a peaceful democratic transition.

Finally, the kind of ruling coalition that emerges in the course of democratization depends a great deal on the incentives created by the international environment. Both Germany and Japan started on the path toward liberal, stable democratization in the mid-1920s, encouraged by abundant opportunities for trade with and investment by the advanced democracies and by credible security treaties that defused nationalist scaremongering in domestic politics. When the international supports for free trade and democracy were yanked out in the late 1920s, their liberal coalitions collapsed. For China, whose democratization may occur in the context of expanding economic ties with the West, a steady Western commercial partnership and security presence is likely to play a major role in shaping the incentives of proto-democratic coalition politics.

In the long run, the enlargement of the zone of stable democracy will probably enhance prospects for peace. In the short run, much work remains to be done to minimize the dangers of the turbulent transition.❷

Toward Post-Heroic Warfare

Edward N. Luttwak

THE OBSOLESCENCE OF TOTAL WAR

ONLY ONE thing could possibly link the protracted warfare in the former Yugoslavia, the destruction of Grozny, and the recent border fighting between Ecuador and Peru. Once more, as in centuries past, wars are rather easily started and then fought without perceptible restraint. When belligerents see that no particular penalty is paid for opening fire first or using any and all means of warfare—even the wholesale destruction of cities by aerial or artillery bombardment—self-imposed restraints on the use of force are everywhere eroded. The border fighting between Ecuador and Peru had only just begun when tactical bombing was employed, as if it were no more consequential than one more infantry skirmish.

This new season of war is upon us as one more consequence of the passing of the Cold War. The latter induced or intensified a number of hot wars in the contested zones between each camp as each superpower provided allies and clients with weapons and expertise far beyond their own capacities. Thus the Middle East especially became something of a preferred battleground by proxy.

At the same time, however, the fear that escalation could eventually reach the nuclear level inhibited any direct combat whatsoever by the superpowers themselves in Europe or anywhere else, even on the smallest scale. Above all, the Cold War suppressed many potential shooting wars in a great part of the world because neither superpower would tolerate them within its own camp. Both, moreover, were notably vigilant in controlling the form and geographic scope of the wars they fought in Korea,

---

EDWARD N. LUTTWAK is a Senior Fellow at the Center for Strategic and International Studies.

Vietnam, and Afghanistan, and also the wars their allies and clients fought, again for fear of an escalation to direct clash and nuclear war.

The concept of war governing those encounters has long been so strongly entrenched that it is not even commonly recognized as particular, but rather is seen as the only possible concept for now and always. It envisages only wars fought for great national purposes that can evoke public fervor, by armed forces that represent the aroused nation rather than merely a body of professionals going about their business. Yet that is only one concept of war, as even casual readers of military history well know. Far from an eternal verity, the concept is a rather modern innovation, associated with a particular phase of fairly recent history. Before the French Revolution, most wars were fought for much less than imperative purposes that rarely evoked popular enthusiasm, with prudent strategies and tactics to conserve expensive professional forces. While no great purposes at hand could motivate the entire nation in war, there is much justification for some eighteenth-century warfare of our own, with modest purposes and casualty avoidance as the controlling norm.

THE NEW CULTURE OF WAR

THE COLD War culture of intense but controlled tension, which required disciplined constraints on the use of force, seems to have influenced even nonaligned nations such as India and Pakistan. To use force at all during the Cold War came to be seen almost everywhere as a very grave decision indeed, to be made only after the fullest deliberation, usually after all other means had been exhausted. Further decisions to escalate to regular infantry combat rather than deniable guerrilla operations, armored warfare and artillery support rather than infantry, aerial bombing rather than ground warfare were deemed worthy of distinct political decisions at the highest levels instead of being left, as in the past, to the discretion of military commanders. The latter complained, sometimes loudly, but they obeyed, thus affirming the new culture of restraint.

Restraint did not prevent 138 wars between 1945 and 1989, by the most expansive count, which killed as many as 23 million people. But in the previous 44 years, which included two world wars, many more were killed. In the absence of any restraint arising from strategic prudence, internal repression killed many more people over the years 1945-89 than all 138 wars combined.

Now that the Cold War no longer suppresses hot wars, the entire culture of disciplined restraint in the use of force is in dissolution. Except for Iraq's wars, the consequences have chiefly been manifest within the territories that had been Soviet, as well as Yugoslav. The protracted warfare, catastrophic destruction, and profuse atrocities of eastern Moldavia, the three Caucasian republics, parts of Central Asia, and lately Chechnya, Croatia, and Bosnia have certainly horrified and moved many Americans. But this diverse violence derives from the same postimperial devolution of epic, unprecedented scale or from purely localized sources. Hence one could still hope that the new readiness to start unrestrained wars would at least be geographically confined, if only within an area already vast.

The fighting between Ecuador and Peru, the mounting recklessness manifest between Greece and Turkey, and also perhaps Pakistan's increasing boldness over Kashmir suggest the more sinister possibility that a new, much less restrained culture of war is emerging and spreading far and wide. Nothing is now countering a number of perverse precedents. Aggression and willful escalation alike remain unpunished; victors remain in possession of their gains; the defeated are abandoned to their own devices. It was not so during the Cold War, when most antagonists had a superpower patron with its own reasons to control them, victors had their gains whittled down by superpower compacts, and the defeated were often assisted by whichever superpower was not aligned with the victor.

One may wonder what precedents the Ecuador-Peru fighting will set. Without knowing its map-changing results, one cannot assert that other dormant Latin American border disputes will be revived. But it would be most surprising if those disputes were not now undergoing some reappraisal, if only by politicians interested in defining ultranationalist stances for themselves. Moreover, some deceleration, if not an outright reversal, is certain to occur in the downward trend in military spending by many Latin American countries. That most positive development of recent years, which yielded important political and economic benefits, is now endangered. The Ecuador-Peru war could turn out far more costly for Latin America as a whole and indirectly for the United States too than its limited dimensions might suggest.

Edward N. Luttwak

THE MEANING OF "WAR"

CAN THE United States counter perverse precedents and the new culture of wars easily started and fought without restraint? Beyond diplomacy is the controversial remedy of armed intervention, with or without a multilateral framework, with or without foreign auxiliaries. But aside from its suitability in any particular setting (in some it is unimaginable), military force collides with the general refusal of the American public to sanction interventions in place after place without end.

That political given must be accepted, but it is contingent upon the cost in U.S. casualties of a particular concept of war and particular methods of intervention—the only concepts and methods the U.S. military establishment now offers. If these could be changed drastically to minimize the exposure of U.S. military personnel to the risks of combat, the response of public opinion to proposed military interventions should also change. The United States might then do more to dissuade aggression and escalation.

Much is implicit in American political discourse, the official manuals of the U.S. military services, and the popular understanding of the very word "war" when the United States is a protagonist. Quite naturally, the various Weinberger-Powell-Cheney doctrines, which set out to define several preconditions for any decision to send U.S. military forces into combat, are based squarely, tacitly, and without discussion on the same concept of war. While the three sets of preconditions differ in detail, they all require vital, fervor-arousing U.S. national interests to be clearly threatened, and that the United States employ forces powerful enough to win not only decisively but also quickly, before the fervor abates and the nation is no longer aroused.

War fought for grand purposes is yet another product of the French and American revolutions. With some chronological laxity, however, I here label it "Napoleonic" because grand purposes often imply the decisive employment of large forces in large operations, in true Napoleonic fashion. The concept originally emerged in reaction to the typical warfare of eighteenth-century Europe, ridiculed by Napoleon and systematically criticized by Carl von Clausewitz.

While fully recognizing that the cautious methods of the prior age of warfare were congruent with their times and the habitually modest aims of what were called "cabinet wars," Clausewitz was scathing in his descriptions. Demonstrative maneuvers meant to induce enemy withdrawals without firing a shot were readily called off if serious fighting ensued. Superior forces avoided battle if there was a risk of heavy casualties even in victory. Prolonged sieges were preferred to determined assaults and circumspect pursuits to all-out exploitation in the wake of battle victories. At the strategic level, elaborately prepared offensives had unambitious objectives, promising campaigns were interrupted by early retreats into winter quarters merely to avoid further losses, and offensive performance was routinely sacrificed to the overriding priority of avoiding casualties and conserving forces for another day, with much effort expended to build and garrison linear defenses and fortifications.

Napoleon triumphed over such cautious military practices with bold strategic offensives powered by the mass and momentum of rapidly concentrated forces, and that was the kind of warfare that Clausewitz advocated. Envisaging only wars fought for great national purposes, and with the unification of Germany in mind, Clausewitz exposed the logical error of half-hearted, risk-avoiding methods likely in the long run to be more costly. To be sure, Clausewitz concurrently derived the strongest argument for strategic prudence from his insistence on the primacy of political considerations, but that did not affect his demonstration of the economy of tactical and operational boldness, a formula for efficacy that can easily become detached from its justifying context of correspondingly ambitious goals.

Complete with profound insights into the eternal mechanics and psychology of war, the teachings of Clausewitz remain unsurpassed. Along with parallel examples of the merits of risk-taking drawn from the successes of the great captains of history (a highly selective list that omits prudent victors, favoring Patton and Hannibal, for example, over Bradley or Fabius Cunctator), they pervade the professional discourse of U.S. service academies and war colleges and can easily be recognized in current field manuals and official doctrinal statements. Many such documents are prefaced by restatements of the principles of "war" (concentration, mass, momentum, etc.) that are actually in large part the Clausewitzian principles of Napoleonic war.

Both were fully appropriate to the circumstances of the two world wars and also of the Cold War as far as the planning of nonnuclear operations was concerned. Neither fits present circumstances, domestic or international. There are no threatening great powers on the current world scene, only a handful of quiescent rogue states, and many lesser wars and internal disorders that cannot arouse the nation, for none of them directly threatens the United States or its compelling interests. The preconditions of Napoleonic war-making, or for that matter of military interventions as specified in the Weinberger-Powell-Cheney doctrines, are therefore absent.

Yet its moral economy is damaged as the United States remains the attentive yet passive witness of aggressions replete with atrocities on the largest scale. Moreover, there is no doubt that the diffusion of the new culture of wars easily started and quickly escalated is damaging U.S. material interests. Commercial opportunities, not all of them small, are being lost every day wherever guns are firing, and many more could be lost in the future.

Given the performance of certain modern weapons, if military planning is appropriately modified to fully exploit their technical potential, it may be possible to emulate the casualty-avoiding methods of eighteenth-century warfare and thus conduct armed yet virtually bloodless interventions. To be sure, U.S. aims would have to be correspondingly modest and remain so, resisting all temptations to achieve more than partial, circumscribed, and often slow results as firmly as any good eighteenth-century general.

At present, by contrast, there is a profound contradiction between the prevailing military mentality, formed by the Napoleonic concept of war with its Clausewitzian adjuncts, and current exigencies. The Somalia intervention came to a sudden end after the bloody failure of a daring helicopter raid in true commando style—a normal occupational hazard of high-risk, high-payoff commando operations. But given the context at hand—a highly discretionary intervention in a country of the most marginal significance for American interests—any high-risk methods at all were completely inappropriate in principle. Nor was what happened the result of an error of judgment, still less of malfeasance. In accordance with the prevailing mentality, the senior military planners allowed a role in the Somalia undertaking to U.S. Special Operations Command, which naturally mounted its own kind of operations, which in turn inherently entail the risk of casualties.

The casualties of war were not a decisive consideration, within reasonable limits, so long as the Napoleonic concept still applied. War fought for great purposes implies a willingness to accept casualties even in large numbers. Moreover, a certain tolerance for casualties was congruent with the demography of preindustrial and early-industrial societies, whereby families had many children and losing some to disease was entirely normal. The loss of a youngster in combat, however tragic, was therefore fundamentally less unacceptable than for today's families, with their one, two, or at most three children. Each child is expected to survive into adulthood and embodies a great part of the family's emotional economy. Even in the past, the United States never had the supply of expendable soldiers that was the fuel of discretionary great power wars fought for colonial aggrandizement or yet more recondite motives. Still less is there such a supply of expendable lives at present, when all other low-birthrate, postindustrial societies refuse to sanction the casualties of any avoidable combat.

How, therefore, can armed forces, staffed by professional, salaried, pensioned, and career-minded military personnel who belong to a nation intolerant of casualties, cope with aggressors inflamed by nationalism or religious fanaticism? Yet to avoid combat and do nothing allows not only aggressive small powers such as Serbia, but even mere armed bands such as those of Somalia, to rampage or impose their victories at will.

Some view the dilemma as unprecedented and irresolvable. Actually it is neither. If we free ourselves from the Napoleonic concept to recognize the historical normality of eighteenth-century warfare, we can find many situations in which the same dilemma arose and was successfully overcome. As far back as two millennia, the professional, salaried, pensioned, and career-minded citizen-soldiers of the Roman legions routinely had to fight against warriors eager to die gloriously for tribe or religion. Already then, their superiors were far from indifferent to the casualties of combat, if only because trained troops were very costly and citizen manpower was very scarce. Augustus, famously, went to his grave still bitterly mourning the three legions Varus lost in Germany years before.

THE ROMAN SIEGE

THE ROMANS relied on several remedies to minimize their troop losses while overcoming enemies from Britain to Mesopotamia. In the first place, it was their standard practice to avoid open-field combat, especially spontaneous engagements, if at all possible, even if their forces were clearly superior. Rather than face the uncertainties of time and place, which could result in an equally unpredictable casualty toll, the Romans routinely allowed their enemies to withdraw to positions of their own choosing, even if well fortified or naturally strong. Having thus turned a fluid situation into a far more controllable set-piece encounter, the Romans would gather forces and assemble equipment and supplies to commence systematic siege operations. Even then their first priority was not to breach enemy defenses but rather to build fairly elaborate fortifications to protect their besieging units, to minimize whatever casualties enemy sallies could inflict. Overall, the siege was the medium in which the Romans could best exploit both their technological superiority in siege craft and their logistic advantage, which normally enabled them patiently to outlast the food supplies of the besieged. A purposeful, calculated patience was a signal military virtue.

Trade embargoes and armed blockades, the modern equivalents of the Roman siege, are not tactical but strategic. But so long as the Napoleonic concept prevails, it is impossible to exploit their full capacity to achieve warlike results without the casualties of war. For the presumption of an aroused nation greatly discounts any results not rapidly achieved, while the effects of embargoes and blockades are cumulative rather than immediate and may be long delayed. Moreover, the Napoleonic concept only recognizes decisive results, while the effects of embargoes and blockades are usually partial rather than complete, even if very much worth having. For example, since 1990 those means have controlled the military resurgence of Saddam Hussein's Iraq. Its armed forces have not been allowed to recover from the equipment losses of 1991 and have instead been steadily weakened as imported weapons destroyed or worn out are not replaced. True, only direct oil exports by tanker or pipeline have been denied, but the lesser quantities Iraq has been able to send out overland have not been enough for rearmament. Nor does the imminent possibility that the United Nations will lift its prohibition on Iraqi oil exports alter the effective containment, without a more active use of force, of a serious threat. Incidentally (in this case), the decisive result that only an all-out war could have achieved would have been even more temporary and indecisive, for the complete destruction of Iraq's military strength would immediately have made containing Iran's threat that much harder.

Likewise, in the former Yugoslavia, amid the utter failure of every other diplomatic or military initiative of the United Nations, European Community, or NATO, only the denial of Serbian and Montenegrin imports and exports—notoriously incomplete though it has been—has had positive effects. In addition to the certain if unmeasurable impact on Serbian and Montenegrin war capabilities, the trade embargo has moderated the conduct of Belgrade's most immoderate leadership. The embargo dissuaded at least the more blatant forms of combat and logistic support for the Serb militias of Bosnia-Herzegovina, Slavonia, and Krajina and also induced whatever slight propensity has been shown to negotiate, if only in the hope of securing the lifting of the arms embargo. The prospect of perpetuating the embargo has almost certainly helped to avert an invasion of Macedonia, still now precariously vulnerable to Serb expansion aided and abetted by Greek malevolence.

Even by the most optimistic reckoning, those results are sadly inadequate. Nevertheless, without any cost in blood or treasure, the trade embargo has achieved much more than the expensive and ineffectual U.N. armed intervention or the tens of thousands of yet more expensive NATO air patrols over Bosnia, flown by heavily armed fighter-bombers that hardly ever fight or bomb, even as the carnage below them continues.

Against those two instances of at least partial success, in the entire record of blockades and embargoes, many outright failures can be cited. But quite a few of them only came to be considered failures because of the premise that results must be rapid to be at all worthwhile. It would take a new (or rather renewed) concept of war that esteems a calculated, purposeful patience to allow the full exploitation of embargoes and blockades, or of any slow and cumulative form of combat. As it is, the Napoleonic and Clausewitzian emphasis on sheer tempo and momentum unconsciously induces an almost compulsive sense of urgency, even when there are no truly imperative reasons to act quickly. British Field Marshal Bernard Law Montgomery was not the first nor the last general to achieve success where others had failed simply by insisting on thorough preparations where others had hurriedly improvised.

A compulsive sense of urgency was much in evidence during the first weeks of the 1991 Persian Gulf War, when the systematic air attack of strategic targets in Iraq was viewed with unconcealed impatience by many of the subordinate military commanders on the scene. News accounts duly conveyed their skepticism about the value of strategic bombing and their corresponding eagerness to see the air attack diverted to Iraqi army units and other tactical targets to open the way for a ground offensive as soon as possible.

Edward N. Luttwak

The most senior officers resisted this upward pressure on the chain of command, which reflected no objective imperatives but only deeply rooted instinct as well as more obvious bureaucratic urges. But the pressure could not be completely denied. Well before strategic bombing was virtually stopped to provide air support for the ground campaign, which began on the 39th day of the war, many of the aircraft best suited to continue the methodical destruction of Iraqi research, development, production, and storage facilities for conventional and nonconventional weapons were instead diverted to attack some 4,000 individual armored vehicles.

The diversion of the air effort from strategic to tactical targets was to have unhappy consequences. In the aftermath, many important nuclear, biological, and chemical warfare installations remained undestroyed. For in spite of the great abundance of U.S. combat aircraft, less than 200 were fully equipped to attack strategic targets with precision weapons. That number, as it turned out, was simply too small to exhaust in less than 39 days a long list of targets, which included command and control, electrical supply, telecommunication, air defense, and oil refining and storage facilities, as well as air and naval bases, rail and road bridges, and any number of supply depots.

The same compulsive urgency almost certainly played some role in shaping the decision to launch the ground offensive on the 39th day of the war instead of, say, the 49th. By the former date the air campaign had thoroughly hollowed out Iraq's military strength, not least by cutting off most supplies to frontline units. Hence it cannot be argued that the decision to start the ground offensive sooner rather than later caused any more U.S. and allied casualties than the incidentals of war would in any case have claimed, the total number being so very small. But had the air campaign been prolonged just ten more days, 2,000 more sorties could have been flown against strategic targets. The novel instrument of precision air attack on a strategic scale, so slow in its methodical sequence but so effective in its cumulative results, so costly to acquire but so exceedingly economical in U.S. lives, was simply not allowed enough time to realize its full potential.

The central importance attributed in the immediate aftermath of the war to the swiftly victorious ground offensive was also suggestive of the dominant influence of the Napoleonic concept on civilian opinion. Though little more than a mopping-up operation, it resonated with the prevailing mentality much more than the air campaign because it was both rapidly executed and visibly decisive.

PATIENT AIR POWER

THE KEYprofessional argument advanced by the most senior U.S. military chiefs to reject all proposals to employ U.S. offensive air power in Bosnia rested on the implicit assumption that only rapid results are of value. After first noting that anything resembling area bombing would inevitably kill many civilians, the chiefs argued that the potential targets were simply too elusive, or too easily camouflaged in the rugged Bosnian terrain, to allow effective precision attacks. They took it for granted that any air operation would have to be swiftly concluded, or even amount to no more than a one-time attack. Any one precision air strike certainly can easily fail because the assigned targets are concealed by bad weather, are no longer where last spotted, or are successfully camouflaged. There is no doubt that weapons such as the 120-millimeter mortars much used by Serb militias to bombard Sarajevo can be quickly moved and readily camouflaged; even much more elaborate howitzers and field guns can be elusive targets.

But this argument utterly obscured the drastic difference between a one-time strike, or any brief operation for that matter, and a patiently sustained air campaign with sorties flown day after day, week after week. If one sortie fails because of dense clouds, the next one, or the one after that, will have clear visibility. If one sortie misses a howitzer just moved under cover, the next might spot another actually firing. If one sortie is called off because the target is too close to civilians, another can proceed to completion. What was the great hurry to finish an air operation quickly? The fighting in Bosnia continues even now, years after the use of U.S. air power was originally rejected on the grounds that nothing much could be achieved in a few days.

But of course the other presumption of the Napoleonic concept of war—that only decisive results are worth having—was even more consequential. As the most senior U.S. military chiefs correctly pointed out, air strikes alone could not end the war in the former Yugoslavia, nor save the Bosnian state from its enemies, nor safeguard civilians from rape, murder, or forcible deportation. Therefore, it was argued by implication, air power alone was useless. Actually it would be much worse than that because the Serb militias would immediately retaliate against U.N. troops, thereby causing the withdrawal of U.N. contingents from Bosnia, which might in turn force the United States to send its own troops.

Given the dubious assumption that U.N. troops were in fact usefully protecting vulnerable civilians, and the prior assessment that air attacks alone would be useless, the conclusion was inevitable. True, air attacks alone could not possibly end the war nor save Bosnia. But a sustained air campaign could most certainly have reduced the use of artillery against cities, a particularly devastating form of warfare. That would have sufficed to ameliorate a tragic situation and demonstrate the active concern of the United States—much less than a total remedy, but much more than nothing.

CASUALTY-FREE WARFARE

A FURTHER aspect of Roman military practice is relevant for current acquisition policies as well as tactical doctrines. It is enough to recall images of legionary troops to see how far offensive performance was deliberately sacrificed to reduce casualties. The large rectangular shield, sturdy metal helmet, full breastplate, shoulder guard, and foot grieves were so heavy that they greatly restricted agility. Legionnaires were extremely well protected but could hardly chase enemies who ran away, nor even pursue them for long if they merely retreated at a quick pace. Moreover, to offset the great weight of armor, only a short stabbing sword was issued. The Romans evidently thought it much more important to minimize their own casualties than to maximize those of the enemy.

Much better materials than iron and leather are available today, but it is symptomatic of an entirely different order of priorities that till now very little research and development funding has been allocated to advanced body armor. In fact the best such items now available have been privately developed for sale to law enforcement agencies.

The modern equivalent of Roman fortifications is not to build walls or forts with modern techniques, but rather to emulate the underlying Roman priorities. That applies to weapons as much as tactics. Most notably, current cost-effectiveness criteria do not yet reflect the current sensitivity to casualties. In setting overall budget priorities, alternative force categories—ground, maritime, and air—are still evaluated by cost and combat performance, without treating casualty exposure as a coequal consideration. Yet the risk of suffering casualties is routinely the decisive constraint, while the exposure to casualties for different kinds of forces varies quite drastically, from the minimum of offensive air power to the maximum of army and marine infantry. Also revealing is the entire debate on stealth aircraft, which are specifically designed to evade radar and infrared detection. When judged very expensive, stealth planes are implicitly compared to non-stealth aircraft of equivalent range and payload, not always including the escorts the latter also require, which increase greatly the number of fliers at risk. Missing from such calculations is any measure of the overall foreign policy value of acquiring a means of casualty-free warfare by unescorted bomber, a weapon of circumscribed application but global reach. Casualty avoidance is not yet valued at current market prices.

Present circumstances call for even more than a new concept of war, but for a new mentality that would inject unheroic realism into military endeavor precisely to overcome excessive timidity in employing military means. A new post-Napoleonic and post-Clausewitzian concept of war would require not only a patient disposition, but also a modest one, so as to admit the desirability of partial results when doing more would be too costly in U.S. lives, and doing nothing is too damaging to world order and U.S. self-respect.@

Pivotal States
and U.S. Strategy

Robert Chase, Emily Hill, and Paul Kennedy

THE NEW DOMINOES

HALF A DECADE after the collapse of the Soviet Union, American policymakers and intellectuals are still seeking new principles on which to base national strategy. The current debate over the future of the international order—including predictions of the "end of history," a "clash of civilizations," a "coming anarchy," or a "borderless world"—has failed to generate agreement on what shape U.S. policy should take. However, a single overarching framework may be inappropriate for understanding today's disorderly and decentralized world. America's security no longer hangs on the success or failure of containing communism. The challenges are more diffuse and numerous. As a priority, the United States must manage its delicate relationships with Europe, Japan, Russia, and China, the other major players in world affairs. However, America's national interest also requires stability in important parts of the developing world. Despite congressional pressure to reduce or eliminate overseas assistance, it is vital that America focus its efforts on a small number of countries whose fate is uncertain and whose future will profoundly affect their surrounding regions. These are the pivotal states.

The idea of a pivotal state—a hot spot that could not only determine the fate of its region but also affect international stability—has a distinguished pedigree reaching back to the British geographer Sir Halford Mackinder in the 1900s and earlier. The classic example of a pivotal state throughout the nineteenth century was Turkey, the epicenter of the so-

ROBERT CHASE is a Ph.D. candidate in economics at Yale University. EMILY HILL is a Ph.D. candidate in history at Yale University. PAUL KENNEDY is Professor of History at Yale University.

called Eastern Question; because of Turkey's strategic position, the disintegration of the Ottoman Empire posed a perennial problem for British and Russian policymakers.

Twentieth-century American policymakers employed their own version of a pivotal states theory. Statesmen from Eisenhower and Acheson to Nixon and Kissinger continually referred to a country succumbing to communism as a potential "rotten apple in a barrel" or a "falling domino." Although the domino theory was never sufficiently discriminative—it worsened America's strategic overextension—its core was about supporting pivotal states to prevent their fall to communism and the consequent fall of neighboring states.

Because the U.S. obsession with faltering dominoes led to questionable policies from Vietnam to El Salvador, the theory now has a bad reputation. But the idea itself—that of identifying specific countries as more important than others, for both regional stability and American interests—is sensible. The United States should adopt a discriminative policy toward the developing world, concentrating its energies on pivotal states rather than spreading its attention and resources over the globe.

Indeed, the domino theory may now fit U.S. strategic needs better than it did during the Cold War. The new dominoes, or pivotal states, no longer need assistance against an external threat from a hostile political system; rather, the danger is that they will fall prey to internal disorder. A decade ago, when the main threat to American interests in the developing world was the possibility that nations would align with the Soviets, the United States faced a clear-cut enemy. This enemy captured the American imagination in a way that impending disorder does not. Yet chaos and instability may prove a greater and more insidious threat to American interests than communism ever was. With its migratory outflows, increasing conflict due to the breakdown of political structures, and disruptions in trade patterns, chaos undoubtedly affects bordering states. Reacting with interventionist measures only after a crisis in one state threatens an important region is simply too late. Further, Congress and the American public would likely not accept such actions, grave though the consequences might be to U.S. interests. Preventive assistance to pivotal states to reduce the chance of collapse would better serve American interests.

A strategy of rigorously discriminate assistance to the developing world would benefit American foreign policy in a number of ways. First, as the world's richest nation, with vast overseas holdings and the most to lose from global instability, the United States needs a conservative strategy. Like the British Empire in the nineteenth and early twentieth centuries, the interests of the United States lie in the status quo. Such a strategy places the highest importance on relations with the other great powers: decisions about the expansion of NATO or preserving amicable relations with Russia, China, Japan, and the major European powers must remain primary. The United States must also safeguard several special allies, such as Saudi Arabia, Kuwait, South Korea, and Israel, for strategic and domestic political reasons.

Second, a pivotal states policy would help U.S. policymakers deal with what Sir Michael Howard, in another context, nicely described as "the heavy and ominous breathing of a parsimonious and pacific electorate." American policymakers, themselves less and less willing to contemplate foreign obligations, are acutely aware that the public is extremely cautious about and even hostile toward overseas engagements. While the American public may not reject all such commitments, it does resist intervention in areas that appear peripheral to U.S. interests. A majority also believes, without knowing the relatively small percentages involved, that foreign aid is a major drain on the federal budget and often wasted through fraud, duplication, and high operating costs. Few U.S. politicians are willing to risk unpopularity by contesting such opinions, and many Republican critics have played to this mood by attacking government policies that imply commitments abroad. Statesmen responsible for outlining U.S. foreign policy might have a better chance of persuading a majority of Congress and the American public that a policy of selective engagement is both necessary and feasible.

Finally, a pivotal states strategy might help bridge the conceptual and political divide in the national debate between "old" and "new" security issues. The mainstream in policy circles still considers new security issues peripheral; conversely, those who focus on migration, overpopulation, or environmental degradation resist the realist emphasis on power and military and political security.

In truth, neither the old nor the new approach will suffice. The traditional realist stress on military and political security is simply inadequate—it does not pay sufficient attention to the new threats to American national interests. The threats to the pivotal states are not communism or aggression but rather overpopulation, migration, environmental degradation, ethnic conflict, and economic instability, all phenomena that traditional security forces find hard to address. The "dirty" industrialization of the developing world, unchecked population growth and attendant migratory pressures, the rise of powerful drug cartels, the flow of illegal arms, the eruption of ethnic conflict, the flourishing of terrorist groups, the spread of deadly new viruses, and turbulence in emerging markets—a laundry list of newer problems—must also concern Americans, if only because their spillover effects can hurt U.S. interests.

Yet the new interpretation of security, with its emphasis on holistic and global issues, is also inadequate. Those who point to such new threats to international stability often place secondary importance (if that) on U.S. interests; indeed, they are usually opposed to invoking the national interest to further their cause. For example, those who criticized the Clinton administration in the summer of 1994 for not becoming more engaged in the Rwandan crisis paid little attention to the relative insignificance of Rwanda's stability for American interests. The universal approach common to many advocates of global environmental protection or human rights, commendable in principle, does not discriminate between human rights abuses in Haiti, where proximity and internal instability made intervention possible and even necessary, and similar abuses in Somalia, where the United States had few concrete interests.

Furthermore, the new security approach cannot make a compelling case to the American public for an internationalist foreign policy. The public does not sense the danger in environmental and demographic pressures that erode stability over an extended period, even if current policies, or lack thereof, make this erosion inexorable and at some point irreversible. Finally, the global nature of the new security threats makes it tempting to downplay national governments as a means to achieving solutions.

A pivotal states strategy, in contrast, would encourage integration of new security issues into a traditional, state-centered framework and lend greater clarity to the making of foreign policy. This integration may make some long-term consequences of the new security threats more tangible and manageable. And it would confirm the importance of working chiefly through state governments to ensure stability while addressing the new security issues that make these states pivotal.

HOW TO IDENTIFY A PIVOT

ACCORDING TO which criteria should the pivotal states be selected? A large population and an important geographical location are two requirements. Economic potential is also critical, as recognized by the U.S. Commerce Department's recent identification of the "big emerging markets" that offer the most promise to American business. Physical size is a necessary but not sufficient condition: Zaire comprises an extensive tract, but its fate is not vital to the United States.

What really defines a pivotal states is its capacity to affect regional and international stability. A pivotal state is so important regionally that its collapse would spell transboundary mayhem: migration, communal violence, pollution, disease, and so on. A pivotal state's steady economic progress and stability, on the other hand, would bolster its region's economic vitality and political soundness and benefit American trade and investment.

For the present, the following should be considered pivotal states: Mexico and Brazil; Algeria, Egypt, and South Africa; Turkey; India and Pakistan; and Indonesia. These states' prospects vary widely. India's potential for success, for example, is considerably greater than Algeria's; Egypt's potential for chaos is greater than Brazil's. But all face a precarious future, and their success or failure will powerfully influence the future of the surrounding areas and affect American interests. This theory of pivotal states must not become a mantra, as the domino theory did, and the list of states could change. But the concept itself can provide a necessary and useful framework for devising American strategy toward the developing world.

A WORLD TURNING ON PIVOTS

To UNDERSTAND this idea in concrete terms, consider the Mexican crisis a year ago. Mexico's modernization has created strains between the central and local governments and difficulties with the unions and the poorest groups in the countryside, and it has damaged the environment. Like the other pivotal states, Mexico is delicately balanced between progress and turmoil.

Given the publicity and political debate surrounding the Clinton administration's rescue plan for Mexico, most Americans probably understood that their southern neighbor is special, even if they were disturbed by the means employed to rescue it. A collapse of the peso and the consequent ruin of the Mexican economy would have weakened the U.S. dollar, hurt exports, and caused convulsions throughout Latin America's

Southern Cone Common Market and other emerging markets. Dramatically illustrating the potency of new security threats to the United States, economic devastation in Mexico would have increased the northward flow of illegal immigrants and further strained the United States' overstretched educational and social services. Violent social chaos in Mexico could spill over into this country. As many bankers remarked during the peso crisis, Mexico's troubles demonstrated the impossibility of separating "there" from "here."

Because of Mexico's proximity and its increasing links with the United States, American policymakers clearly needed to give it special attention. As evidenced by the North American Free Trade Agreement, they have. But other select states also require close American attention.

EGYPT

EGYPT'S LOCATION has historically made its stability and political alignment critical to both regional development and relationships between the great powers. In recent decades, its proximity to important oil regions and its involvement in the Arab-Israeli peace process, which is important for the prosperity of many industrialized countries, has enhanced its contribution to stability in the Middle East and North Africa. Furthermore, the government of President Muhammad Hosni Mubarak has provided a bulwark against perhaps the most significant long-term threat in the region—radical Islamic fundamentalism.

The collapse of the current Egyptian regime might damage American interests more than the Iranian revolution did. The Arab-Israeli peace process, the key plank of U.S. foreign policy in this region for the past 20 years, would suffer serious, perhaps irreparable, harm. An unstable Egypt would undermine the American diplomatic plan of isolating fundamentalist "rogue" states in the region and encourage extremist opposition to governments everywhere from Algeria to Turkey. The fall of the Mubarak government could well lead Saudi Arabia to reevaluate its pro-Western stance. Under such conditions, any replay of Operation Desert Storm or similar military intervention in the Middle East on behalf of friendly countries such as Kuwait or Jordan would be extremely difficult, if not impossible. Finally, the effect on oil and financial markets worldwide could be enormous.

Robert S. Chase, Emily B. Hill, and Paul Kennedy

Egypt's future is not only vital, but very uncertain. While some signs point to increasing prosperity and stability—birth rates have declined, the United States recently forgave $7 billion of debt, and Egypt's international reserves reached $16 billion in 1995—the preponderance of evidence paints a dimmer picture. Jealously guarding its power base and wary that further privatization would produce large numbers of resentful former state employees, the government fears losingcontrol over the economy. Growth rates lurch fitfully upward and, although reform has improved most basic economic indicators, it has also widened the gap between rich and poor. Roughly one-third of the population now lives in poverty, up from 20-25 percent in 1990.

A harsh crackdown on fundamentalism has reduced the most serious short-term threat to the Mubarak regime, but a long-term solution may prove more elusive. The government's brutal attack on the fundamentalist movement may ultimately fuel Islam's cause by alienating the professional middle class; such a policy has already greatly strengthened the more moderate Muslim Brotherhood and radicalized the extremist fringe.

Environmental and population problems are growing. Despite the gradually decreasing birthrate, the population is increasing by about one million every nine months, straining the country's natural resources, and is forecast to reach about 94 million by 2025.

Recognizing Egypt's significance and fragility, successive U.S. administrations have made special provisions to maintain its stability. In 1995 Egypt received $2.4 billion from the U.S. government, making it the second-largest recipient of American assistance, after Israel. That allocation is primarily the result of the Camp David accords and confirms Egypt's continuing importance in U.S. Middle East policy. Current attempts by American isolationists to cut these funds should be strongly resisted. On the other hand, the U.S. government and Congress should seriously consider redirecting American aid. F-16 fighters can do little to help Egypt handle its internal difficulties, but assistance to improve infrastructure, education, and the social fabric would ease the country's troubles.

INDONESIA

WHILE EGYPT'sprospects for stability are tenuous, Indonesia's future appears brighter. By exercising considerable control over the population and the economy for the last several decades, Indonesia's authoritarian regime has engineered dramatic economic growth, now expected to be about 7 percent annually for the rest of the decade. Poverty rates have dropped drastically, and a solid middle class has emerged. At first glance, Indonesia's development has been a startling success. However, the government now confronts strains generated by its own efforts.

Along with incomes, education levels, and health status, Indonesia's population is increasing dramatically. With the fourth-largest population in the world and an extra three million people added each year, the country is projected to reach 260 million inhabitants by 2025. The main island of Java, one of the most densely populated places on earth, can scarcely accommodate the new bodies. In response, the government is forcing many citizens to migrate to other islands. This resettlement program is the focal point for a host of other tensions concerning human rights and the treatment of minorities. The government's brutal handling of the separatist movement in East Timor continues to hinder its efforts to gain international respect. President Suharto's regime has made a point of cooperating with Chinese entrepreneurs to boost economic expansion, but ethnic differences remain entrenched. Finally, the government's favoring of specific businesses has produced deep-rooted corruption.

Because of the government's tight control, it can maintain stability even while pursuing these questionable approaches to handling its people. However, as a more sophisticated middle class emerges, Indonesians are less willing to accept the existing concentration of economic and political power. These opposing forces, one for continued central control and one for more dispersed political power, will clash when Suharto leaves office, probably after the 1998 elections.

A reasonable scenario for Indonesia would be the election of a government that shares power more broadly, with greater respect for human rights and press freedoms. The new regime would maintain Indonesia's openness to foreign trade and investment, and it would end favoritism toward certain companies. Better educated, better paid, and urbanized for a generation, Indonesians would have fewer children per family. Indonesia would continue its leadership role in the Association of Southeast Asian Nations (ASEAN) and the Asia-Pacific Economic Cooperation forum (APEC), helping foster regional growth and stability.

The possibility remains, however, that the transfer of power in Jakarta could trigger political and economic instability, as it did in 1965 at the end of President Sukarno's rule. A new regime might find it more difficult to overawe the people while privately profiting from the economy. Elements of the electorate could lash out in frustration. Riots would then jeopardize Indonesia's growth and regional leadership, and by that stage the United States could do nothing more than attempt to rescue its citizens from the chaos.

Instability in Indonesia would affect peace and prosperity across Southeast Asia. Its archipelago stretches across key shipping lanes, its oil and other businesses attract Japanese and U.S. investment, and its stable economic condictions and open trade policies set an example for ASEAN, APEC, and the region as a whole. If Indonesia, as Southeast Asia's fulcrum, falls into chaos, it is hard to envisage the region prospering. It is equally hard to imagine general distress if Indonesia booms economically and maintains political stability.

Despite the difficulty, the United States must have a strategy for encouraging Indonesia's stability. Part of this will involve close cooperation with Japan, which is by far the largest donor to Indonesian development. A more sensitive aspect of the strategy will be encouraging the regime to respect human rights and ethnic differences. The strategy also calls for calibrated pressure on Indonesia to decrease its widespread corruption, which in any case is required to achieve the country's full integration into the international business world.

BRAZIL

B RAZIL BORDERS every country in South America except Ecuador and Chile, and its physical size, complex society, and huge population of 155 million people are more than enough to qualify it as a pivotal state.

Brazil's economy appears to be recovering from its 1980s crisis, although the indicators for the future are inconsistent. President Fernando Henrique Cardoso's proposals for economic reform, which include deregulation and increased openness to foreign investment in key industries, have advanced in Brazil's congress. Many basic social and economic indexes point to a generally improving quality of life, including the highest industrial growth since the 1970s (6.4 percent in 1994), declining birth and death rates, increasing life expectancy, and an expanding urban infrastructure. In the longer term, however, Brazil must address extreme economic inequality, poor educational standards, and extensive malnutrition. These realities, together with a burgeoning current account deficit and post–peso crisis skittishness, help diminish investor confidence.

Were Brazil to founder, the consequences from both an environmental and an economic point of view would be grave. The Amazon basin contains the largest tropical rain forest in the world, boasting unequaled biodiversity. Apart from aesthetic regrets about its destruction, the practical consequences are serious. The array of plants and trees in the Amazon is an important source of natural pharmaceuticals; deforestation may also spread diseases as the natural hosts of viruses and bacteria are displaced to other regions.

A social and political collapse would directly affect significant U.S. economic interests and American investors. Brazil's fate is inextricably linked to that of the entire South American region, a region that before its debt and inflation crises in the 1970s bought large amounts of U.S. goods and is now potentially the fastest-growing market for American business over the decades to come. In sum, were Brazil to succeed in stabilizing over the long term, reducing the massive gap between its rich and poor, further opening its markets, and privatizing often inefficient state-run industries, it could be a powerful engine for the regional economy and a stimulus to U.S. prosperity. Were it to fail, Americans would feel the consequences.

APARTHEID'S END makes South Africa's transition particularly dramatic. So far, President Nelson Mandela's reconciliation government has set an inspiring example of respect for ethnic differences, good governance, and prudent nurturing of the country's economic potential. In contrast to other conflicts, in which different groups have treated each other with so much acrimony that they could not negotiate, the administration has successfully overcome some of its political divisions: it includes both former apartheid president Frederik Willem de Klerk and Zulu Chief Mangosuthu Buthelezi. Moreover, South Africa is blessed with a strong infrastructure, a sound currency, and vast natural resources. These assets make its economy larger and more vital than any other on the continent, accounting for a colossal 75 percent of the southern

African region's economic output. No longer an international pariah, it is working to develop robust trade and financial links around the region and the globe. A hub for these connections, South Africa could stimulate growth throughout the southern cone of Africa.

There are indications, however, that South Africa could succumb to political instability, ethnic strife, and economic stagnation. Power-sharing at the cabinet level belies deep ethnic divisions. Any one of several fissures could collapse this collaboration, plunging the country into civil war. Afrikaner militias may grow increasingly intransigent, traditional tribal leaders could raise arms against their diminished influence, and when Mandela no longer leads the African National Congress, the party may abandon its commitment to ethnic reconciliation.

As Mandela's government struggles to improve black living standards and soothe ethnic tensions, the legacy of apartheid creates a peculiar dilemma. It will be hard to meet understandable black expectations of equity in wages, education, and health, given the country's budget deficits and unstable tax base. As racial inequalities persist, blacks are likely to grow impatient. Yet if whites feel they are paying a disproportionate share for improved services for blacks, they might flee the country, taking with them the prospects for increased foreign direct investment.

While the primary threats to South Africa's stability are internal, its effectiveness in containing them will have repercussions beyond its borders. Even before apartheid ended, South Africa had enormous influence over the region's political and economic development, from supporting insurgencies throughout the "front-line states" to providing mining jobs for migrant workers from those same countries. If South Africa achieves the economic and political potential within its grasp, it will be a wellspring of regional political stability and economic growth. If it prospers, it can demonstrate to other ethnically tortured regions a path to stability through democratization, reconciliation, and steadily increasing living standards. Alternatively, if it fails to handle its many challenges, it will suck its neighbors into a whirlpool of self-defeating conflict.

Although controlling the sea-lanes around the Cape of Good Hope would be important, especially if widespread trouble were to erupt in the Middle East, American strategic interests are not otherwise endangered in southern Africa. Yet because South Africa is the United States' largest trading partner in Africa and possesses vast economic potential, its fate would affect American trading and financial interests that have invested there. It would also destabilize key commodity prices, especially in the gold, diamond, and ore markets. More generally, instability in South Africa, as in Brazil and Indonesia, would cast a large shadow over confidence in emerging markets.

American policy toward South Africa should reflect its importance as a pivotal state. While recognizing South Africa's desire to solve its problems without external interference, the United States should promote South Africa's economic and political stability. Of $10.5 billion in American economic aid given in 1995, a mere one percent ($135 million) was for South Africa. A strategy that acknowledges this nation's importance to American interests would surely be less parsimonious.

ALGERIA AND TURKEY

ALGERIA'S geographical position makes its political future of great concern to American allies in Europe, especially France and Spain. A civil war and the replacement of the present regime by extremists would affect the security of the Mediterranean sea-lanes, international oil and gas markets, and, as in the case of Egypt, the struggle between moderate and radical elements in the Islamic world. All the familiar pressures of rapid population growth and drift to the coastal cities, environmental damage, increasing dependence on food imports, and extremely high youth unemployment are evident. Levels of violence remain high as Algerian government forces struggle to crush the Islamist guerrilla movement.

While a moderate Islamist government might prove less disturbing than the West fears, a bloody civil war or the accession of a radical, anti-Western regime would be very serious. Spain, Italy, and France depend heavily on Algerian oil and gas and would sorely miss their investments, and the resulting turbulence in the energy markets would certainly affect American consumers. The flood of middle-class, secular Algerians attempting to escape the bloodshed and enter France or other parts of southern Europe would further test immigration policies of the European Union (EU). The effects on Algeria's neighbors, Morocco and Tunisia, would be even more severe and encourage radical Islamic elements everywhere. Could Egypt survive if Algeria, Morocco, Tunisia, and Muammar al-Qaddafi's Libya collaborated to achieve fundamentalist goals? Rumors of an Algerian atomic bomb are probably premature, but the collapse of the existing regime would undoubtedly reduce security in the entire western Mediterranean. All the more reason for the United States to buttress the efforts of the International Monetary Fund and for the Europeans to improve Algeria's well-being and encourage a political settlement.

Although Turkey is not as politically or economically fragile as Algeria, its strategic importance may be even greater. At a multifold crossroads between East and West, North and South, Christendom and Islam, Turkey has the potential to influence countries thousands of miles from the Bosporus. The southeast keystone of NATO during the Cold War and an early (if repeatedly postponed) applicant to enlarged EU membership, Turkey enjoys solid economic growth and middle-class prosperity. However, it also shows many of the difficulties that worry other pivotal states: population and environmental pressures, severe ethnic minority challenges, and the revival of radical Islamic fundamentalism, all of which test the country's young democratic institutions and assumptions. There are also a slew of external problems, ranging from bitter rivalries with Greece over Cyprus, various nearby islands' territorial boundaries, and Macedonia, to the developing quarrel with Syria and Iraq over control of the Euphrates water supply, to delicate relationships with the Muslim-dominated states of Central Asia. A prosperous, democratic, tolerant Turkey is a beacon for the entire region; a Turkey engulfed by civil wars and racial and religious hatreds, or nursing ambitions to interfere abroad, would hurt American interests in innumerable ways and concern everyone from pro-NATO strategists to friends of Israel.

INDIA AND PAKISTAN

CONSIDERED separately, the challenges facing the two great states of South Asia are daunting enough. Each confronts a population surge that is forecast to take Pakistan's total (123 million in 1990) to 276 million by 2025, and India's (853 million in 1990) to a staggering 1.45 billion, thus equaling China's projected population. While such growth taxes rural environments by causing the farming of marginal lands, deforestation, and depletion of water resources, the urban population explosion is even more worrisome. With 46 percent of Pakistan's and 35 percent of India's population under 15 years old, according to 1990 census figures, tens of millions of young people enter the job market each year; the inadequate opportunities for them further strain the social fabric. All this forms an ominous backdrop to rising tensions, as militant Hindus and Muslims, together a full fifth of the population, challenge India's democratic traditions, and Islamic forces stoke nationalist passions across Pakistan.

The shared borders and deep-rooted rivalry of India and Pakistan place these pivotal states in a more precarious position than, for example, Brazil or South Africa. With three wars between them since each gained independence, each continues to arm against the other and quarrel fiercely over Kashmir, Pakistan's potential nuclear capabilities and missile programs, and other issues. This jostling fuels their mutual ethnic-cum-religious fears and could produce another bloody conflict that neither government could control. What effect a full-scale war would have on the Pakistan-China entente is hard to predict, but the impact of such a contest would likely spread from Kashmir into Afghanistan and farther afield, and Pakistan could find support in the Muslim world. For many reasons, and perhaps especially the nuclear weapons stakes, the United States has a vital interest in encouraging South Asia's internal stability and external peace.

Could this short list of important states in the developing and emerging-markets regions of the globe include others? Possibly. This selection of pivotal states is not carved in stone, and new candidates could emerge over the next decades. Having an exact list is less important than initiating a debate over why, from the standpoint of U.S. national interests, some states in the developing world are more important than others.

BETTER WISE THAN WIDE

THE UNITED STATES needs a policy toward the developing world that does not spread American energies, attention, and resources too thinly across the globe, but rejects isolationist calls to write it off. This is a realistic policy, both strategically and politically. Strategically, it would permit the United States, as the country that can make the greatest contribution to world security, to focus on supporting pivotal states. Politically, given the jaundiced view of Americans and their representatives toward overseas engagements, a strategy of discrimination is the strongest argument against an even greater withdrawal from the developing world than is now threatened.

As the above case studies suggest, each pivotal state grapples with an intricate set of interrelated problems. In such an environment, the

Robert S. Chase, Emily B. Hill, and Paul Kennedy

United States has few clear-cut ways to help pivotal states succeed. Therefore, it must develop a subtle, comprehensive strategy, encompassing all aspects of American interaction with each one. Those strategies should include appropriate focusing of U.S. Agency for International Development assistance, promoting trade and investment, strengthening relationships with the country's leaders, bolstering country-specific intelligence capabilities and foreign service expertise, and coordinating the actions of government agencies that can influence foreign policy. In short, the United States must use all the resources at its disposal to buttress the stability of key states around the globe, working to prevent calamity rather than react to it. Apart from avoiding a great-power war, nothing in foreign policy could be more important.

This focus on the pivotal states inevitably means that developing states not deemed pivotal would receive diminished attention, energy, and resources. This will seem unfair to many, since each of the pivotal states examined above enjoys a higher per capita GDP than extremely poor nations like Mali and Ethiopia. Ideally, U.S. assistance to the entire developing world would significantly increase, but that will not happen soon. A pragmatic refocusing of American aid is better than nothing at all being given to the developing world, which may happen if the isolationist mood intensifies.

Such a refocusing could improve the American public's confidence that its money can be used effectively abroad. Relative to what other states give for development, the American contribution is declining. By continuing to spread those resources across a broad swath of developing countries, the United States might further diminish the impact of its assistance in many countries. In contrast, concentrating on a few pivotal states would increase American influence in them and improve the chances of convincing the public to spend resources overseas.

Current patterns of assistance to developing and emerging countries do not reflect American global security interests and in many cases seem glaringly inconsistent with U.S. strategic priorities. While conceding that by far the largest amounts of American aid will go to Israel and Egypt, is it not curious that India, like South Africa, receives less than one percent of total U.S. assistance? Pakistan receives virtually nothing. Algeria receives nothing. Brazil is given one-fifth of the aid awarded to Bolivia. Turkey gets less than Ethiopia (although, like Egypt, Ankara is given a large amount of military assistance that is hard to explain in the post–Cold War environment). Surely this requires serious examination?

In changing these patterns, diplomatic and political objections will be inevitable. Questions will arise about countries not on the list, particularly when one of them faces a crisis. Some will plead that exceptions be made for states that have been encouraged to undertake internal political changes, like Haiti, El Salvador, and the Philippines. Foreign service professionals will caution against making this strategy part of the declared policy of the United States, for that could indicate likely American reactions in a crisis. The more critics raise these problems, the more controversial this idea will become.

However, the pivotal states strategy merits such a debate, and it is high time for such a policy discussion to begin. As Mackinder pointed out, democracies find it difficult to think strategically in times of peace. All the above-mentioned problems and reservations, far from weakening the case for helping pivotal states, point to the importance of identifying how better to order U.S. policies in different parts of the world. A debate over pivotal states would also provide a way of checking the extent to which American agencies already carry out a discriminative strategy and the degree to which they recognize that the traditional types of external threats are not the only sources of danger to countries important to U.S. interests.

Would this formula solve all of America's foreign policy challenges? By no means. Priority should always be given to managing relations with the other great powers. In view of the international convulsions of the past 10 years, who would be rash enough to predict American relations with Russia, Japan, and China a decade or more hence and the dire implications if they go badly? Yet even if those countries remain our primary concern, the developing world still needs a place in U.S. global strategy. By identifying pivotal states to Congress and the public and providing the greatest possible support to those countries, this strategy has a greater chance of coherence and predictability than vague and indiscriminate assurances of good will to all developing countries, large and small. America's concern about traditional security threats would then be joined by a heightened awareness of the newer, nonmilitary dangers to important countries in the developing world and the serious repercussions of their collapse. Whichever administration steers the United States into the next century, American priorities would be ordered, and its foreign policy toward the developing world would have a focus—that of supporting those pivotal states whose future affects the fate of much of the planet.☯

On American Principles

George F. Kennan

AT A LARGE dinner given in New York in recognition of his ninetieth birthday, the author of these lines ventured to say that what our country needed at this point was not primarily policies, "much less a single policy." What we needed, he argued, were principles—sound principles—"principles that accorded with the nature, the needs, the interests, and the limitations of our country." This rather cryptic statement could surely benefit from a few words of elucidation.

The place that principle has taken in the conduct of American foreign policy in past years and decades can perhaps best be explained by a single example from American history. In the aftermath of the Napoleonic wars, and particularly in the period beginning about 1815-25, there set in a weakening of the ties that had previously held the Spanish empire together, and demands were raised by certain of the American colonies for complete independence. Pressure was brought on Washington to take the lead not only in recognizing their independence at an early stage, but also in giving them political and presumably military aid in their efforts to consolidate their independence in the face of whatever resistance might be put up by the Spanish government.

These questions presented themselves with particular intensity when James Monroe was president (1817-25). At that time the office of secretary of state was occupied by John Quincy Adams. In view of his excep-

GEORGE F. KENNAN is Professor Emeritus in the School of Historical Studies at the Institute for Advanced Study in Princeton, N.J. This is his nineteenth article for *Foreign Affairs*. His first, "The Sources of Soviet Conduct," appeared in July 1947 under the pseudonym X. Copyright 1995 by George F. Kennan.

tional qualities and experience, and the high respect with which he was held in Washington and throughout the country, much of the burden of designing the U.S. response to those pressures rested on him.

Adams realized that the U.S. historical experience left no choice but to welcome and give moral support to these South American peoples in their struggle for the recognition and consolidation of their independence. But he had little confidence in the ability of the new revolutionary leaders to shape these communities at any early date into mature, orderly, and firmly established states. For this reason, he was determined that America not be drawn too deeply into their armed conflicts with Spain, domestic political squabbles, or sometimes complicated relationships with their neighbors. Adams took this position, incidentally, not just with regard to the emerging South American countries, but also in relation to similar conflicts in Europe, particularly the efforts of Greek patriots to break away from the Turkish empire and establish an independent state.

These attitudes on Adams' part did not fail to meet with opposition in portions of the American political establishment. Some people, including the influential speaker of the House, Henry Clay, remembering America's own recent struggle for independence, felt strongly that the United States should take an active part in the similar struggles of other peoples. This, of course, was directly opposed to Adams' views. For this reason, Adams felt the need to take the problem to a wider audience and enlist public support for his views. In 1823, when he was invited by a committee of citizens to deliver a Fourth of July address in the nation's capital, he promptly agreed. The address was delivered in the premises of the House of Representatives, although not before a formal session of that body. The talk was presented as a personal statement, not an official one; and Adams took care to see that the text was printed and made widely available to the public.

A considerable part of the address was devoted to the questions I have just mentioned. On this subject Adams had some firm views. America, he said, had always extended to these new candidates for statehood "the hand of honest friendship, of equal freedom, and of generous reciprocity." It had spoken to them in "the language of equal liberty, of equal justice, and of equal rights." It had respected their independence. It had abstained from interference with their undertakings even when these were being conducted "for principles to which she [America] clings, as to the last vital drop that visits the heart." Why? Because, he explained, "America goes not abroad in search of monsters to destroy. She is the well-wisher to the freedom and independence of all. She is the champion and vindicator only of her own. She will recommend the general cause by the countenance of her voice, and the benignant sympathy of her example. She well knows that by once enlisting under other banners than her own, were they even the banners of foreign independence, she would involve herself beyond the power of extrication, in all the wars of interest and intrigue, of individual avarice, envy, and ambition, which assumed the colors and usurped the standards of freedom .... She might become the dictatress of the world. She would be no longer the ruler of her own spirit."

The relevance of this statement to many current problems—in such places as Iraq, Lebanon, Somalia, Bosnia, Rwanda, and even Haiti—is obvious. But that is not the reason why attention is being drawn to the statement at this point. What Adams was doing in those passages of his address was enunciating a principle of American foreign policy: namely, that, while it was "the well-wisher to the freedom and independence of all," America was also "the champion and vindicator only of her own." Those words seem to provide as clear an example as any of what the term "principle" might mean in relation to the diplomacy of this country or any other.

THE IDEAL VS. REALITY

HOW, THEN, using Adams' statement as a model, would the term "principle" be defined? One might say that a principle is a general rule of conduct by which a given country chooses to abide in the conduct of its relations with other countries. There are several aspects of the term, one or two of them touched on in this definition, others not, that require elucidation.

A principle was just defined as a general rule of conduct. That means that whoever adopts a principle does not specify any particular situation, problem, or bilateral relationship to which this rule should apply. It is designed to cover the entirety of possible or presumptive situations. It merely defines certain limits, positive and negative, within which policy, when those situations present themselves, ought to operate.

A principle, then, is a rule of conduct. But it is not an absolute one. The possibility is not precluded that situations might arise—unforeseeable situations, in particular—to which the adopted principle might not seem applicable or to the meeting of which the resources of the government in question were clearly inadequate. In such cases, exceptions might have to be made. This is not, after all, a perfect world. People make mistakes in judgment. And there is always the unforeseeable and unexpected.

But as new situations and challenges present themselves, and as government is confronted with the necessity of devising actions or policies with which to meet them, established principle is something that should have the first and the most authoritative claim on the attention and respect of the policymaker. Barring special circumstances, principle should be automatically applied, and whoever proposes to set it aside or violate it should explain why such violation seems unavoidable.

Second, a principle is, by definition, self-engendered. It is not something that requires, or would even admit of, any sort of communication, negotiation, or formal agreement with another government. In the case of the individual person (because individuals have principles, just as governments do), the principles that guide his life are a matter of conscience and self-respect. They flow from the individual's view of himself, the nature of his inner commitments, and his concept of the way he ought to behave if he is to be at peace with himself.

Now, the principles of a government are not entirely the same as those of an individual. The individual, in choosing his principles, engages only himself. He is at liberty to sacrifice his own practical interests in the service of some higher and more unselfish ideal. But this sort of sacrifice is one that a responsible government, and a democratic government in particular, is unable to take upon itself. It is an agent, not a principal. It is only a representative of others.

When a government speaks, it speaks not only for itself but for the people of the country. It cannot play fast and loose with their interests. Yet a country, too, can have a predominant collective sense of itself—what sort of a country it conceives itself or would like itself to be—and what sort of behavior would fit that concept. The place where this self-image finds its most natural reflection is in the principles that a country chooses to adopt and, to the extent possible, to follow. Principle represents, in other words, the ideal, if not always, alas, the reality, of the rules and restraints a country adopts. Once established, those rules and restraints require no explanation or defense to others. They are one's own business.

A drawing that appeared in *The New Yorker* magazine many years ago showed a cringing subordinate standing before the desk of an irate officer, presumably a colonel, who was banging the desk with his fist and saying: "There is no reason, damn it; it's just our policy."

Well, as a statement about policy, this was ridiculous. But had the colonel been referring to a principle instead of a policy, the statement might not have been so out of place. It would not be unusual, for example, for someone in authority in Washington today to say to the representative of a foreign government, when the situation warranted it, "I am sorry, but for us, this is a matter of principle, and I am afraid we will have to go on from there."

Let me also point out that principles can have negative as well as positive aspects. There can be certain things that a country can make it a matter of principle not to do. In many instances these negative aspects of principle may be more important than the positive ones. The positive ones normally suggest or involve action; actions have a way of carrying over almost imperceptibly from the realm of principle into that of policy, where they develop a momentum of their own in which the original considerations of principle either are forgotten or are compelled to yield to what appear to be necessities of the moment. In other words, it is sometimes clearer and simpler to define on principle the kinds of things a country will not go in for—the things that would fit with neither its standards nor its pretensions—than it is to define ways in which it will act positively, whatever the circumstances. The basic function of principles is, after all, to establish the parameters within which the policies of a country may be normally conducted. This is essentially a negative, rather than a positive, determination.

Another quality of a principle that deserves notice is that it is not, and cannot be, the product of the normal workings of the political process in any democratic country. It could not be decided by a plebiscite or even by legislative action. You would never get agreement on it if it came under that sort of debate, and whatever results might be achieved would deprive the concept of the degree of flexibility it requires to serve its purpose.

A principle is something that can only be declared, and then only by a political leader. It represents, of necessity, his own view of what sort of a country his is, and how it should conduct itself in the international arena. But the principle finds its reality, if it finds it at all, in the degree of acceptance, tacit or otherwise, that its proclamation ultimately receives from the remainder of the political establishment and from the populace at large. If that acceptance and support are not forthcoming in sufficient degree, a principle ceases to have reality. The statesman who proclaims it, therefore, has to be reasonably confident that, in putting it forward, he is interpreting, appealing to, and expressing the sentiment of a large proportion of the people for whom he speaks. This task of defining a principle must be seen as not just a privilege, but also a duty of political leadership.

Adams' statement certainly had this quality. The concept was indeed his own. But his formulation of it met wide and enthusiastic support among the people of his time, as he probably thought it would. The same could be said of similar declarations of principle from a number of other American statesmen, then and later. One has only to think, for example, of George Washington's statements in his farewell address, Thomas Jefferson's language in the Declaration of Independence, or Abraham Lincoln's in his Gettysburg speech. In each of those instances, the leaders, in putting forward their idea of principle, were speaking from their own estimate—a well-informed estimate—of what would find a sufficient response on the part of a large body, and not just a partisan body, of American opinion.

In no way other than by advocacy or proclamation from high office could such professions of principle be usefully formulated and brought forward. The rest of us may have our thoughts from time to time about the principles America ought to follow in its relations with the world, but none of us could state these principles in a manner that would give them significance for the behavior of the country at large.

THE POWER OF EXAMPLE

So MUCH, then, for the essential characteristics of a principle and the manner in which it can be established. But there are those who will not be content with this abstract description of what a principle is, and who will want an example of what a principle valid for adoption by the United States of our day might look like.

The principle cited from Secretary Adams' Fourth of July speech was one that was applicable, in his view, to the situation then. The world now is, of course, different from his in many respects. There are those who will hold the gloomy view that such is the variety of our population and such are the differences among its various components, racial, social, and political, that it is idle to suppose that there could be any consensus among them on matters of principle. They have too little in common. There is much to be said for that view. This writer has at times been inclined to it himself. But further reflection suggests that there are certain feelings that we Americans or the great majority of us share, living as we do under the same political system and enjoying the same national consciousness, even though we are not always aware of having them. One may further suspect that if the translation of these feelings into principles of American behavior on the world scene were to be put forward from the highest governmental levels and adequately explained to the people at large, it might evoke a surprisingly strong response.

But this understanding and support cannot be expected to come spontaneously from below. It will not be likely to emerge from a public media dominated by advertisers and the entertainment industry. It will not be likely to emerge from legislative bodies extensively beholden to special interests, precisely because what would be at stake here would be the feelings and interests of the nation as a whole and not those of any particular and limited bodies of the citizenry. An adequate consensus on principles, in other words, could come from below only by way of response to suggestions from above, brought forward by a leadership that would take responsibility for educating and forming popular opinion, rather than merely trying to assess its existing moods and prejudices and play up to them.

Now, coming back to the model of Adams' Fourth of July speech, the problems now facing this country show a strong resemblance to ones Adams had in mind when he gave that address in 1823. At that time the dissolution of the great empires was only just beginning, and few—at the most half a dozen—of the newly emerging states were looking to us for assistance. In the period between Adams' time and our own, and particularly in the wake of the Second World War, the process of decolonization has proceeded at a dizzying pace, casting onto the surface of international life dozens of new states, many of them poorly prepared, as were those of Adams' time, for the responsibilities of independent statehood. This has led to many situations of instability, including civil wars and armed conflicts with neighbors, and there have been, accordingly, a great many appeals to us for political, economic, or military support.

To what extent, then, could Adams' principle of nonintervention, as set forth in 1823, be relevant to our situation today?

One cannot ignore the many respects in which our present situation differs from that which Adams was obliged to face. This writer is well aware of the increasingly global nature of our problems and the myriad involvements connecting our people and government with foreign countries. I do not mean to suggest a great reduction in those minor involvements. But what is at stake here are major political-military interventions by our government in the affairs of smaller countries. These are very different things.

First of all, we do not approach these questions with entirely free hands. We have conducted a number of such interventions in recent years, and at least three of these—Korea, Iraq, and Haiti—have led to new commitments that are still weighty and active.

There are several things to note about these interventions and commitments. First, while some may well have helped preserve peace or promote stability in local military relationships, this has not always been their stated purpose; in a number of instances, in particular, where we have portrayed them as efforts to promote democracy or human rights, they seem to have had little enduring success.

Second, lest there be any misunderstanding about this, the interventions in which we are now engaged or committed represent serious responsibilities. Any abrupt withdrawal from them would be a violation of these responsibilities; and there is no intention here to recommend anything of that sort. On the contrary, it should be a matter of principle for this government to meet to the best of its ability any responsibilities it has already incurred. Only when we have succeeded in extracting ourselves from the existing ones with dignity and honor will the question of further interventions present itself to us in the way that it did to Mr. Adams.

Third, instances where we have undertaken or committed ourselves to intervene represent only a small proportion of the demands and expectations that have come to rest on us. This is a great and confused world, and there are many other peoples and countries clamoring for our assistance. Yet it is clear that even these involvements stretch to the limit our economic and military resources, not to mention the goodwill of our people. And even if this were not a compelling limitation, there would still be the question of consistency. Are there any considerations being presented as justifications for our present involvements that would not, if consistently applied, be found to be relevant to many other situations as well? And if not, the question arises: If we cannot meet all the demands of this sort coming to rest upon us, should we attempt to meet any at all? The answer many would give to this question would be: yes, but only when our vital national interests are clearly threatened.

And last, beyond all these considerations, we have the general proposition that clearly underlay John Quincy Adams' response to similar problems so many years ago—his recognition that it is very difficult for one country to help another by intervening directly in its domestic affairs or in its conflicts with its neighbors. It is particularly difficult to do this without creating new and unwelcome embarrassments and burdens for the country endeavoring to help. The best way for a larger country to help smaller ones is surely by the power of example. Adams made this clear in the address cited above. One will recall his urging that the best response we could give to those appealing to us for support would be to give them what he called "the benign sympathy of our example." To go further, he warned, and try to give direct assistance would be to involve ourselves beyond the power of extrication "in all the wars of interest and intrigue, of individual avarice, envy, and ambition, which assumed the colors and usurped the standards of freedom." Who, today, looking at our involvements of recent years, could maintain that the fears these words expressed were any less applicable in our time than in his?

These, then, are some of the considerations bearing on the relevance of Adams' principle to the present problems of our country. This writer, for one, finds Adams' principle, albeit with certain adjustments to meet our present circumstances and commitments, entirely suitable and indeed greatly needed as a guide for American policy in the coming period. This examination of what Adams said, and its relevance to the problems of our own age, will in any case have served to illustrate what the word "principle" meant in his time and what it could, in this case or others, mean in our own.

One last word: the example offered above of what a principle might be revolved primarily around our relations with smaller countries that felt, or professed to feel, the need for our help in furthering their places in the modern world. These demands have indeed taken a leading place in our diplomacy of this post-Cold War era. But one should not be left with the impression that these relationships were all that counted in our present problems with diplomacy. Also at stake are our relations with the other great powers, and these place even more important demands on our attention, policies, and resources.

The present moment is marked, most happily, by the fact that there are no great conflicts among the great powers. This situation is without precedent in recent centuries, and it is essential that it be cherished, nurtured, and preserved. Such is the destructive potential of advanced modern weapons that another great conflict between any of the leading powers could well do irreparable damage to the entire structure of modern civilization.

On American Principles

Intimately connected with those problems, of course, is the necessity of restraining, and eventually halting, the proliferation of weapons of mass destruction and of achieving their eventual total removal from national arsenals. And finally, also connected with these problems but going beyond them in many respects, there is the great environmental crisis our world is entering. To this crisis, too, adequate answers must be found if modern civilization is to have a future.

All of these challenges stand before us. Until they are met, even the many smaller and weaker countries can have no happy future. Our priorities must be shaped accordingly. Only when these wider problems have found their answers will any efforts we make to solve the problems of humane and civil government in the rest of the world have hopes of success. ☯

Back to the Womb?

Arthur Schlesinger, Jr.

ISOLATIONISM'S RENEWED THREAT

AMERICAN isolationism is an ambiguous concept. The United States has never been isolationist with regard to commerce. Our merchant vessels roamed the seven seas from the first days of independence. Nor has the United States been isolationist with regard to culture. Our writers, artists, scholars, missionaries, and tourists have ever wandered eagerly about the planet. But through most of its history, the republic has been isolationist with regard to foreign policy. From the start, Americans sought to safeguard their daring new adventure in government by shunning foreign entanglements and quarrels. George Washington admonished his countrymen to "steer clear of permanent alliances," and Thomas Jefferson warned them against "entangling alliances."

Only a direct threat to national security could justify entry into foreign wars. The military domination of Europe by a single power has always been considered such a threat. "It cannot be to our interest," Jefferson observed when Napoleon bestrode the continent, "that all Europe should be reduced to a single monarchy." America would be forever in danger, he said, should "the whole force of Europe [be] wielded by a single hand." But between Napoleon and the kaiser, no such threat arose, and Americans became settled in their determination to avoid ensnarement in the corrupt and corrupting world. Isolationism, in this political sense, was national policy.

Then World War I revived the Jeffersonian warning. Once again, as

ARTHUR SCHLESINGER, JR., is Professor Emeritus in the Humanities at the Graduate School and University Center, the City University of New York. This article is drawn from his George W. Ball Lecture, delivered at Princeton University in April.

in the time of Napoleon, the force of Europe might have been wielded by a single hand. A balance of power in Europe served American interests as it had served British ones. The United States entered the Great War in its own national interest. But for Woodrow Wilson, national interest was not enough to excuse the sacrifice and horror of war. His need for a loftier justification led him to offer his country and the world a strikingly bold American vision.

The position of the United States had changed since the days of the founding fathers. Where Washington and Jefferson had seen independence, Wilson saw interdependence. His aim was to replace the war-breeding alliance system and the bad old balance of power with a "community of power" embodied in a universal League of Nations. The establishment of the League, Wilson said, promised a peaceful future. Should this promise not be kept, Wilson warned in Omaha in September 1919, "I can predict with absolute certainty that within another generation there will be another world war."

For a glorious moment, Wilson was the world's prophet of peace. No other American president—not Lincoln, not F.D.R., not J.F.K., not Reagan—has ever enjoyed the international acclaim that engulfed Wilson. But Wilson was a prophet without much honor in his own country. His vision of a community of power implied a world of law. It rested on the collective prevention and punishment of aggression. Article X of the league covenant imposed on member nations the "obligation" to "preserve against external aggression the territorial integrity and existing political independence of all members of the league." This meant, or seemed to mean, that American troops might be sent into combat not just in defense of the United States but in defense of world order. U.S. soldiers would have to kill and die for what many would regard as an abstraction and do so when the life of their own nation was not in danger.

The commitment of troops to combat became the perennial obstacle to American acceptance of the Wilsonian dream. It is a *political* obstacle: how to explain to the American people why their husbands, fathers, brothers, or sons should die in conflicts in remote lands where the local outcome makes no direct difference to the United States? And it is a *constitutional* obstacle: how to reconcile the provision in the constitution giving Congress exclusive power to declare war with the dispatch of American troops into hostilities at the behest of a collective security organization?

Wilson's fight for the League of Nations foundered in the Senate on these obstacles. So America, after the two-year Wilsonian internationalist binge, reverted to familiar and soothing isolationism. Disenchantment over the Great War accelerated the return to the womb. Revisionist historians portrayed American entry into the war as a disastrous mistake brought about by sinister forces—international bankers, munitions makers, British propagandists—and by Wilsonian deceptions and delusions. Novelists and playwrights depicted the sacrifice of war as meaningless. The onset of the Great Depression further confirmed the isolationist impulse.

By the early 1930s, even Wilsonians abandoned the League as a lost cause. Isolationism set the terms of the foreign policy debate. Franklin D. Roosevelt had no illusions about the threats to peace posed by Nazi Germany and imperial Japan. Although he was a mighty domestic president, he could not, for all his popularity and all his wiles, control an isolationist Congress when it came to foreign policy. Congress rejected American membership in the World Court. It passed rigid neutrality legislation that, by denying the president authority to discriminate between aggressor and victim, nullified any American role in restraining aggression. In sum, it put American foreign policy in a straitjacket during the critical years before World War II.

I refer to this history to illustrate the continuing strength of the isolationist faith. Roosevelt meanwhile began a campaign of popular education to awaken the nation to international dangers. In 1939, the outbreak of war in Europe fulfilled Wilson's Omaha prediction and justified Roosevelt's warning. But it did not destroy isolationism. Rather, it ushered in the most savage national debate of my lifetime—more savage than the debate over communism in the late 1940s, more savage than the debate over McCarthyism in the early 1950s, more savage than the debate over Vietnam in the 1960s. The debate between interventionists and isolationists in 1940-41 had an inner fury that tore apart families, friends, churches, universities, and political parties. As late as August 1941, the extension of the draft passed the House by only a single vote.

Pearl Harbor settled that particular debate. But in vindicating internationalism, it did not vanquish isolationism. In the 1942 congressional election, despite a major campaign by internationalists, only 5 of 115 legislators with isolationist records were beaten. The predominantly isolationist Republicans gained 44 seats in the House and 9 in the Senate—

their best performance in years. Secretary of State Cordell Hull told Vice President Henry Wallace that "the country was going in exactly the same steps it followed in 1918."

ARTICLE X

FOR ROOSEVELT, the critical task in 1943-45, beyond winning the war, was to commit the United States to postwar international structures before peace could return the nation to its old habits. "Anybody who thinks that isolationism is dead in this country is crazy," F.D.R. said privately. "As soon as this war is over, it may well be stronger than ever."

So he moved methodically to prepare the American people for a continuing world role. By the end of 1944, F.D.R. had organized a series of conferences setting up international machinery to deal with the post-war world. These conferences, held mostly at American initiative and dominated mostly by American agendas, came up with postwar blueprints for international organization (Dumbarton Oaks); international finance, trade, and development (Bretton Woods); food and agriculture (Hot Springs); civil aviation (Chicago); and relief and reconstruction (Washington).

Above all, F.D.R. saw the United Nations, in the words of Charles E. Bohlen, as "the only device that could keep the United States from slipping back into isolationism." He was determined to put the United Nations in business while the war was still on and the American people were still in an internationalist mood; hence the founding conference in San Francisco, which took place after his death but before victory. And, as Winston Churchill emphasized, the new international organization "will not shrink from establishing its will against the evil-doer or evil-planner in good time and *by force of arms*" (italics mine).

Once again, there arose the Article X question that had so bedeviled Wilson. Could the new United Nations on its own order American troops into war in defense of world order and the peace system? Washington's veto in the Security Council ensured that U.S. soldiers could not be sent into combat over a president's objection. But if a president favored U.S. participation in a U.N. collective security action, must he go to Congress for specific authorization? Or could the U.N. Charter supersede the U.S. Constitution?

Arthur Schlesinger, Jr.

The U.N. Participation Act of 1945 came up with an ingenious solution. It authorized the United States to commit limited force through congressionally approved special agreements as provided for in Article 43 of the U.N. Charter. Presidents could not enter into such agreements on their own. If more force was required than the agreement specified, the president must return to Congress for further authorization. This formula offered a convincing way to reconcile the charter and the Constitution. Unfortunately, the Article 43 special agreement procedure soon withered on the vine. When Harry S Truman sent troops into Korea five years later, he sought neither an Article 43 agreement nor a congressional joint resolution, thereby setting the precedent that persuaded several successors that presidents possess the inherent power to go to war when they choose.

At the same time, the Cold War aborted the resurgence of isolationism so much feared by Roosevelt and Hull. Within a few years, the Truman Doctrine, the Marshall Plan, NATO, other security pacts, and overseas troop deployments bound the United States to the outside world in a way isolationists, in their most pessimistic moments, could hardly have envisaged. In two hot wars fought on the mainland of East Asia under the sanction of the Cold War, the United States lost nearly 100,000 people. Even the traditionally isolationist Republican Party joined in support of the United Nations and collective action. At last, it seemed, Americans had made the great turning and would forever after accept collective responsibilities. The age of American isolationism, it was supposed, was finally over.

In retrospect, that seems an illusion. It is now surely clear that the upsurge in American internationalism during the Cold War was a reaction to what was seen as the direct and urgent Soviet threat to the security of the United States. It is to Joseph Stalin that Americans owe the 40-year suppression of the isolationist impulse. The collapse of the Soviet threat faces us today with the prospect that haunted Roosevelt half a century ago—the return to the womb in American foreign policy.

This suggestion requires immediate qualification. The United States will never—unless Republican presidential candidate Pat Buchanan has his way—return to the classical isolationism of no "entangling alliances." It will continue to accept international political, economic, and military commitments unprecedented in its history. It will even enlarge some, as in the curious mania to expand NATO, which would commit U.S. forces to the defense of Eastern Europe from, presumably, the menace of a

Russian army that cannot even beat Chechnya. But such enlargement hinges on the assumption that other nations will do as we tell them. The isolationist impulse has risen from the grave, and it has taken the new form of unilateralism.

THE REPUBLICAN REJECTION

THE CLINTON administration began by basing its foreign policy on the premise that the United States could not solve the world's troubles all by itself. "Many of our most important objectives," Secretary of State Warren Christopher has said, "cannot be achieved without the cooperation of others." The key to the future, in the Clintonian view, was collective action through the building of international institutions and through multilateral diplomacy in the spirit of Wilson and F.D.R.

But as the Soviet threat faded away, the incentives for international collaboration faded away too. The Republican capture of Congress last year gave unilateralism new force and momentum. In a perhaps ill-judged attempt at conciliation, President Clinton issued Presidential Directive 25, which restricted U.S. participation in collective security operations and declared that "the United States does not support a standing U.N. Army, nor will we earmark specific U.S. military units for participation in U.N. operations." Predictably, this retreat failed to appease House Speaker Newt Gingrich, who promptly accused Clinton of still cherishing the "multinational fantasy" and of a continued desire "to subordinate the United States to the United Nations." Nor did it appease Senate Majority Leader Robert Dole, who argued that international organizations too often "reflect a consensus that opposes American interests or does not reflect American principles and ideals."

The House has already passed a Gingrich-backed bill with the Orwellian title of the National Security Revitalization Act. This bill would cut U.S. financial support for current U.N. peacekeeping operations by more than $1 billion and limit the president's ability to approve new peacekeeping missions. The effect, should the bill be enacted into law, would be to eviscerate the American role in collective security.

For its part, the Senate has under consideration Dole's Peace Powers Act, which would amend the U.N. Participation Act of 1945 to give Congress a statutory role in the relationship between the United States and the United Nations. This bill, Dole tells us, "imposes significant new limits on peacekeeping policies which have jeopardized American interests, squandered American resources—and cost lives." Among other things, the Dole bill would generally forbid U.S. troops to serve under foreign commanders and, in the words of *The Washington Post*, "would make it difficult if not impossible for the president to commit U.S. troops to new or expanded U.N. operations or even continue support for ongoing activities." "The American people," Dole says, "will not tolerate American casualties for irresponsible internationalism."

Sir Nicholas Henderson, the distinguished former British ambassador to Washington, characterizes the present situation as "the rejection by the Republicans of the main plank of U.S. foreign policy for the last 50 years." And it is not as if America is at present deeply involved in collective security. The United States stands 20th on the list of nations making troop contributions to U.N. operations, well behind such world powers as Bangladesh, Ghana, and Nepal. Jordan, for example, with a population of less than two percent of the United States, is contributing more than three times as many troops to U.N. peacekeeping.

In foreign aid, despite the popular impression that it is a major charge on the U.S. budget, the Organization for Economic Cooperation and Development recently reported that the United States, once the world's top aid donor, has cut back its allocation today to a mere 0.15 percent of its gross domestic product, placing it by that measure last among the 21 industrial nations. If the Gingrich Congress has its way, foreign aid will be cut still further. And the new mood has already forced the administration to abandon its intention to rejoin the reformed U.N. Educational, Scientific, and Cultural Organization.

Nor can it be said that this recoil from collective security misrepresents American popular sentiment. The latest public opinion survey by the Chicago Council on Foreign Relations and the Gallup Organization shows that, while Americans are still ready to endorse euphonious generalities in support of internationalism, there is a marked drop-off when it comes to committing not just words but money and lives. Defending the security of American allies, rated very important by 61 percent of the public in 1990, fell to 41 percent in the most recent survey. Public support for the protection of weaker nations against foreign aggression fell from 57 to 24 percent. There was a 24 percent decline in support for the promotion of human rights and a 19 percent decline in support for efforts to improve living standards in underdeveloped countries.

This wave of neo-isolationism draws strength in part from the understandable desire to concentrate on improving things at home—a desire justified by the neglect of domestic problems during the Reagan-Bush years. The neo-isolationist enthusiasm also results from waning popular confidence in the United Nations, its bureaucracy, its competence, and its peacekeeping skills. And it draws strength from the recoil against all-out internationalists, who would set the nation on a crusade to establish human rights and democracy.

Neo-isolationism gains further support as America—and indeed all nations—confronts the ultimate price of collective security. For the essence of collective security remains, as Churchill said, the readiness to act against evildoers "by force of arms." Denied military enforcement, and with economic sanctions of limited effect, the international community's effort to restrain aggressors becomes hortatory.

THE NEO-ISOLATIONIST IMPULSE

ARE AMERICANS today prepared to take a major collective security role in enforcing the peace system? The U.N. Participation Act of 1945 provided a way to overcome the constitutional obstacle, but no president has gone down the special agreement path, and the old struggle between presidents and their Congresses remains. This is a political battle fought in constitutional terms, and the political obstacle is more potent than ever. How to persuade the housewife in Xenia, Ohio, that her husband, brother, or son should die in Bosnia or Somalia or some other place where vital U.S. interests are not involved? Nor is it just the Xenia housewife who must be persuaded. How many stalwart internationalists in the Council on Foreign Relations would send their own sons to die in Bosnia or Somalia?

Dying for world order when there is no concrete threat to one's own nation is a hard argument to make. For understandable reasons, our leaders are not making it. We have a professional army made up of men and women who volunteered for the job; and the job, alas, may include fighting, killing, and dying. But let a few American soldiers get killed, and the congressional and popular demand for withdrawal becomes almost irresistible. Nor is the United States alone in this reaction. When two French soldiers were killed in Sarajevo in April, the French government, on the eve of its presidential election, threatened to withdraw its 4,350 peace-keeping troops from Bosnia. Terrorists recognize this vulnerability of democracies and know now how a couple of accurate snipers can drive peacekeeping forces from their land.

Surely this flinching from military enforcement calls for a reexamination of the theory of collective security. Despite two grievous hot wars, a draining Cold War, and a multitude of smaller conflicts, the Wilsonian vision is as far from realization today as it was three-quarters of a century ago. In the United States, neo-isolationism promises to prevent the most powerful nation on the planet from playing any role in enforcing the peace system. If we refuse a role, we cannot expect smaller, weaker, and poorer nations to ensure world order for us. We are not going to achieve a new world order without paying for it in blood as well as in words and money.

Perhaps our leaders should put the question to the people: what do we want the United Nations to be? Do we want it to avert more killing fields around the planet? Or do we want it to dwindle into impotence, leaving the world to the anarchy of nation-states?

Perhaps we might reduce the constitutional and political obstacles to a collective security role by reviving the Article 43 special agreements and asking members of the armed forces to volunteer for consequent U.N. assignments. Or perhaps we might consider the proposal recently made by that distinguished international civil servant Sir Brian Urquhart for a U.N. volunteer army, a foreign legion recruited from idealists, adventurers, and mercenaries that could serve the Security Council as a rapid deployment force.

If we cannot find ways of implementing collective security, we must be realistic about the alternative: a chaotic, violent, and ever-more dangerous planet. Maybe the costs of military enforcement are too great. National interest narrowly construed may be the safer rule in an anarchic world. But let us recognize, as we return to the womb, that we are surrendering a magnificent dream.

Foreign Policy
as Social Work

Michael Mandelbaum

THE CLINTON RECORD
THE SEMINAL events of the foreign policy of the Clinton administration were three failed military interventions in its first nine months in
office: the announced intention, then failure, to lift the arms embargo
against Bosnia's Muslims and bomb the Bosnian Serbs in May 1993; the
deaths of 18 U.S. Army Rangers at the hands of a mob in Mogadishu, Somalia, on October 3; and the turning back of a ship carrying military
trainers in response to demonstrations in Port-au-Prince, Haiti, on
October 12. Together they set the tone and established much of the
agenda of the foreign policy of the United States from 1993 through 1995.

These failed interventions expressed the view of the worldwide role
of the United States that the members of the Clinton foreign policy team
brought to office. Their distinctive vision of post–Cold War American
foreign policy failed because it did not command public support. Much
of the administration's first year was given over to making that painful
discovery. Much of the next two years was devoted to coping with the
consequences of the failures of that first year.

Bosnia, Somalia, and Haiti were not, as the administration claimed,
problems it had inherited. The Bush administration had sent troops to
Somalia for the limited purpose of distributing food and not, as the Clinton administration's ambassador to the United Nations, Madeleine

---

MICHAEL MANDELBAUM is Christian A. Herter Professor of
American Foreign Policy at the Paul H. Nitze School of Advanced
International Studies, The Johns Hopkins University, and Director of the Project on East-West Relations at the Council on Foreign Relations.

Albright, put it, "for the restoration of an entire country."[1] As for Bosnia and Haiti, during the 1992 presidential campaign Clinton promised to change the Bush policies by using air power to stop ethnic cleansing in the Balkans and by discontinuing the repatriation of Haitian refugees fleeing to the United States.

The Clinton campaign promises, however, cannot be properly understood merely as tactical maneuvers designed to secure electoral advantage. Although they certainly were that, they also reflected the convictions of W. Anthony Lake, the campaign's foreign policy coordinator who became President Clinton's national security adviser. The campaign commitments may have been expedient, but they were not cynical. Nor were they challenged by Warren Christopher, who became the secretary of state, the office from which American foreign policy has generally been directed.

The abortive interventions shared several features. Each involved small, poor, weak countries far from the crucial centers that had dominated American foreign policy during the Cold War. Whereas previous administrations had been concerned with the powerful and potentially dangerous members of the international community, which constitute its core, the Clinton administration turned its attention to the international periphery.

In these peripheral areas the administration was preoccupied not with relations with neighboring countries, the usual subject of foreign policy, but rather with the social, political, and economic conditions within borders. It aimed to relieve the suffering caused by ethnic cleansing in Bosnia, starvation in Somalia, and oppression in Haiti. Historically the foreign policy of the United States has centered on American interests, defined as developments that could affect the lives of American citizens. Nothing that occurred in these three countries fit that criterion. Instead, the Clinton interventions were intended to promote American values.

Lake characterized this approach, incorrectly, as "pragmatic neo-Wilsonianism." While Woodrow Wilson, like Bill Clinton, favored the spread of democracy, so has every other president since the founding of the republic. While Wilson sought to promote democracy in Europe to prevent a repetition of World War I, the absence of democracy in Bosnia, Somalia, and Haiti was not going to lead to World War III. And while Wilson had a formula for spreading democracy—the establishment of

---

[1] Paul Lewis, "U.N. Will Increase Troops in Somalia," *The New York Times*, March 27, 1993, p. 3.

sovereign states on the basis of national self-determination—that principle was precisely what the Clinton administration was determined to prevent the Serbs from applying in the Balkans.

Lake himself supplied a better analogy. "I think Mother Teresa and Ronald Reagan were both trying to do the same thing," he said in suggesting that the Clinton foreign policy encompassed both, "one helping the helpless, one fighting the Evil Empire."[2] In fact, they were trying to do different things. Reagan conducted a traditional foreign policy with a strong ideological overlay. He was in the business of pursuing the national interest of the United States as he understood it. Mother Teresa, by contrast, is in the business of saving lives, which is what Lake and his colleagues tried in 1993 to make the cornerstone of American foreign policy. They tried, and failed, to turn American foreign policy into a branch of social work.

While Mother Teresa is an admirable person and social work a noble profession, conducting American foreign policy by her example is an expensive proposition. The world is a big place filled with distressed people, all of whom, by these lights, have a claim to American attention. Putting an end to the suffering in Bosnia, Somalia, and Haiti would have involved addressing its causes, which would have meant deep, protracted, and costly engagement in the tangled political life of each country.

When the time came to carry out the commitment to do so at the risk of American lives, the president balked. He refused to bomb in Bosnia, withdrew U.S. troops from Somalia, and recalled the ship from Haiti, thereby earning a reputation for inconstancy that haunts his presidency. In each case, however, he did not have, nor was he likely to get, the political support in the United States necessary to rearrange the political and economic lives of the three countries so as to end their misery and uphold American values.

THE COLD WAR DIFFERENCE

THE NEW American foreign policy that surfaced and sank in the first nine months of 1993 was the product of an unusual set of circumstances that created a void: a public and a president less interested in interna-

---

2 Jason DeParle, "The Man Inside Bill Clinton's Foreign Policy," *The New York Times Magazine*, August 20, 1995, p. 35.

tional affairs than at any time in the previous six decades combined with the disappearance of the familiar foreign policy guideposts of the Cold War. Into that void stepped a group of people who, during the Carter administration, had been uncomfortable with and unsuccessful at waging the global conflict with the Soviet Union but who believed they could take the political capital the public had furnished for 40 years to oppose the Soviets and put it to uses they deemed more virtuous.

In this they were wrong. The American public had supported intervention in poor, distant reaches of the Third World during the Cold War, and would no doubt do so again, but only on behalf of traditional American national interests.

This was the great lesson to emerge from the fiascoes of Clinton's first year. It can be illustrated by comparing two Caribbean invasions, ten years apart, in which the United States sought to remove an unfriendly government: the Reagan administration's dispatch of forces to Grenada in 1983 and the Clinton administration's efforts to intervene in Haiti in 1993 and 1994. By most criteria Haiti is the more important of the two: larger, closer, a source of refugees, and a country that the United States had occupied from 1915 to 1934. Yet the invasion of Grenada was less controversial.

The reason was that the first invasion was part of the Cold War. The radical Grenadan government was aligned with Cuba, an ally of the Soviet Union, with which the United States was locked in a mortal struggle. The intervention in Grenada could thus be portrayed as an act of self-defense, albeit at several removes, and self-defense is a cause for which Americans have always been willing to sacrifice. The invasion of Haiti could not be presented in that light. Grenada could be seen as affecting American interests. With the end of the Cold War, Haiti could not. It was the conflict with the Soviet Union that connected the international periphery to American interests.

In the wake of their initial failures, administration officials lamented that the conduct of foreign policy had been easier for their predecessors. This is not true. There has never been a formula for deciding on military intervention, and Cold War presidents had to make that decision with the specter of nuclear conflict with the Soviet Union hovering in the background, an experience the Clinton administration was spared.

But if the decision to intervene was not easier during the Cold War, it was simpler: U.S. presidents did not necessarily know when to use force, but they always knew why—to combat the Soviet Union, its allies, and its clients, and thus defend American interests. The argument for intervention was not always universally persuasive, but it was always plausible. In Bosnia, Somalia, and Haiti in 1993 it was not even plausible.

Lake provided an epitaph for the foreign policy of Mother Teresa, one that captured the motive for its rise and the reason for its demise: "When I wake up every morning and look at the headlines and the stories and the images on television of these conflicts, I want to work to end every conflict, I want to work to save every child out there," he said. "But neither we nor the international community have the resources nor the mandate to do so."[3]

COMEDY, TRAGEDY, AND HAITI

WHILE THE administration withdrew from Somalia, the problems of Haiti and Bosnia lingered on, pieces of unfinished business, reminders of the humiliations of 1993.

In both, the administration followed the same pattern. First it adopted policies that made things worse. Then, in 1994 in Haiti and in 1995 in Bosnia, it finally used force. But the motivation was not, as in 1993, to "help the helpless," in Lake's words. Rather it was to bolster the administration's political standing, which was suffering from the failure to resolve these problems. Both interventions achieved a measure of success, but in each case the success was provisional, fragile, and reversible.

In Haiti, the Clinton administration first tried to dislodge the junta led by Brig. Gen. Raoul Cédras by imposing an ever-tighter trade embargo, ultimately cutting off almost all Haitian contact with other countries. The embargo devastated Haiti, destroying its small manufacturing sector and leading to predictions of starvation by the end of 1994. That prospect, combined with the continuing exodus of refugees, the insistence of the Congressional Black Caucus that the elected Haitian president Jean-Bertrand Aristide be restored to power, and a hunger strike protesting the failure to do this by American political activist Randall Robinson, persuaded the administration to use force. Finally, in October 1994, troops from the United States landed in Haiti, the junta's leaders departed, and Aristide returned.

The triumph, however, was conditional. For the administration had

---

[3] Elaine Sciolino, "New U.S. Peacekeeping Policy Deemphasizes Role of the U.N.," *The New York Times*, May 6, 1994, p. A1.

promised not simply to return Aristide but to restore (or, to put it more accurately, create) democracy and help the country lift itself out of destitution, which required the establishment of a stable political system, the rule of law, and a freely functioning market economy.

Because Haiti lacked all three, the administration's goals could not be accomplished overnight. To give Haiti a chance to reach them required a substantial American commitment. This the Clinton administration was not able to give. The stay of the American and U.N. troops was to be short, ending in February 1996. Their mission was limited; they did not make a serious effort to disarm the country. Financial aid would not be long-term.

All this reduced the capacity of the United States to help ensure that Aristide would leave office, as he promised, in February 1996, that an orderly democratic succession would take place, and that economic reforms would be carried out. At the end of 1995, therefore, Haiti's long-term prospects for democracy and prosperity were uncertain.

The administration lacked leverage in Haiti because it lacked political support in the United States. The American public was opposed to the dispatch of troops. The president did not ask for congressional approval of the operation because he would not have received it. Economic assistance to the country was unpopular with the Republican congressional majority.

The weakness of the administration's political position was demonstrated by the unusual role accorded former President Jimmy Carter. Along with retired General Colin Powell and Senator Sam Nunn (D-Ga.), he negotiated an agreement with the Haitian junta for U.S. troops to enter the country peacefully and for the junta to leave. Carter's function was to negotiate terms and make concessions that the Clinton administration, because of its political weakness, found it impolitic to make publicly.

The Clinton administration tried to make a case for invading Haiti, falling back on the kinds of arguments that had justified the use of force during the Cold War. J. Brian Atwood, the director of the U.S. Agency for International Development, attempted to connect autocratic rule in Haiti with American interests by asserting that it was "an assault on the progress toward democracy that has been made throughout the hemisphere."[4]

The argument was inappropriate in a way that was both comic and

---

[4] J. Brian Atwood, "On the Right Path in Haiti," *The Washington Post*, October 14, 1994, p. A27.

tragic: comic because it was ludicrous to contend that the fate of a small, impoverished half of a Caribbean island would affect Mexico, Argentina, or Brazil, tragic in that it was precisely because Haiti was so isolated that its political and economic conditions had become—had been allowed to become—so miserable.

That appeal to national interest failed because the United States had no interest in Haiti. Haiti was, however, one place where an appeal to values might have generated support. Because it was nearby, poor, weak, had once been occupied by the United States, and was populated by descendants of African slaves, the United States had reason to be concerned about its fate. A serious effort to put Haiti on a path toward decent politics and rational economics could have been presented as a good deed in the neighborhood at manageable cost and justified by the fact that America is a rich, powerful, and generous country. The Clinton administration, however, did not try to make that case.

THE EXIT IS THE STRATEGY

BOSNIA WAS more complicated than Haiti because it involved relations with America's European allies, Britain and France, with whom for 30 months the Clinton administration was at odds. The Europeans deemed the conflict a civil war, to be ended as soon as possible even at the cost of a settlement unfavorable to Bosnia's Muslim government in Sarajevo. They supported the three proposed peace accords of the period: the Vance-Owen Plan of 1992, the Owen-Stoltenberg Plan of 1993, and the Contact Group Plan of 1994. The Clinton administration, in contrast, viewed the war as Serbian aggression against Bosnia. Its goal was justice for the Bosnian government even at the price of prolonging the war. It favored air strikes against the Serbs.

The Americans and the Europeans were each able to veto the policy the other wanted. The United States prevented the implementation of the peace plans; the Europeans blocked all but token bombing. The war dragged on. More and more people were killed or displaced, transatlantic acrimony mounted, and the gap between bellicose pronouncements and timid actions made the Western powers look increasingly inept.

In the summer of 1995 the United States launched a diplomatic initiative in the Balkans. The motive, as it had been with Haiti the previous year, was concern about the damage the war was doing to President Clinton's domestic political standing. The House and Senate voted, against the president's wishes, to end the arms embargo against the former Yugoslavia, but delayed a vote to override the president's veto to give diplomacy a chance. The president would have suffered embarrassment if, as seemed likely, his veto had been overridden. Moreover, the end of the embargo would likely have provoked the withdrawal of the British and French peacekeepers in Bosnia, triggering the dispatch of U.S. troops to the war zone to help extricate them and risking American casualties.

The course of the war turned out to favor American diplomacy. Bosnian Serb ethnic cleansing in eastern Bosnia and military victories by the Croatian army in the west removed the U.N. peacekeepers from easy reach of the Bosnian Serbs—who on occasion had held U.N. troops hostage—paving the way for a compromise between the Americans and the Europeans. With their peacekeepers no longer at risk, the Europeans consented to a vigorous campaign of bombardment against the Bosnian Serbs in late August and early September of 1995. At the same time, the United States accepted the European preferences on the division of territory between the three contending groups in Bosnia—ethnic cleansing had made different parts of the country more homogeneous ethnically—and agreed to the Bosnian Serbs' demand that they be permitted to federate with Serbia, just as the Bosnian Croats had been allowed to federate with Croatia under the terms of the American-brokered Croat-Muslim alliance of the year before. Perhaps because of the American bombing, certainly because of the American concessions, a cease-fire was achieved, and a conference convened in Dayton, Ohio, in November 1995 that produced a peace settlement.

Where flimsy political support had forced the Clinton administration to compromise on the implementation of its goals in Haiti in 1994, in Bosnia in 1995 political weakness compelled compromise on the goals themselves. Indeed, the principles that the administration had said were at stake in Bosnia were all but abandoned: the settlement rewarded what the administration had termed Serb aggression and ratified the results of ethnic cleansing. The United States negotiated directly with Serbian President Slobodan Milŏsević, whom the administration had initially considered a war criminal. Bosnia was partitioned along ethnic lines, subverting the principles of undiluted sovereignty and ethnic pluralism that members of the Clinton administration had insisted, in 1993 and 1994, were inviolable.

The single indisputable American accomplishment in the Balkans between 1993 and 1995 was to assist Croatia in gaining control of some additional territory in Bosnia and all the territory it had included as a Yugoslav republic. This, however, was hardly a victory for American values. The Croats had practiced ethnic cleansing on a scale comparable to the Bosnian Serbs and were just as ardent about ethnic homogeneity and intolerance of Muslims. The federation between Croats and Muslims in Bosnia that the United States had brokered in 1994 was a partition between the two groups in all but name.

Prior to the Dayton negotiations, the administration had promised to send as many as 25,000 American troops to Bosnia as part of a peace settlement, and, as it had with the invasion of Haiti, struggled to find a rationale for this. As with Haiti, interests were said to be at stake, specifically the interest in avoiding a larger conflict. "If war reignites in Bosnia," President Clinton said, "it could spark a much wider conflagration. In 1914, a gunshot in Sarajevo launched the first of two world wars."[5]

The conditions that had led to World War I, however, were absent eight decades later. The assassination of the heir to the Hapsburg throne in 1914 was the occasion for rival great powers to settle their differences by war. There is no such rivalry for the Balkan conflicts of the 1990s to ignite. Indeed, post–Cold War Europe lacks great European military powers to prosecute such a rivalry: Russia is not great, Germany is not military, and the United States is not European. The people of the former Yugoslavia were allowed to fight over its territory precisely because their wars did not pose a threat to the rest of Europe.

The United States, its European allies, and the Soviet Union would not have allowed Yugoslavia to disintegrate during the Cold War, the end of which had made Europe safe for war in the Balkans. Because Bosnia could not plausibly be connected to interests the American public would consider worthy of sacrificing blood and treasure to defend, the support for dispatching American troops to enforce the Dayton accords was bound to be weak. As in Haiti, therefore, the chief purpose of an American expeditionary force in Bosnia would be to leave as soon as possible, with as few casualties as possible, rather than to do whatever was necessary, for as long as necessary, to keep (or make) peace.

---

[5] President Bill Clinton, "Why Bosnia Matters to America," *Newsweek*, November 13, 1995, p. 55.

Michael Mandelbaum

At the end of the Cold War, General Powell proposed a set of precepts for the use of force abroad that included the need for both a clear mission and a clear exit strategy. The Clinton interventions in Haiti in 1994 and prospectively in Bosnia in 1996 modified the Powell doctrine by conflating the two: the exit strategy became the mission.

WARD POLITICS, WORLD STAKES

BOSNIA AND Haiti were the centerpieces of American foreign policy in 1994 and 1995, but there were other issues to be addressed. With the rejection in 1993 of the vision it had brought to office, the administration needed some basis for dealing with them. It found such a basis in domestic politics. Clinton administration policy toward much of the world beyond Bosnia, Somalia, and Haiti was made by responding to the concerns and wishes of particular groups in American society.

The pattern is a familiar one for American politicians. With its close attention to Ireland and Israel (Italy was unaccountably omitted), the Clinton administration was pursuing the foreign policy of many a big-city mayor. With its emphasis on securing contracts abroad for American firms, it was conducting the international economic policy common to governors. Such an approach to foreign policy is normal: all presidents have catered to important domestic constituencies. It is natural: foreign policy is a branch of politics, and the president is a professional politician. In the post–Cold War era, without an overarching principle to guide the nation's foreign relations, it is all but inevitable: the promotion of domestic interests is the default strategy of American foreign policy.

Nor is the primacy of domestic considerations in foreign policy necessarily a mistake. Profits for American corporations, jobs for American workers, and a settlement of the long-running conflict in Northern Ireland are all desirable. In its immersion in the Middle East peace process, moreover, the administration was pursuing a goal that transcends the preferences of particular segments of American society and that has thus been central to American diplomacy for two decades.

Making American foreign policy by attending to the wishes of American interest groups did, however, interfere with the pursuit of larger American interests in the cases of Japan, North Korea, and Russia.

The administration placed the reduction of Japan's trade surplus at the center of its policy toward America's most important Asian ally, for a time seeking to establish quotas for Japanese-American trade. Opening Japanese markets is important, and not only for the United States. But the way the administration went about it had unfortunate side effects. It ran counter to the principles of free trade, of which the United States had long been the global champion and on which the world's trading system is based. It contributed to the false impression in the United States that the American trade deficit was due mainly to Japanese protectionism rather than to imbalances in the domestic American economy. And it left the related misimpression that the object of trade policy must be a trade surplus, a proposition dubious in theory and, as a universal principle, impossible to achieve.

Putting relations with Japan on this basis also hampered the administration in dealing with North Korea's nuclear program. This was a genuine threat to American interests and a problem that actually was inherited from the Bush administration. In 1994 the administration put together, again with the participation of former President Carter, what amounted to a standstill agreement with the communist government in Pyongyang. The accord was flawed, providing no way to determine whether North Korea had already diverted spent fuel to bomb-making. It was, however, defensible, freezing the most dangerous parts of the North Korean nuclear program and avoiding, or at least postponing, a military confrontation.

The optimal approach, however, would have been to assemble a coalition of the United States and North Korea's two most important neighbors, Japan and China, to exert pressure on the communist regime to give up its nuclear program. That would have involved intensive consultations with Tokyo and Beijing, which Secretary of State Christopher never undertook, and giving priority in America's East Asian policy to opposing nuclear proliferation rather than to the aims that the Clinton administration, responding to domestic constituencies, chose to emphasize: the trade imbalance with Japan and human rights violations in China.

Finally, the administration's cultivation of domestic groups distorted its policy toward the nation's most important international commitment, NATO, and toward Russia. In the first weeks of 1994, having earlier rejected the idea, President Clinton declared that NATO would extend membership to the nations of Central Europe. A principal reason, according to press accounts, was to win favor with American voters of Central European descent.[6]

The sudden announcement annoyed the Western European members of NATO, who had just agreed to a more modest change known as the Partnership for Peace. It infuriated the Russians, especially Russian democrats, who believed that it was based on the assumption—which was indeed widely shared among its proponents in Central Europe and the West—that its democratic experiment would inevitably fail and Russia would revert to threatening its neighbors. The Clinton administration, however, had adopted policies based on the opposite view, committing itself to the success of Russian democracy. NATO expansion, therefore, not only jeopardized the American interest in the peaceful integration of Russia into Europe and the international community, it also contradicted Clinton's own Russia policy.

NATIONAL INTERESTS

IN JAPAN, Korea, and Russia, the American stakes were larger than, and different from, the preferences of particular American interest groups. The United States continues to have national interests, although they can no longer be expressed simply as opposition to the Soviet Union. Perhaps the most important task the Clinton administration faced as it entered office was to state these interests in a way that would guide the foreign policy bureaucracy, inform the international community, and persuade the American public. Although senior officials gave occasional speeches, and some of the policies the administration carried out were compatible with the nation's central purposes in the post–Cold War world, it never offered a clear, persuasive account of just what those purposes are, sometimes even denying that such an account is possible.

It is possible, and it begins with the maintenance of an American military presence in Europe and in the Asia-Pacific region. The goal has changed. During the Cold War the mission of American forces abroad was to deter the Soviet Union. Today it is to reassure all countries in both regions that there will be no sudden change in the military balance. This is especially important for Germany and Japan. Without the assurance of

---

[6] See, for example, Rick Atkinson and John Pomfret, "East Looks to NATO to Forge Links to West," *The Washington Post*, July 6, 1995, p. A1.

American protection, they might feel the need for stronger military forces, ultimately including nuclear weapons. The suspicion that the two might adopt such policies would alarm their neighbors, who would feel the need to adopt military policies that would, in turn, alarm Germany and Japan. American forces serve as a barrier to such dangerous chain reactions. It is therefore important to keep some of them in place.

The United States does have a major security interest on the periphery of the international system: preventing the spread of nuclear weapons. A North Korean nuclear arsenal would upset the balance of power in East Asia; a bomb in the hands of Iraqi dictator Saddam Hussein would jeopardize American interests in the Middle East and Europe. A campaign against nuclear proliferation is a complicated, open-ended task that requires extensive international cooperation. The United States is the indispensable leader of that campaign.

A third principal post–Cold War purpose of American foreign policy, the one the administration best promoted and explained despite its neomercantilist initiatives toward Japan, is trade. It engineered the passage of the General Agreement on Tariffs and Trade and the North American Free Trade Agreement, both of which expanded the international trading system that has contributed mightily to global economic growth for five decades.

Trade was related to another policy the Clinton administration intermittently practiced, one that lent coherence to a seemingly disparate set of initiatives and provided a justification for the most controversial of them. American economic engagement for the promotion of liberal economic policies that would create wealth and expand freedom was a common feature of the Clinton administration's decision to grant normal trading status to China, economic assistance to Russia, and diplomatic recognition to Vietnam.

During the Cold War, each of these countries posed a threat to American interests. Reducing their power through economic isolation was then the proper policy. With the end of the Cold War, American policy could safely and appropriately be reoriented toward promoting freer domestic politics. Market reforms in China, Russia, and Vietnam have had that effect. This rationale justifies a policy of economic engagement with them and with Cuba in the event of real market reforms there, but not with Iran or Iraq, whose governments continue to threaten American interests.

Michael Mandelbaum

AFTER THREE YEARS the Clinton administration had not articulated a clear foreign policy doctrine for the post–Cold War world, but it had compiled a foreign policy record. How good was it?

During the Cold War, the yardstick was straightforward: how well the nation was doing in the worldwide struggle against the Soviet Union. In the wake of the Cold War, three different criteria for judgment are available: the one important to the Clinton foreign policy team, the one important to the country, and the one of most immediate importance to President Clinton himself.

By the standards of Mother Teresa, the Clinton foreign policy could claim modest success. At the end of 1995 Haitians and Bosnians were better off, or at least less likely to be killed, than had been the case 15 months earlier. (Of the administration's three abortive interventions in 1993, the one in which the United States may have accomplished the most was Somalia, where, by some estimates, American intervention saved half a million lives. That had been the aim and was thus partly the achievement of the Bush administration.)

On the other hand, the Clinton team did not succeed in establishing Lake's commitment to "helping the helpless" as the dominant principle of American foreign policy. Meanwhile, political support for the organization it had hoped would be an instrument of its new foreign policy, the United Nations, fell sharply, in part because the administration sought to deflect responsibility for its own failures in Bosnia and Somalia onto the international organization.

The more traditional standard by which the foreign policy of a great power is evaluated is its relations with the most important members of the international system. Here the Clinton performance could not be judged a success. The real legacy of the Bush administration was not Bosnia, Somalia, and Haiti. It was, instead, unprecedentedly good American relations with all the other major centers of power: Western Europe, Japan, China, and Russia. Three years later, those relations were worse in every case.

This is not, in and of itself, an indictment. The purpose of foreign policy is not to cultivate good relations with other countries under any circumstances. It is, rather, to maintain the best possible relations consistent with the nation's interests. Sometimes it is necessary to sacrifice goodwill for the sake of more important goals. But the Clinton administration alienated others to no good effect. The political capital it expended brought nothing in return.

The acrimony with the Western Europeans over Bosnia made no contribution to the defense of the values the administration had said were at stake there. The friction with Japan did not have an appreciable effect on the trade balance between the two countries. The offense given to Beijing by the inconsistent approach to linking trade to human rights and by the decision to admit Taiwan's President Lee Teng-hui to the United States after assuring China's foreign minister that this would not occur, did nothing for the cause of human rights in China or Taiwan's security.

The relationship with Russia deserves special mention. Much of what the administration did turned out well, or at least not badly. American economic assistance gave a boost to extensive privatization in Russia. While tacit support for Boris Yeltsin during his confrontation with members of the Russian parliament in October 1993 cost the United States some goodwill among the Russian public, had Yeltsin's adversaries prevailed the damage to American interests would have been worse. Belatedly, the administration recognized the importance of preserving an independent Ukraine and protecting and implementing the arms treaties negotiated by its predecessors: the two Strategic Arms Reduction Treaties and the accord on Conventional Forces in Europe.

Between the beginning of 1993 and the end of 1995, relations with Russia deteriorated sharply, but this was largely unavoidable, the result of Russians' delayed anger at their reduced international status and economic disintegration. However, the clumsy exclusion of Moscow from much of the diplomacy surrounding Bosnia and the commitment to expand NATO made the inevitable deterioration unnecessarily worse.

NATO expansion had the potential to alienate Russia from the post–Cold War settlement in Europe and make the goal of overturning that settlement central to Russian foreign policy, even as the infamous Clause 231 of the Versailles Treaty, assigning guilt for World War I to Germany, helped set the Germans on the course that led to World War II. In that worst case, the Clinton policy would rank with America's two greatest twentieth-century foreign policy blunders: the failure to remain politically engaged in Europe after World War I and the Vietnam war.

Still, at the end of 1995, while relations with the major centers of power were worse than they had been when the Clinton administration took office, they were not catastrophically or irretrievably worse. That meant that in 1996, for the president and the country, the immediate test of the Clinton foreign policy would be its impact on his prospects for reelection.

Polls consistently showed that the administration's foreign policy performance was held in low esteem by the American public. The same polls showed that, in the public's ranking of issues important to the country, those having to do with foreign policy were consistently at the bottom. Nonetheless, foreign policy was likely to be part of the 1996 election in a way unhelpful to the president.

Clinton's political difficulties, as he entered the election season, could be divided into two parts. On the ideological spectrum he had drifted too far to the left for many voters during his first two years. A gifted, energetic politician, he subsequently devoted himself to moving nearer to the center. But another problem afflicted him: doubt about whether he measured up to the job of chief executive and commander in chief. The conduct of foreign policy was only one part of this problem, but it was likely to prove more convenient as a metaphor for issues of character and leadership than the details of his personal life.

In this sector of the political battlefield, therefore, his early vacillation on military intervention, his dispatch of troops abroad without political support at home, his failure to spell out a clear set of priorities for post–Cold War American foreign policy, his visible discomfort in dealing with international issues, and his choice of senior foreign policy officials who proved unable to establish their authority either at home or abroad, were likely to come back to haunt him. As election day approached, his political opponents would have every reason to portray Bill Clinton as what he had never wanted to be and had gone to great lengths to avoid becoming: a foreign policy president.

Making Peace with the Guilty

The Truth about Bosnia

Charles G. Boyd

> English persons, therefore, of humanitarian and reformist disposition constantly went out to the Balkan Peninsula to see who was in fact ill-treating whom, and, being by the very nature of their perfectionist faith unable to accept the horrid hypothesis that everybody was ill-treating everybody else, all came back with a pet Balkan people established in their hearts as suffering and innocent, eternally the massacree and never the massacrer.
>
> Rebecca West
> *Black Lamb and Grey Falcon*, 1938

REBECCA WEST loved the peoples of the Balkans, but she is not the only traveler to return from there with some measure of cynicism. For more than two years, I have found myself increasingly consumed and frustrated by events in the former Yugoslavia. I have traveled to the region on several occasions and have had the advantage of hearing the personal views of young men and women in Croatia and Macedonia assigned to the American forces, the U.N. Protection Force (UNPROFOR), and the U.N. High Commissioner for Refugees.

The views I share here are the product of seeing this war up close, almost continuously, in all its ugliness. These views differ from much of the

---

GENERAL CHARLES G. BOYD, USAF (RET.), was the Deputy Commander in Chief, U.S. European Command, from November 1992 to July 1995. A fighter pilot and combat veteran of Vietnam, he held many senior command and staff positions throughout his 35-year military career.

conventional wisdom in Washington, which is stunted by a limited understanding of current events as well as a tragic ignorance or disregard of history. Most damaging of all, U.S. actions in the Balkans have been at sharp variance with stated U.S. policy.

The linchpin of the U.S. approach has been the underinformed notion that this is a war of good versus evil, of aggressor against aggrieved. From that premise the United States has supported U.N. and NATO resolutions couched in seemingly neutral terms—for example, to protect peacekeepers—and then has turned them around to punish one side and attempt to affect the course of the war. It has supported the creation of safe areas and demanded their protection even when they have been used by one warring faction to mount attacks against another. It has called for a negotiated resolution of the conflict even as it has labeled as war criminals those with whom it would negotiate. It has pushed for more humanitarian aid even as it became clear that this was subsidizing conflict and protecting the warring factions from the natural consequences of continuing the fighting. It has supported the legitimacy of a leadership that has become increasingly ethnocentric in its makeup, single-party in its rule, and manipulative in its diplomacy.

To take one example: recently more than 90 percent of the Serbs in western Slavonia were ethnically cleansed when Croatian troops overran that U.N.-protected area in May. As of this writing this Croatian operation appears to differ from Serbian actions around the U.N. safe areas of Srebrenica and Zepa only in the degree of Western hand-wringing and CNN footage the latter have elicited. Ethnic cleansing evokes condemnation only when it is committed by Serbs, not against them.

We must see things in the Balkans as they are, not as we wish them to be. We must separate reality from image. Is it possible that all sides have legitimate interests and fears, or does legitimacy remain the special province of only one or two factions? We need a healthy skepticism about accepted "wisdom," and above all, we need to tell the truth, if only to ourselves.

THE OBJECTIVES

ALL FACTIONS in the former Yugoslavia have pursued the same objective—avoiding minority status in Yugoslavia or any successor state—and all have used the tools most readily available to achieve that end. For the Croats that meant a declaration of independence from a Yugoslav feder-

ation increasingly dominated by Serb nationalism and an appeal to the
European Union for recognition. The new state identified itself and full
citizenship within it as Croatian and claimed sovereignty extending to the
boundaries of the old Croat Republic of the Yugoslav federation. Bosnia's
Muslims had no such option as they were a plurality, not a majority, on
their territory. They were also considerably less enthusiastic about leaving
the federation, recognizing that with its explosive population mix, Bosnia
seemed to make more sense as part of a larger multiethnic Yugoslavia than
as a stand-alone entity. The secession of Slovenia and Croatia left a rump
Yugoslavia formed around Serbia and Montenegro an even less hospitable
home, however, and Bosnia's Muslims too opted for secession.

In recognizing the new Bosnian state, the international community
demanded, and Bosnia's Muslims (and some of their Serb and Croat
neighbors) delivered, a commitment to democracy and individual rights
that made the nations of the West comfortable with their own commitment to the new Bosnian state. Their approach was tactically sound and,
as a practical matter, the only course available to Bosnia's well-educated
but under-armed Muslim plurality if it was to preserve its newly proclaimed independence. Pointing this out does not diminish the essential
nobility of this course, nor the obvious moral advantage it gave the new
state in comparison with some of its neighbors.[1]

In this atmosphere of fear, uncertainty, and resurgent nationalism,
first the Croatian and then the Bosnian Serbs—with Serbian support—
took up arms to do what international recognition had done for the
Croats of Croatia and the Muslims of Bosnia: ensure that they would not
be a minority in a state they perceived to be hostile. What is frequently
referred to as rampant Serb nationalism and the creation of a greater
Serbia has often been the same volatile mixture of fear, opportunism, and
historical myopia that seems to motivate patriots everywhere in the
Balkans. Much of what Zagreb calls the occupied territories is in fact land
held by Serbs for more than three centuries, ever since imperial Austria
moved Serbs to the frontier (the Krajina) to protect the shopkeepers of

---

[1] Regrettably, the Bosnian polity had organized itself into political parties based largely on ethnic identity. As the world moved toward recognition of the Bosnian state, Bosnian President Alija Izetbegović's Party of
Democratic Action and its Croat and Serb counterparts exercised near-ab-
solute control over regions where their ethnic groups were in the majority.
Izetbegović's party today runs Bosnia as a one-party state.

Vienna (and Zagreb) from the Ottomans. The same is true of most Serb land in Bosnia, what the Western media frequently refers to as the 70 percent of Bosnia seized by rebel Serbs. There were only 500,000 fewer Serbs than Muslims in Bosnia at independence, with the more rural Serbs tending toward larger landholdings. In short, the Serbs are not trying to conquer new territory, but merely to hold on to what was already theirs.

These are not minor historical points. The twin poles of much of Western diplomacy in the Balkans and elsewhere have been self-determination and the inviolability of borders. In the cases of Croatia and Bosnia, as well as Slovenia and Macedonia, Western nations suffered a temporary lapse in their concern over borders, accepting the dissolution of a U.N. member nation in favor of self-determination. That policy contributed to stability where the will of the population was most clear—ethnically homogeneous Slovenia—and led to catastrophic destabilization where the will of the population was most ambiguous—ethnically mixed Bosnia. One-third of Bosnia's population boycotted the referendum on independence and made it unmistakably clear that it would take up arms if the new state was created and recognized.

There are legitimate concerns over what constitutes an appropriate unit of self-determination; the United States cannot possibly support ever-shrinking pockets of ethnic preference. But the United States hobbles its understanding of this conflict if it imputes its global concerns to the local players. As one Serb officer confided to a member of my staff, he did not understand why his people had been "satanized" for insisting on the same right of self-determination that had been accorded virtually all others in the former Yugoslavia.

War in Bosnia and Croatia was not the inevitable product of centuries of ethnic hatreds. It was created from ambition, fear, and incompetence—local and international.

THE CONDUCT OF THE WAR

No one of conscience can ignore the moral dimension of this crisis. Unspeakable acts have been perpetrated on the innocent. I have flown over Bosnian villages and seen the results, not of combat, but of ethnically based criminal violence, homes within a village selectively and systematically destroyed as the majority population—Muslim, Serb, or Croat—cleansed its community of now unwanted minorities. I have walked the streets of villages like Gornji Vakuf and seen the faces of angry, armed young men staring at one another across city squares and streets transformed into ethnic confrontation lines. No one can visit Mostar and witness the city's historic center—made rubble by small arms fire—and not feel and fear how thin the veneer of civility must be for us all. And as one turns every corner in Sarajevo to be greeted by more destruction, it is difficult to escape the questions, what manner of man is in those hills, and what possessed him to pull the lanyard on his artillery?

But to make rational judgments of policy requires a depth of understanding that goes beyond a transient image or sound bite. For some, the war in Bosnia has become a tragedy of proportions that parallel the Holocaust, an example of plain good against stark evil. For these people, the Serbs are the forces of darkness, responsible for most if not all of the atrocities, the ethnic cleansing, mass rapes, concentration camps, and indiscriminate killing.

Regrettably, that behavior is not unprecedented in Balkan conflicts, and to say that it is peculiarly Serb behavior says more about the observer than the Balkans. If one comes into the movie in 1991 or 1992, a case can be made that the Serbs indeed are the villains of this picture, but to ignore the previous reels will, at a minimum, impair divining the ultimate plot line. And let me dare to suggest that my observations tell me that even today's picture is more complex than is generally regarded. The public view of this war has come largely through the eyes of one party, a people, as Rebecca West warned, whose status as victim has been a valuable and jealously protected tool of war. Make no mistake: Serb behavior has been reprehensible. The question is how bad? On what scale? And how unique? Analysis of what has happened is not a claim of moral equivalence, nor is it a justification for the actions being examined.

How bad has this war been? When one drives past the destroyed speed-skating rink and the Olympic stadium in Sarajevo, the eye involuntarily turns to row upon row of markers atop fresh graves dug in the new and largest cemetery in the capital. Clearly, thousands have died in Sarajevo. How many people have died in this war overall? Nobody knows. The Bosnian government has an interest in portraying the number as high as possible: it is a testament to the savagery of their opponent, a cry for assistance and at the same time an indictment of a cautious international community. Until recently the government claimed the number of dead and missing to be about 250,000. Many have been skeptical of that figure, with some suggesting the real number could be as low as 25,000, although other estimates—including my own—are more frequently in the 70,000 to 100,000 range. In April the government lowered its estimate to just over 145,000, about 3 percent of the prewar population. That is a sobering number, but even accepting it at face value and granting that it is unevenly distributed across the population, does that total after 38 months of warfare make charges of genocide a meaningful contribution to policy debate?

Sarajevo is instructive. The government estimate puts the death toll in the capital just above 10,000. Someone has calculated that the city has been hit by 600,000 shells, and some 60 percent of its buildings have been destroyed or severely damaged. Recent fighting, shelling, and harassment of humanitarian convoys have once again increased the city's suffering and isolation. What normalcy that exists there is a tribute to international relief efforts and, above all, the courage and resilience of the city's population.

The city's actual suffering, however, does not change the reality that the image of Sarajevo, battered and besieged, is a valuable tool for the Bosnian government. As that government was commemorating the thousandth day of the siege, local markets were selling oranges, lemons, and bananas at prices only slightly higher than prices in western Europe. At the same time the commercial price of gasoline in Sarajevo was 35 percent cheaper than gasoline in Germany. A World Food Programme survey in May 1994 found that, after a tough winter for Sarajevo, no one in the city was malnourished, and only a small percentage of the population was undernourished. Even the rate of violent deaths had gone down considerably in 1994 (324 for the year according to the United Nations; the per capita rate was comparable to some North American cities and slightly lower than Washington, D.C.), although press coverage and government statements gave the image of unrelenting siege.

Some of the city's suffering has actually been imposed on it by actions of the Sarajevo government. Some were understandable policies, like the restriction on travel to prevent the depopulation of the city during those periods when movement was possible. Others were the by-product of government weakness, like relying on the Sarajevo underworld for the initial defense of the city, thereby empowering criminal elements that took their toll on the population, especially Serbs. Still others were intentional; whether out of individual greed or official policy is unclear.

Government soldiers, for example, have shelled the Sarajevo airport, the city's primary lifeline for relief supplies. The press and some governments, including that of the United States, usually attribute all such fire to the Serbs, but no seasoned observer in Sarajevo doubts for a moment that Muslim forces have found it in their interest to shell friendly targets. In this case, the shelling usually closes the airport for a time, driving up the price of black-market goods that enter the city via routes controlled by Bosnian army commanders and government officials. Similarly, during the winter of 1993-94, the municipal government helped deny water to the city's population. An American foundation had implemented an innovative scheme to pump water into the city's empty lines, only to be denied permission by the government for health reasons. The denial had less to do with water purity than with the opposition of some Sarajevo officials who were reselling U.N. fuel donated to help distribute water. And, of course, the sight of Sarajevans lining up at water distribution points, sometimes under mortar and sniper fire, was a poignant image.

The war has also redrawn the demographic map of Bosnia; fear, combat, and nationalist extremism have displaced upwards of two million people. Much of this displacement has been forced population movements, the engine for much of which has been Serbian—Serb fear, Serb security demands, and Serb cruelty. When the Serbs took up arms in the spring of 1992, their immediate aim was to secure their communities from real and imagined threats from their non-Serb neighbors. With this accomplished, they moved to connect Serb areas with secure lines of communication through locations in which other ethnic groups were dominant. In both operations, non-Serbs were viewed as security threats and cleansed from the territory in question. In a campaign that appeared to reflect central direction and planning, Serb excesses were common and well documented.

Less generally known are Serb population movements. During a visit to Sarajevo in February a senior U.N. official told me that there may be as few as 500,000 Serbs on Serb-held territory in Bosnia. Combined with the 200,000 Serbs that he estimated are living on Bosnian-controlled land, the Serb population in Bosnia may be only about half its prewar total. Like their former neighbors, Bosnia's Serbs can point to fear, combat, and forced expulsion as the reasons for their movement, although the proportions are likely different.

Serbian people have suffered when hostile forces have advanced, with little interest or condemnation by Washington or CNN correspondent

Christiane Amanpour. Late in 1994, when the Bosnian V Corps broke out of the Bihać pocket, they burned villages as they went and forced several thousand Serbs to flee. The same happened when Bosnian Croat forces pushed up the Livno valley shortly thereafter. If anyone doubts the capacity of Bosnia's non-Serb population to inflict ethnic cruelty, let him or her visit the Croat enclaves around Kiseljak or Vitez. The scarred shells of Catholic churches and Muslim mosques as well as thousands of private homes give ample testimony to the barbarity of Muslim and Croat violence, and these Muslim and Croat troops likely did what they did for much the same reasons as their Serb neighbors: revenge for real and alleged sins of the past and the perceived demands of present security. There are times when the distinctions among the factions appear more a question of power and opportunity than morality.

THE FUTURE COURSE OF THE WAR

THE STRATEGIC situation on the ground has changed substantially since the war began. Three years of fear, combat, and crime masquerading as battle have effected great change. With their enclaves largely preserved, Croats see their future more in their relationship with Zagreb than with Sarajevo. And with the 1993-94 combat and atrocities a fresh memory, they view their Muslim federation partners with distrust, frequently echoing Serb fears of the encroachment of Islam into Christian Europe. Bosnia's Croats joined the federation to get out of the Bosnian war (which they were losing) and have little interest in joining any sustained campaigns against Bosnia's Serbs. This is not true of Bosnia's Muslims and Serbs. Without question, these factions each intend to win this war. The Serbs think they have won already and want the war to end. The Muslims know they have not and are seeking ways to continue it.

Serbs suffer from the general depopulation of the areas they control; economic activity is depressed, and they are hard-pressed to marshal forces. The popular image of this war is one of unrelenting Serb expansion, but much of Bosnia has historically been Serb, and the recent Serb moves against the eastern enclaves represent the only significant changes in their area of control in nearly two years.

Muslims have been largely forced into the central core of the country. This has provided the Sarajevo government with a strong base and internal lines of communication with which to take the fight to extended Serb units. The refugee population that forms the core of the Bosnian army guarantees a numerical advantage (150,000-200,000 to 80,000) and ensures a continued will to fight to recapture lost territory.

Even the Serb advantage in heavy equipment is not what it once was. The closure of the Serbian border by Belgrade is incomplete and imperfect but nonetheless real. It has affected Bosnian Serb access to fuel and equipment. Meanwhile, the flow of armaments passing to Bosnian forces continues almost unremarked upon by the international community. Senate Majority Leader Bob Dole's much-trumpeted desire to lift the embargo would be amusing but for the fact that it would almost certainly lead to the introduction of U.S. ground forces. The embargo has been lifted in all but name, to the delight of much of the U.S. policy elite. To be sure, since supplies must pass through Croatian territory, Zagreb controls the types of weapons that pass to Bosnia and continues to deny the heavy weapons that could challenge it in renewed Muslim-Croat fighting. Nonetheless, the Muslims' forces are vastly better off than they were earlier in the war. The armies in Bosnia—Serb and Muslim—are asymmetrical in their military power, but they are very closely matched. Serbian successes against the eastern enclaves in July were small-scale operations against isolated, demoralized units. That Serbian units did not attack the government army in central Bosnia—Sarajevo's real center of gravity—is a reflection of this new balance. And time is quite likely on the side of the Muslims.

It is a remarkable achievement of Bosnian diplomacy, and one reinforced by the government's rhetoric after the fall of Srebrenica, that the Muslims have been able to gain significant military parity with the Serbs, while nonetheless maintaining the image of hapless victim in the eyes of much of the world community. It is all the more remarkable since, before the Srebrenica attack, the Muslims had been on the strategic offensive for more than a year.

In this campaign the Muslims have consistently tried to use the United Nations and NATO (with the attendant safe areas, no-fly zones, exclusion zones, and demilitarized zones) as a shield, allowing themselves to weaken their forces in one area—depending on the United Nations or the international community to protect it—while concentrating their forces elsewhere. In the winter of 1993-94 the Sarajevo government stripped the capital's defenses to release troops to fight against the Croats in central Bosnia, counting on their public diplomacy efforts to manage the risk to Sarajevo. It was a near-run thing, but in the end the city was protected by the threat of NATO air strikes and the imposition of a heavy-weapons exclusion zone.

This spring and summer the Muslims excoriated the United Nations for failing to protect Sarajevo, or as one U.N. official privately put it, for failing to do their fighting for them. Almost immediately after the Serb shelling of the tunnel under the Sarajevo airport—the only route open for Muslim military supplies and commercial goods—the Bosnian government demanded NATO air strikes, attacked the passive attitude of UNPROFOR , and complained that the genocide was continuing; Sarajevo was still a death camp. Holocaust-like rhetoric was even more prominently featured in government statements following the mid-July fall of Srebrenica.

All of this is designed to enlist active military intervention in support of Muslim war aims. To date this campaign appears to have been successful in guaranteeing the Bosnian government against catastrophic failure in continuing to pursue the military option. The Bosnian army may suffer casualties and even significant defeats, but neither the existence of the Bosnian state nor its control over the core of its territory can be seriously jeopardized without provoking a sharp international response. Beyond this, the Sarajevo government hopes to prod NATO and particularly the United States into even more active intervention. French President Jacques Chirac's challenge to President Clinton to help the Bosnians defend Goražde and the latter's willingness to consider helicopter and air support for the operation suggest that the effort might yet bear fruit.

Last fall's action around Bihać—a portion of which is a U.N. safe area—is particularly instructive. The situation in this pocket is complex, even by Balkan standards. The Bosnian government unit there, the V Corps, was opposed by both Bosnian Serb forces and troops loyal to Fikret Abdić, usually described in Western press accounts as renegade Muslim units. Actually Abdić, a powerful local businessman, was a member of the Bosnian collective presidency (he outpolled Izetbegović in national elections) and had been expelled from the government (or broke with it, depending on your point of view) when Sarajevo rejected an internationally brokered peace agreement. Eager for profit and familiar with operating on the gray side of the law, Abdić established his own state and mutually profitable relationships with his Serb and Croat neighbors. These ties were one of the few examples of successful multi-ethnic cooperation in the Balkans.

The Bosnian V Corps was still a fighting force, however, and in a series of well-conducted campaigns it defeated Abdić's largely mercenary army. The V Corps then turned its attention to the Bosnian Serb forces that surrounded it, broke out of the pocket, and captured several hundred square kilometers of territory from a shaken Serb opponent.

Serb forces were hard-pressed, and to mount a counterattack they had to rely not only on forces in Bosnia but units in the Krajina of Croatia as well. Slowly the Serbs pushed the V Corps back to approximately the original lines of confrontation. The V Corps gave ground but was never defeated and remains an effective fighting force to this day. During the counterattack, however, the Bosnian government and many in the international community demanded that the United Nations and NATO protect the Bihać safe area from Serb aggression. A common theme was the impending humanitarian catastrophe if strong steps were not taken—even though this was a fight that the Muslim army had picked, there was limited damage to the safe area, and Bihać was the headquarters and garrison town of the Bosnian units that had mounted the attack. Finally, rather than work toward a cease-fire to fend off the looming tragedy, Bosnian government actions were clearly orchestrated to create the conditions for NATO air strikes, not a cessation of hostilities.

HOW TO MAKE PEACE

I BELIEVE that the U.S. approach to the war in Bosnia is torn by a fundamental contradiction. The United States says that its objective is to end the war through a negotiated settlement, but in reality what it wants is to influence the outcome in favor of the Muslims. The United States, for example, watched approvingly as Muslim offensives began this spring, even though these attacks destroyed a ceasefire Washington has supported. This duplicity, so crude and obvious to all in Europe, has weakened America's moral authority to provide any kind of effective diplomatic leadership. Worse, because of this, the impact of U.S. action has been to prolong the conflict while bringing it no closer to resolution.

The United States recognized the secession of Bosnia reluctantly, but having done that, it embraced the new state and both praised and supported its multiethnic character. Whether this character was ever real or had a reasonable chance of success is a fair subject of debate, but no reasonable person can believe that a unitary, multiethnic Bosnia is possible today. Nonetheless, Washington treats the Bosnian government as it—and perhaps the best of the Bosnian leadership—hoped and dreamed the country would be. It is not. It is the representative of one warring faction.

More balanced American diplomats admit privately that the Bosnian Serbs—like their Muslim and Croat neighbors—are not without legitimate interests and concerns in this conflict. The United States rarely addresses the problem in this light and for much of the past three years has based its approach more on excluding than including the Serbs. Former President Jimmy Carter made this point following his December visit to Sarajevo and Pale when he commented to the author that negotiating with one side, condemning the other, and issuing ultimatums was unlikely to lead to any agreement.

It is worse than that. Isolation and privation have helped legitimize in the eyes of Serbs the worst of the Serb nation, to make acceptable to the broader population the faction that said the world was their enemy, that they were history's victims and Europe's protectors, that so great was their danger that any measures were appropriate to their defense. Demonization has unleashed demons.

How then is the United States to make tomorrow better than today? The most imporant change is to start telling the truth. The result will be, aside from restoring some moral stature, to reduce the fighting.

To think with clarity about the former Yugoslavia that exists rather than the one the U.S. administration would prefer and then to speak with honesty about it will be very difficult given the distance this government has traveled down the road of Serb vilification and Muslim and Croat approval. But until the U.S. government can come to grips with the essential similarities between Serb, Croat, and Muslim and recognize that the fears and aspirations of all are equally important, no effective policy can possibly be crafted that would help produce an enduring peace. This truth, however difficult to acknowledge publicly at this late date, must at the very least be recognized privately so that a revamp of policy can proceed from clear and accurate premises.

The first step is for the United States to announce, and then follow through by its actions, that it really does oppose a military solution. That would require a cessation of all the nonsense rhetoric about lifting an embargo that has in reality long since been lifted and about leveling a playing field that is as nearly level as it is likely to get. As long as the free flow of arms through Croatia to Bosnia continues to be taxed by the Croats in terms of a percentage of the total plus a prohibition on most heavy weapons (which the Croats understandably do not want to face the next time they square off against the Muslims), the strategic balance that now exists in Bosnia will likely remain.

By turning a blind eye to these arms deliveries while screeching at Belgrade to stop whatever still continues across the Drina to the Bosnian Serbs, the United States does two things: one, it disqualifies itself as the fair and balanced intermediary in the peace process, and two, it sends a powerful signal to the Muslims that a military solution is acceptable and perhaps preferred, notwithstanding solemn public statements in support of the diplomatic process.

Once established as actually supporting the arms embargo, the United States can gain credibility by opposing military activity irrespective of the source. Strong public denunciation must follow all attacks by Bosnian Serbs, Bosnian government forces, or for that matter Croatian campaigns such as that against the Krajinian Serbs in the western sector. The quiet approval by the United States when the Muslim forces broke the Cessation of Hostilities Agreement must change to condemnation just as stern as that directed at the Bosnian Serbs as they captured Srebrenica. Moreover, an absolutely impartial use of NATO air power against any faction that violates a U.N. sanction, not just the Serbs, must also become the expected response that the United States supports if the antagonists are to be persuaded that violence is not acceptable. This, if nothing else, will certainly help reduce the dying.

The second step is to reinforce peace and cooperation where they are found. The Bosnian federation is a starting point. The slow progress of building Muslim-Croat cooperation highlights the difficulties ahead, but the major failing of the federation is not the pace of its progress but its biethnic nature. It includes none of the Serbs in Bosnia, many of whom live in government-controlled lands. If the United States is not anti-Serb—merely against criminals and those who would choose war over peace—it must address the status of these citizens. Making peace with the Serbs in federation territory and giving them an identity, political voice, and the potential for constitutional options comparable to Bosnia's Croats would send a powerful signal to those in Bosnian Serb territory that there are options beyond war and isolation.

The third major step is to restart the negotiation process. In the Washington agreement that led to the federation, the United States treated Bosnia's Croats and Muslims as separate entities, accorded their leaders legitimacy, brokered a deal between the two that largely stopped the killing, sought the ratification of that deal from a foreign power (Croatia), and recognized the validity of constitutional ties from one of those ethnic communities to another state (again, Croatia). The Contact Group's approach to Bosnia's Serbs (largely driven by U.S. pressure) has been decidedly different—a take-it-or-leave-it map. Under these circumstances there are no incentives for the Bosnian government to negotiate or compromise. That leaves the Serbs with three choices: accept the Contact Group plan, respond to government military action, or drastically increase the level of violence to force a military decision. The current map is unacceptable, so the fighting continues.

A key to restarting the negotiation process may lie with the nation that has quietly, but continuously, been marginalized: Russia. The United States' apparent desire to minimize Russia's involvement in the peace process is difficult to comprehend but may be rooted in two fears: that Russia would balk at using the peace process to advance for the Muslims diplomatically what they could not achieve militarily; and that Russia, currently on the sidelines in the international community, would gain considerable prestige and renewed diplomatic status from a success in brokering a solution to the conflict.

Whether these fears existed or were justified in the past is no longer relevant. The United States has now reached the point where the Russians may be its best hope for facilitating a diplomatic solution. The United States, for reasons of credibility, cannot do so; it can talk effectively with only two sides and therefore is not in a position to lead the diplomatic effort. Likewise, the United States has co-opted the other players of the Contact Group, except Russia. In this regard, the Russians are untainted and have more credibility with the Serbs. Perhaps only they can address the Serbs' deepest fears and give them the confidence no other party has been interested in providing. And the Russians may like this new role. It would give them foreign policy stature in the wake of their debacle in Chechnya and a chance to prove their willingness and ability to play a constructive diplomatic role. More important, it would give the West new hope for settling the conflict diplomatically where no other option seems viable. This significant role comes with a risk, but at this stage it is a worthwhile price the United States may have to pay to stop the war. If the marginalization of Russia has not alienated the latter beyond redemption, the United States should seek its full partnership immediately.

The hour is late in Bosnia. By the time you read this, the United States may not be able to prevent the withdrawal of U.N. forces; it may even be beyond its ability to resist the pressures to deploy American ground troops, goaded by a strangely bellicose press and anxious allies. But if the United States is to insert itself, it should do so without illusion. Without a determined policy choice to the contrary, it would in fact be entering not to reinforce the peace, but rather to help one faction win, a faction that has been maneuvering for such intervention since the Bosnian state was created. It would be allowing its European allies who, until now, have had the lead militarily in the Balkans, to transfer the tar now stuck to their fingers to the United States' and force America to assume the moral responsibility for the outcome of the conflict.

All this will be at considerable cost because in this conflict only very large numbers of troops on the ground will make a difference. Despite its appeal to the amateur strategist, a reliance on air power alone—the strike option—in this type of terrain with these kinds of targets has never held any real promise of conflict resolution. Given the political dynamics that developed after the fall of Srebrenica and Žepa and as Goražde seemed threatened, a strong response from NATO was necessary if further erosion of its credibility was to be avoided. And indeed, the use of "robust" air power can have an effect on Serb behavior, particularly if it is used without regard for civilian casualties. But it cannot make the Serbs want to live as an ethnic minority in a nation they perceive to be hostile. It can only reinforce the paranoia that drives them to continue the fight so relentlessly even now.

Pushing NATO to agree to the robust use of its air power, then, as with most of the other U.S. policy moves in the former Yugoslavia, is linked more to the immediacy of the evening newscasts than to a rational overall political objective. For that reason it can have no more than a near-term effect. At the end of the day the United States must face the reality that it cannot produce an *enduring* solution with military force—air or ground—only one that will last until it departs.

There is an alternative: proceed from the premise that all factions to the conflict have legitimate needs, not just Muslims and Croats. Lever-

Charles G. Boyd

age Belgrade and Zagreb equally to stop the flow of arms to Bosnia. Denounce the use of military force with equal indignation toward all perpetrators. Pressure the Bosnians to negotiate in good faith or risk true abandonment. Enlist the Russians both to represent and dampen Serb demands. Enforce a ceasefire impartially.

There need be no illusions about the future. Given the horrors of the last three years, rebuilding trust in Bosnia will take a very long time. True healing is beyond our means. The best we can hope for is to create the conditions for Bosnia to heal itself. The U.S. can aid in this process but only if it is willing to be honest, at least to itself.

The Last Ambassador

Warren Zimmerman

A MEMOIR OF THE COLLAPSE OF YUGOSLAVIA

IN EARLY 1989, shortly after I was confirmed as the new—and as it turned out the last—U.S. ambassador to Yugoslavia, I sought out Lawrence Eagleburger. Eagleburger had been named deputy secretary of state for the incoming Bush administration but had not yet been approved by the Senate. His temporary office was in the small back room adjoining the opulent deputy secretary's office, and there he could be found inhaling a cigarette, which, as an asthma sufferer, he was not supposed to have.

Larry Eagleburger remains one of the foremost American experts on the Balkans. Like an unusually large number of Foreign Service officers—myself included—he served twice in Yugoslavia. He and I shared a love of the country and its people. As we talked, we discovered a mutual view that the traditional American approach to Yugoslavia no longer made sense, given the revolutionary changes sweeping Europe.

By 1989 the world had changed dramatically. The Cold War was over and the Soviet Union was breaking up. The East European countries had already slipped Moscow's leash, and Poland and Hungary had achieved quasi-Western political systems, with Czechoslovakia soon to follow. In such circumstances, Eagleburger and I agreed that in my introductory calls in Belgrade and the republican capitals, I would deliver a new message: Yugoslavia no longer enjoyed the geopolitical importance that the United States had given it during the Cold War. Then, Marshal Josip Tito had made Yugoslavia a model for independence from the Soviet Union as well as for a brand of communism that was more open politically and less centralized economically.

WARREN ZIMMERMANN was Ambassador to Yugoslavia from 1989 to 1992. He is now a Senior Consultant at RAND.

Warren Zimmermann

Now Yugoslavia had been surpassed by both Poland and Hungary in economic and political openness. In addition, human rights had become a major element of U.S. policy, and Yugoslavia's record on that issue was not good—particularly in the province of Kosovo, where an authoritarian Serbian regime was systematically depriving the Albanian majority of its basic civil liberties. Finally, I was to reassert the traditional mantra of U.S. support for Yugoslavia's unity, independence, and territorial integrity. But I would add that the United States could only support unity in the context of democracy; it would strongly oppose unity imposed or preserved by force.

Thus equipped, my wife and I arrived in Belgrade on March 9, 1989, after an absence of 21 years. The city had not changed much from the dusty half-Slav, half-Turkish town we remembered. Everybody still talked politics in the outdoor cafés, shaded by splendid chestnut trees. Belgrade was an acquired taste, and I had acquired it. What had changed was the character of the Serbian politics that people were busy discussing. Slobodan Milošević, an ambitious and ruthless communist party official, had clawed his way to power several years before. In early 1989, his efforts were focused on Kosovo.

Kosovo is to Serbs what Jerusalem is to Jews—a sacred ancestral homeland. In the postwar period, the Albanians in Kosovo—about 90 percent of the population—had carved out a dominant position in the province. Milošević was intent on wresting back that control, and he had no qualms about doing it unconstitutionally. Working through the intimidating powers of the communist apparatus, he took over or suspended Kosovo's governing bodies. He replaced bureaucratic and party incumbents with Serbs or pliant Albanians, one of whom, party chief Rahman Morina, sweated through his shirt during each of my meetings with him. Morina was later carried off prematurely by a heart attack brought on, no doubt, by stress.

On Kosovo, the message that Eagleburger and I had worked out was simple: if Yugoslavia wanted to continue its close relations with the United States, it would have to curb human rights abuses in the province. The point was naturally welcomed by the Albanians in Kosovo and also by Slovenia, an already democratic republic, which was proclaiming that Kosovo was the most egregious example of Milošević's dictatorial rule. Milošević, on the other hand, took my criticism personally; he later cited it as the reason he waited nearly a year before agreeing to meet me.

The Last Ambassador

AN OBSESSION WITH HISTORY

MILOŠEVIČ's Serbia was at the heart of the complex of issues that destroyed Yugoslavia. Serbs are a naturally talented and ebullient people with an instinctive liking for Americans that is based partly on a shared garrulity and partly on a military alliance spanning both world wars. Their tragic defect is an obsession with their own history; their hearts are in the past, not the future. In the Balkans, intellectuals tend to be the standard-bearers of nationalism; in Serbia, this is carried to fetishistic lengths.

A lugubrious, paranoid, and Serbocentric view of the past enables the Serbs to blame everyone but themselves for whatever goes wrong. They had a real grievance against Tito, in some measure justified, for creating a postwar Yugoslavia that denied them a role that they believed their large population (40 percent of the nation—similar to Russians in the old Soviet Union) and historical mission entitled them. When Tito died, leaving a Yugoslavia too decentralized for any ethnic group to dominate, it became inevitable that a Serbian nationalist would rise up to redress the perceived wrongs dealt his people. It was a tragedy for Serbia, its neighbors, and Europe as a whole that the nationalist turned out to be Slobodan Milošević.

After the year from the spring of 1989 to 1990 in which Milošević left me cooling my heels, I grew to know him well. We had many long conversations, all of them contentious but none of them shouting matches. "You see, Mr. Zimmermann," he would say, "only we Serbs really believe in Yugoslavia. We're not trying to secede like the Croats and Slovenes and we're not trying to create an Islamic state like the Muslims in Bosnia. They all fought against you in World War II. We were your allies." On Kosovo, Milošević painted a picture without shadings: "Kosovo has always been Serbian, except for a brief period during World War II. Yet we have given the Albanians their own government, their own parliament, their own national library, and their own schools [none of these assertions was true at the time he made them to me]. We have even given them their own academy of sciences. Have you Americans given your blacks their own academy of sciences?"

Milošević makes a stunning first impression on those who do not have the information to refute his often erroneous assertions. Many is the U.S. senator or congressman who has reeled out of his office exclaiming, "Why, he's not nearly as bad as I expected!" One congressman even invited him to a White House prayer breakfast. Milošević knows how to act with Americans. He dresses in the Western style (he spent considerable time in New York in his banking days), drinks Scotch on the rocks, and smokes Italian cigarillos. His cherubic cheeks do not fit the strongman image; in fact, he has to work hard at looking tough for his public posters. His manner is affable and displays his light side. Unfortunately, the man is almost totally dominated by his dark side.

Milošević began his career as a communist apparatchik of extremely authoritarian mien, even for Serbia. He rose to the leadership of the Serbian party by betraying the man who gave him his chance in politics, Ivan Stambolić, whose purge Milošević organized. Milošević is an opportunist, not an ideologue, a man driven by power rather than nationalism. He has made a Faustian pact with nationalism as a way to gain and hold power.

He is a man of extraordinary coldness. I never saw him moved by an individual case of human suffering; for him, people are groups (Serbs, Muslims) or simply abstractions. Nor did I ever hear him say a charitable or generous word about any human being, not even a Serb. This chilling personality trait made it possible for Milošević to condone, encourage, and even organize the unspeakable atrocities committed by Serbian citizens in the Bosnian war. It also accounts for his habitual mendacity, as in his outrageous distortion of Serbian behavior in Kosovo. For Milošević, truth has only a relative value. If it serves his objectives, it is employed; if not, it can be discarded.

When the unity of Yugoslavia was threatened in the late 1980s by Slovenia—Yugoslavia's only Serbless republic—Milošević cast himself as the apostle of unity. Not interested in unity per se, he wanted a unity that Serbia could dominate, working through the Yugoslav People's Army, whose officer corps was over 50 percent Serbian. Milošević's concept of unity did not extend to democracy or power-sharing with other national groups.

In fact, in his verbal attacks on Slovenia and Croatia and his subsequent trade sanctions against them, he became the major wrecker of Yugoslavia. When the Slovenian and Croatian independence movements, together with Milošević's own disruptive actions in the name of unity, made the preservation of Yugoslavia impossible, he fell back on an even more aggressive approach. If Yugoslavia could not encompass all Serbs, then Serbia would. The Serbian populations of Croatia, Bosnia, Montenegro, and possibly Macedonia would be incorporated—along with generous pieces of territory—into a Milošević-dominated "Yugoslavia." His rallying cry was that all Serbs have the right to live in a single state—a doctrine that, if applied globally, would cause the disintegration of dozens of multinational states.

WORST-CASE SCENARIOS

FROM THE beginning of my ambassadorship in Yugoslavia, I pressed the talented and highly professional group of political and economic officers in the U.S. embassy in Belgrade and the consulate general in Zagreb, Croatia, to consider worst-case scenarios for Yugoslavia. The worst case we could think of was the breakup of the country. We reported to Washington that no breakup of Yugoslavia could happen peacefully. The ethnic hatred sown by Milošević and his ilk and the mixture of ethnic groups in every republic except Slovenia meant that Yugoslavia's shattering would lead to extreme violence, perhaps even war. Thus we favored at least a loose unity while encouraging democratic development. The new Yugoslav prime minister, Ante Marković, a dynamic Croatian committed to economic reform and other Western policies, was pressing for both these objectives. The United States supported him and persuaded the West European governments to do so as well.

The U.S. policy of unity and democracy was not controversial within the Bush administration or initially in Western Europe. But it faced vehement criticism, led by Senator Robert Dole (R-Kans.), in the U.S. Congress. Critics of the policy charged that our efforts to hold together a country that was falling apart helped Milošević and hurt the democratic forces in Slovenia and Croatia. The critics did not understand that democratic unity favored Marković, not Milošević, who had no interest in unity on a democratic reformist basis. In the end, the dissolution of Yugoslavia did lead to war (and to Serbian territorial gains), and thus confirmed that unity and democracy were the Siamese twins of Yugoslavia's fate. The loss of one meant that the other would die.

In January 1990, the communist party created by Tito breathed its last; a party congress split by quarreling was adjourned, never to meet again. Yugoslavia lurched into its first democratic elections. The two most anti-Yugoslav republics, Slovenia and Croatia, were the first to vote. By the end of the year the four southern republics had voted as well. Even the Serbian government held elections, despite Milošević's occasional assertions to me that Serbia's needs were much better met by a one-party system.

The republican elections turned out to be a disaster for those who hoped to keep Yugoslavia together in a democratic framework. People had no opportunity to vote on a Yugoslavia-wide level once Prime Minister Marković failed to win approval for federal elections. They vented their pent-up frustrations by voting for nationalists who hammered on ethnic themes. The elections became a test of ethnic loyalty. Ethnic parties won power in five of the six republics, all but Macedonia.

NATIONALISM UNLEASHED

BY BRINGING nationalism to power almost everywhere, the elections helped snuff out the very flame of democracy that they had kindled. Nationalism is by nature uncivil, antidemocratic, and separatist because it empowers one ethnic group over all others. If the elections weakened the democratic element so necessary for Yugoslavia, they also weakened the necessary unifying element. I visited all six republics to evaluate the new leaders. I found that not only was the country breaking up into different power centers, but each local region was developing a nationalist ideology, each different from the other. The age of naked nationalism had begun.

Slovenian nationalists, now in power, quickly broke almost all Slovenia's remaining political and economic ties with the Yugoslav government. The Slovenes' separatist nationalism was unique in Yugoslavia—it had no victims and no enemies; while the Slovenes hated Milošević, they built no ideology against him. They practiced a "Garbo nationalism"—they just wanted to be left alone. Their virtue was democracy and their vice was selfishness. In their drive to separate from Yugoslavia they simply ignored the 22 million Yugoslavs who were not Slovenes. They bear considerable responsibility for the bloodbath that followed their secession.

No Yugoslav republic was more transformed by the elections of 1990 than Croatia. The decisive victory of the Croatian Democratic Union in May brought to the presidency an implacable nationalist, Franjo Tudjman. I first met Tudjman in Zagreb on the morning of his victory; before then I had avoided him because of the extreme nature of some of his campaign statements. If Milošević recalls a slick con man, Tudjman resembles an inflexible schoolteacher. He is a former general and communist, expelled from the party under Tito and twice jailed for nationalism. Prim steel eyeglasses hang on a square face whose natural expression is a scowl. His mouth occasionally creases into a nervous chuckle or mirthless laugh. In our first meeting, he treated the colleagues who accompanied him with extreme disdain. Then, on the spot, he appointed two of them to high-ranking positions—to their surprise, since the venue for this solemn act was the breakfast table of the American consul general.

Tudjman's temper flared when I asked him about his remark during the campaign that he was glad his wife was neither a Serb nor a Jew. He launched into a ten-minute defense of his ethnic humanity, claiming, among other things, that some of his best friends were Serbs. While he didn't profess similar affinities with Jews (and his earlier writings had denigrated the Holocaust), he did promise to make restitution to the Zagreb Jewish community for the destruction of its synagogue by Croatian fascists during World War II. He kept that promise.

Unlike Milošević, who is driven by power, Tudjman is obsessed by nationalism. His devotion to Croatia is of the most narrow-minded sort, and he has never shown much understanding of or interest in democratic values. He presided over serious violations of the rights of Serbs, who made up 12 percent of the population of Croatia. They were dismissed from work, required to take loyalty oaths, and subjected to attacks on their homes and property. I have sat at Tudjman's lunch table and listened to several of his ministers revile Serbs in the most racist terms. He didn't join in, but he didn't stop them either. He has also stifled the independence of the press as much as Milošević, and maybe even more.

Tudjman's saving grace, which distinguishes him from Milošević, is that he really wants to be a Western statesman. He therefore listens to Western expressions of concern and criticism and often does something about them. For better or worse, Croatian nationalism is defined by Tudjman—intolerant, anti-Serb, and authoritarian. These attributes—together with an aura of wartime fascism, which Tudjman has done nothing to dispel—help explain why many Serbs in Croatia reject Croatian rule and why the core hostility in the former Yugoslavia is still between Serbs and Croats.

During 1990, Serbian nationalism under Milošević became even more aggressive. No longer was it enough for Serbs living outside Serbia to have their rights protected. They also had to own and control the territory they inhabited, regardless of prior sovereignty. These Serbian claims had no consistent principles behind them. Where Serbs were a

Warren Zimmermann

minority, as in Kosovo, they asserted a historical, rather than a numerical, right to rule. Where no such historical right was plausible, as in the Krajina area of Croatia, they claimed self-determination on the majority principle. Revealingly, Milošević was unwilling to give the Albanians in Kosovo the same right of self-determination that he demanded for Serbs in Croatia and Bosnia.

In the Serbian elections of December 1990, Milošević made nationalism the litmus test: if you didn't vote for him, you were not a good Serb. The Serbian opposition, overwhelmed by the superior organization of Milošević's still-intact communist apparatus and a near-total media blackout, foundered on whether to play the nationalist game or reject it. Milošević won in a tainted but convincing landslide. The one-party system, beloved by the Serbian leader, survived. Milošević simply modernized it by giving it multiparty trimmings.

Albanian nationalism was, like Croatian nationalism, to some degree a reaction to Milošević's aggressive tactics. As the Serbs pressed, the Albanians stiffened. They boycotted the Serbian elections, despite U.S. counsel that a determined parliamentary minority could wield much political leverage. Milošević's strong-arm approach had launched the Albanians on a path of no return toward complete independence from the Serbs.

By December 1990, there were few Kosovo Albanians who did not insist either on an independent Kosovo or a Kosovo linked with Albania. The psychological break was complete. Any provocation launched by either side had the potential to blow the province apart. In these volatile circumstances, I urged Milošević to meet with the disciplined and impressive Albanian leader Ibrahim Rugova, who was urging a policy of peaceful resistance. Rugova agreed. Milošević refused, saying of the leader of some two million Albanian subjects of Serbia, "Who does he represent?"

The most interesting opposition figure in Serbia was Vuk Drašković, a flamboyant and talented novelist, who leaped onto the political stage as a pro-Serbian extremist, complete with Old Testament beard, racist ideas, and the persona of a Serbian peasant. Once he found his political sea legs, however, Drašković turned into a staunch defender of an open political system and free press. On March 9, 1991, he used his talent for motivating people to stage a mass rally in Belgrade against Milošević's control of the press. Clumsy handling by the police and the army led to two deaths—a demonstrator and a policeman—and to Drašković's arrest and brief detention. Many observers felt that the rally, which has now entered Serbian folklore, came close to dethroning Milošević. While this is doubtful, the courage of nearly 100,000 spontaneous demonstrators was a moving tribute to the democratic vibrancy of many Serbs.

Many new opposition figures within the former republics of Yugoslavia took a clear stand against nationalism. In speaking out, they paid a price in ransacked offices, bombings, death threats, beatings, and arrests. With my strong support, Western human rights groups helped many opposition organizations and publications to survive. The investment, however long-term, will pay off one day. The people being helped, and those who will succeed them, are part of the "other Serbia" and the "other Croatia"—the core of the democratic revival that in time must replace the current nationalist hysteria.

Neither Milošević nor Tudjman could understand why we cared so much about people who were murdered, tortured, abused, or harassed. Milošević would listen patiently, then ask, "Why do you waste time on these individuals, who are mostly criminals anyway, when Serbs as a nation have been abused for years?" Tudjman would often erupt in fury when I had the temerity to suggest that Croatian authorities were not always model democrats. When it came to results, however, Milošević almost never delivered; Tudjman sometimes did.

ELEVENTH-HOUR MANEUVERS

THE LAST YEAR of Yugoslavia's existence—1991—saw the unfolding of unilateral and conflicting nationalist strategies. Slovenia, where a December 1990 referendum showed overwhelming popular support for independence, announced its decision to secede in June 1991 if a loose confederal solution was not found. Wittingly making his republic a hostage to Slovenian policy, Tudjman said Croatia would do what Slovenia did. Milošević countered that the breakup of Yugoslavia would lead to Serbia's incorporating all Serbs into a single state. Bosnian leader Alija Izetbegović argued that the survival of Yugoslavia in some form was essential to Bosnia's survival as well.

Izetbegović was mild-mannered, deferential, and perpetually anxious; he wore the mantle of leadership with great discomfort. A devout Muslim but no extremist, he consistently advocated the preservation of a multinational Bosnia. Ironically, it was Milošević and Tudjman, in their professed desire for Bosnian Serbs and Bosnian Croats to live apart from Muslims, who laid the philosophical groundwork for a separate Muslim entity. Bosnia had a strong multiethnic character and the highest percentage of ethnically mixed marriages of any republic. While its history since the fifteenth-century Turkish occupation was no more bloody than the history of England or France, Bosnia was the major Balkan killing ground during World War II. Izetbegović was succinct with me: "If Croatia goes independent, Bosnia will be destroyed."

In early 1991, the supporters of a unified and democratic Yugoslavia were becoming marginalized. The leaders of the two republics with the most to lose from the breakup of Yugoslavia—Alija Izetbegović of Bosnia and Kiro Gligorov of Macedonia—proposed to hold it together in an even weaker configuration. Milošević gave their plan lip service; the Croats and Slovenes rejected it flatly for leaving too many powers with the central government.

During this period the Yugoslav People's Army (JNA in its Serbo-Croatian acronym) emerged as a major political player, an unusual role for a communist army. I met regularly with the defense minister, General Veljko Kadijević, a brooding, humorless officer who spoke with antipathy about Slovenes and Croats and with paranoia about Germans, whom he saw as bent on incorporating the Balkans into a Fourth Reich. The JNA enjoyed a proud tradition, with roots in Tito's Partisan fighters, who stood up to the Germans in World War II. The fifth-largest army in Europe, well supplied by the Soviet Union and an enormous domestic arms industry, it was seen by many as the most important unifying institution in Yugoslavia. Its officer corps, however, had a Serbian majority who, when events forced them to choose, followed Milošević.

The JNA was soon on a collision course with the breakaway republics. Both Croatia and Slovenia were trying to create their own military forces by calling on their young men to desert the JNA and by weakening the JNA's control over the republican Territorial Defense Forces, a sort of national guard. The JNA went berserk over this proliferation of armies. "How many armies does the United States have?" Kadijević stormed at me. In early 1991, the JNA tried to force the Yugoslav presidency—a comically weak, collective, eight-person chief of state—to declare a national emergency and authorize the army to disarm the Slovenian and Croatian militaries. This bid, which amounted to a military coup, was frustrated politically by the democratically inclined presidency members from Macedonia and Slovenia, Vasil Tupurkovski and Janez Drnovšek. The defeat led

Milošević to use the four votes he controlled in the eight-member presidency to subvert the scheduled rotation of its "president" from a Serb to
a Croat. I asked Milošević several days before the May 15 election by the
presidency if he would block the accession of the Croat Stipe Mesić, even
though it was called for by constitutional precedent. "Serbia will always
act in the spirit of the highest democratic principles," replied Milošević,
who was always at his most mellifluous when expatiating on his devotion
to democracy. "There will be a democratic vote in the presidency."

"But are you going to accept a fair transition from a Serb to a Croat
president?" I pursued. "Mr. Zimmermann," he said, "you can tell your
government that it has absolutely nothing to worry about." I cabled
Washington that Mesić was not a sure thing. Two days later Milošević's
allies on the presidency blocked Mesić's ascension, throwing Yugoslavia
into a constitutional crisis. When I accused Milošević later of lying to
me, he asserted that he had not actually promised that Mesić would be
named. The incident illustrated three important traits of Milošević's
character: his cynicism about Yugoslavia's unity and institutions, his natural mendacity, and the pains he always took to avoid direct responsibility for aggressive actions. The third trait was to become particularly relevant to Milošević's hidden hand in the Bosnia crisis.

ENTER BAKER

IT WAS IN the context of Milošević's move against the Yugoslav presidency and its Croatian president-designate, Croatian actions against the
jobs and property of Serbs in Croatia, growing violence between Serbs
and Croats, and the threat by both Slovenia and Croatia to withdraw
from Yugoslavia at midyear that Secretary of State James Baker arrived
in Belgrade on June 21, 1991.

During his one-day visit Baker had nine consecutive meetings: with
the Albanian leaders from Kosovo, with all six republican leaders, and
twice with Yugoslav Prime Minister Ante Marković and Foreign Minister Budimir Lončar. Listening to Baker deal with these complex and iras-
cible personalities, I felt that I had rarely, if ever, heard a secretary of state
make a more skillful or reasonable presentation. Baker's failure was due
not to his message but to the fact that the different parts of Yugoslavia
were on a collision course.

Baker expressed the American hope that Yugoslavia would hold together behind the reformist Marković, who by that time was seen increasingly as a figurehead or, even worse, a fig leaf. Baker said that it was up to the people of Yugoslavia to determine their future governing structures; the United States would support any arrangement on which they could peacefully agree. Baker told Croatian President Franjo Tudjman and Slovene President Milan Kučan that the United States would not encourage or support unilateral secession; he hoped they would not secede, but if they had to leave, he urged them to leave by negotiated agreement. He argued that self-determination cannot be unilateral but must be pursued by dialogue and peaceful means. To Milošević and (indirectly) the army, Baker made clear that the United States strongly opposed any use of force, intimidation, or incitement to violence that would block democratic change. Yugoslavia could not be held together at gunpoint. In his encounter with Milošević—the most contentious of the nine meetings—Baker hammered the Serb leader on his human rights violations in Kosovo, urged his acquiescence to a looser constitutional arrangement for Yugoslavia, and pressed him to stop destabilizing the Yugoslav presidency.

Never was a green light given or implied to Milošević or the army to invade the seceding republics, as has since been alleged in some press accounts. But was there a red light? Not as such, because the United States had given no consideration to using force to stop a Serbian/JNA attack on Slovenia or Croatia. Nor, at that point, had a single member of Congress, as far as I know, advocated the introduction of American military power. Baker did, however, leave a strong political message. He said to Prime Minister Marković, a conduit to the army, "If you force the United States to choose between unity and democracy, we will always choose democracy."

Baker's message was the right one, but it came too late. If a mistake was made, it was that the secretary of state had not come six months earlier, a time that unfortunately coincided with the massive American preparations for the Persian Gulf War. By June 1991, Baker was making a last-ditch effort. Even so, it is not clear that an earlier visit by Baker would have made a difference. The aggressive nationalism emanating like noxious fumes from the leaders of Serbia and Croatia and their even more extreme advisers, officials, media manipulators, and allies had cast the die for disintegration and violence.

The breakup of Yugoslavia is a classic example of nationalism from the top down—a manipulated nationalism in a region where peace has historically prevailed more than war and in which a quarter of the population were in mixed marriages. The manipulators condoned and even provoked local ethnic violence in order to engender animosities that could then be magnified by the press, leading to further violence. Milošević gave prime television time to fanatic nationalists like Vojislav Šešelj, who once said that the way to deal with the Kosovo Albanians was to kill them all. Tudjman also used his control of the media to sow hate. Nationalist "intellectuals," wrapped in the mantle of august academies of sciences, expounded their pseudo-history of the victimization of Serbs (or Croats) through the ages. One of them seriously asserted to me that Serbs had committed no crimes or moral transgressions at any point in their long history. Worst of all, the media, under the thumb of most republican regimes, spewed an endless daily torrent of violence and enmity. As a reporter for *Vreme*, one of the few independent magazines left in the former Yugoslavia, said, "You Americans would become nationalists and racists too if your media were totally in the hands of the Ku Klux Klan."

SECESSION AND WAR

IN LATE JUNE 1991, just a few days after Baker's departure from Belgrade and almost exactly according to their timetable, Croatia and Slovenia declared independence. Fighting began in Slovenia almost immediately. Contrary to the general view, it was the Slovenes who started the war. Their independence declaration, which had not been preceded by even the most token effort to negotiate, effectively put under their control all the border and customs posts between Slovenia and its two neighbors, Italy and Austria. This meant that Slovenia, the only international gateway between the West and Yugoslavia, had unilaterally appropriated the right to goods destined for other republics, as well as customs revenues estimated at some 75 percent of the Yugoslav federal budget. Even an army less primitive than the jna would have reacted. Worst of all, the Slovenes' understandable desire to be independent condemned the rest of Yugoslavia to war.

The Yugoslav generals, thinking they could intimidate the Slovenes, roared their tanks through peaceful Slovenian streets, slapping aside compact cars as they lumbered through. The Slovenes, trained by the JNA itself in territorial defense, fought back. After ten days, at Milošević's direction or with his acquiescence, the JNA withdrew from Slovenia, leaving the republic effectively independent. Compared to the Croatian and Bosnian wars that followed, the casualty figures in Slovenia seem ludicrously small: 37 JNA and 12 Slovenes killed. They do not bear out the generally held assumption that the Yugoslav army waged an extermination campaign in Slovenia. In provoking war, the Slovenes won the support of the world's television viewers and consolidated their entire population behind independence. Unlike the JNA, they welcomed foreign journalists, to whom they retailed the epic struggle of their tiny republic against the Yugoslav colossus. It was the most brilliant public relations coup in the history of Yugoslavia.

It was no surprise to me that Milošević was willing to let Slovenia go. His policy since 1989 provoked the Slovenes to secede by making it clear that he would not tolerate their liberal, independent ways. With Slovenia out of the game, he and the JNA were now free to take on a Croatia no longer able to count on Slovenia's support.

The fighting in Croatia began with the illusion of evenhandedness. The Yugoslav army would step in to separate the Serbian and Croatian combatants. During the summer of 1991, however, it soon became clear that the JNA, while claiming neutrality, was in fact turning territory over to Serbs. The war in Croatia had become a war of aggression.

As the war grew more bitter through the summer of 1991, the European Community (EC) and the United Nations launched a joint effort to achieve a cease-fire and an agreement among all the Yugoslav republics. Special U.N. envoys Cyrus Vance and Lord Peter Carrington, two former foreign ministers and old friends, shared the Sisyphean task of achieving a peaceful outcome. The determined Vance won the trust of the JNA and succeeded on January 3, 1992, in producing a cease-fire that froze both the military and political status quo in Croatia. The fighting stopped, but the Serbs were left holding about a quarter of the republic. The freeze was unwittingly stabilized by U.N. peacekeepers who arrived in March 1992.

Carrington's job was to get the feuding Yugoslav republics to define the relationship they were prepared to have with each other. He and Vance both argued—as did the U.S. government—that there should be no Western recognition of the independence of any Yugoslav republic until all had agreed on their mutual relationships. If this simple principle had been maintained, less blood would have been shed in Bosnia.

During the fall of 1991, while Vance and Carrington were launching their diplomatic efforts, the JNA shelled the Croatian cities of Vukovar and Dubrovnik, the first major war crimes in Yugoslavia since World War II. The pretty Croatian city of Vukovar, with a mixed population, of which over a third was Serb, first came under JNA shelling in August, apparently because of its location on the Danube River between Serbia and Croatia. For three months the army, shrinking from an attack that might have cost it casualties, sat outside the city and shelled it to pieces. The civilian population of the city—Serbs and Croats alike—huddled in cellars. Over 2,000 civilians were killed before the JNA finally "liberated" the city.

One of the employees in our embassy residence, a young Croatian woman named Danijela Hajnal, was from Vukovar; her mother was trapped in a cellar during the siege. During her stay with my wife and me after Vukovar fell, Danijela's mother described the relations between Serbs and Croats during the attack: "There were a hundred people in that cellar," she said, "half of us Croats and half Serbs. We were friends when we went into the cellar, and three months later when we came out, we were still friends." About the same time I asked Danijela how many Serbs and Croats were in her high school class in Vukovar. She replied that she didn't have the faintest idea. These vignettes, which could be multiplied thousands of times over, show how natural it was for Yugoslavs to get along with each other, despite the ranting of their leaders.

Notwithstanding solemn guarantees by General Kadijević, the JNA in October 1991 also shelled Dubrovnik from the hills and the sea. This medieval town, which glowed in the Adriatic like a piece of pink marble, had withstood the depredations of Turks, Venetians, and many other would-be conquerors. Now it was falling under the guns of an army whose constitutional duty was to defend it. Dubrovnik was not destroyed, but the damage inflicted by the Yugoslav army exceeded the best efforts of any previous marauder. Only Milošević pretended that there was any military objective in Dubrovnik. Denying, as usual, any personal responsibility for what the army did, he told me with a straight face that there were foreign mercenaries hiding in the city. Kadijević didn't even pretend that Dubrovnik was a military target. "I give you my word," he told me, "that the shelling of Dubrovnik was unauthorized. Those who did it will be punished." My repeated requests for the details of their punishment went unanswered.

Shelling civilian populations is a war crime. Vukovar and Dubrovnik led directly to the merciless attacks on Sarajevo and other Bosnian cities. Yet no Western government at the time called on NATO's military force to get the JNA to stop shelling Dubrovnik, although NATO's supreme commander, General John Galvin, had prepared contingency plans for doing so. The use of force was simply too big a step to consider in late 1991. I did not recommend it myself—a major mistake. The JNA's artillery on the hills surrounding Dubrovnik and its small craft on the water would have been easy targets. Not only would damage to the city have been averted, but the Serbs would have been taught a lesson about Western resolve that might have deterred at least some of their aggression against Bosnia. As it was, the Serbs learned another lesson—that there was no Western resolve, and that they could push about as far as their power could take them.

A TAR BABY IN WASHINGTON

SECRETARY OF STATE Baker's failure to head off the Slovenian and Croatian declarations of independence cooled whatever ardor he may have had for projecting the United States into the Yugoslav imbroglio. During the summer of 1991, it had been fair enough to give the EC a chance to deal with what it called a "European problem." But by autumn, the Serbian/JNA plan for taking over parts of Croatia had crystallized in the attacks on Vukovar and Dubrovnik. Threats to the integrity of Bosnia were growing, and the EC, under German cajoling, was stumbling toward recognition of the breakaway republics. Even without threatening force, the United States could have thrown more weight behind the effort to prevent greater violence. However, between July 1991 and March 1992, the United States was not a major factor in the Yugoslav crisis. In the fall of 1991, at a U.S. ambassadors' meeting in Berlin, a friend from the State Department's European Bureau told me that Yugoslavia had become a tar baby in Washington. Nobody wanted to touch it. With the American presidential election just a year away, it was seen as a loser.

Unfortunately, American immobility coincided with growing pressure on Bosnia. Neither Milošević nor Tudjman made any effort to conceal their designs on Bosnia from me. As a place where Serbs, Croats, and Muslims had coexisted more or less peacefully for centuries, Bosnia was an affront and a challenge to these two ethnic supremacists.

At the end of a long meeting with me, Tudjman erupted into a diatribe against Izetbegović and the Muslims of Bosnia. "They're dangerous fundamentalists," he charged, "and they're using Bosnia as a beachhead to spread their ideology throughout Europe and even to the United

States. The civilized nations should join together to repel this threat. Bosnia has never had any real existence. It should be divided between Serbia and Croatia."

I was flabbergasted at this outburst and got the impression that Tudjman's aides who were present were equally surprised. With some heat I asked, "Mr. President, how can you expect the West to help you get back the parts of Croatia taken by the Serbs when you yourself are advancing naked and unsupported claims on a neighboring republic?" There was no answer. I added, "And how can you expect Milošević to respect a deal with you to divide Bosnia when he's trying to annex part of Croatia?" Amazingly, Tudjman answered, "Because I can trust Milošević." On the way down the stairs after this surreal discussion, I asked one of Tudjman's aides if I had gotten too emotional in defending the integrity of Bosnia. "Oh no," he said, "You were just fine."

Milošević's strategy for Bosnia, unlike Tudjman's, was calculating rather than emotional. When Slovenia and Croatia declared independence and stopped participating in the Yugoslav government, Milošević, notwithstanding all he had done to destroy Yugoslavia, now claimed to be its heir. He contended that all those who wanted to "remain" in Yugoslavia should have the right to do so. This included, of course, the Serbs of Croatia and the Serbs of Bosnia. As Milošević explained this to me, he added that while the Muslims in Bosnia tended to live in cities, the Serbs were a rural people living on 70 percent of the land, to which they therefore had a right. Thus, at least six months before the Bosnian Serb army and the irregulars from Serbia shattered the peace in Bosnia, Milošević was laying the groundwork for a Serbian claim. From that moment, in every conversation I had with him I emphasized the strong U.S. opposition to any Serbian power play in Bosnia.

FATAL RECOGNITION

WHEN CROATIA opted for independence in mid-1991, Bosnian President Izetbegović saw the writing on the wall for his republic. He scurried throughout Europe and the United States looking for ways to head off disaster. He pushed, without success, the dying Izetbegović-Gligorov plan for a loosely connected Yugoslavia. He asked for and got EC observers in Bosnia. He asked for, but did not get, U.N. peacekeepers there. Vance and the U.N. leadership in New York took the traditional if puzzling line that peacekeepers are used after a conflict, not before. The U.S. government did not support Izetbegović on the request for peacekeepers either. In a cable to Washington I urged this innovative step, but did not press for it as hard as I should have. As an unsatisfactory compromise, when the U.N. peacekeepers arrived in Croatia in March 1992, they set up their headquarters in Sarajevo.

In the fall of 1991, German Foreign Minister Hans-Dietrich Genscher pressed his EC colleagues to recognize Slovenia and Croatia and to offer recognition to Bosnia and Macedonia. Izetbegović, briefed by the German ambassador to Yugoslavia on how to make his point with Genscher that EC recognition would bring violence to Bosnia, unaccountably failed to do so in his November meeting with the German foreign minister. The omission can only have led Genscher to assume that he had a green light from Izetbegović for recognition.

I was urging Washington to defer recognition, as the EC ambassadors in Belgrade were urging their governments. Although Washington was opposed to premature recognition, U.S. appeals to EC governments were perfunctory. On December 17, 1991, an EC summit decided to grant recognition. Carrington and Vance both complained loudly and publicly. The State Department's statement, to avoid ruffling the EC, was nuanced. War in Bosnia, which had until then been probable, now became virtually inevitable.

A few days after the EC's decision, I had lunch in Belgrade with Izetbegović's deputy, Ejup Ganić, a Muslim hard-liner who had trained at mit. I asked him, "Is Bosnia really going to ask for recognition in the face of all the dangers Izetbegović has repeatedly warned about? Wouldn't it be better to tell the European Community that you need more time to work out the political issues involved?" Ganić looked at me as if I had just dropped out of the sky. He said, "Of course we're going to move ahead on recognition. With Croatia and Slovenia now gone, we can't consign Bosnia to a truncated Yugoslavia controlled by Serbia."

I concluded from the abrupt change of tack by Ganić that Izetbegović was now playing a double game. With the European Community heading toward recognition, he thought he could get away with it under the guns of the Serbs. Perhaps he counted on Western military support, though nobody had promised him that. Whatever his motives, it was a disastrous political mistake. Serbia, Bosnia's vastly more powerful neighbor, now had the pretext it needed to strike—the claim that 1.3 million

Serbs were being taken out of "Yugoslavia" against their will. I believe that Milošević and Bosnian Serb leader Radovan Karadžić had already decided to annex the majority of Bosnia by military force (Milošević had spoken to me of 70 percent). The EC's irresponsibility, the United States' passivity, and Izetbegović's miscalculation made their job easier.

Events took their inexorable course following the EC's recognition decision. Hardly anybody noticed the December 20 resignation of Milošević, so power-less had Yugoslavia's last prime minister become. Although defeated by an ad hoc cabal of nationalists, from the liberal Slovenes to the neo-communist Serbs, Marković still departed as a symbol of everything his country needed: a modern, stable economy, the rule of law, and ethnic tolerance. He had treated Yugoslavia like a patient with a serious cancer—nationalism. A semi-heroic, semi-tragic figure, Marković failed, but at least he had fought the cancer instead of adjusting to it. He had aspired to be Yugoslavia's savior. Instead, he turned out to be the Yugoslavian equivalent of Russia's last leader before the Bolshevik deluge, Aleksandr Kerensky. The war in Croatia, the impending war in Bosnia, and a future that promised a generation of violence in the Balkans were the results of Yugoslavia's demise.

PARTNERS IN CRIME

DURING THE first few months of 1992, events in Bosnia careened down two parallel tracks. On one, the Izetbegović government, following the EC lead, prepared for independence. Its referendum on February 29 and March 1 produced predictable results. Practically all the Muslims and Croats voted for independence, yielding a 64-percent majority, while practically all the Serbs boycotted the election. On the other track, the leaders of the Serbian minority prepared for secession and war. Since the 1990 Bosnian election, I had paid periodic visits to Karadžić. The Bosnian Serb leader is a large man with flamboyant hair, an outwardly friendly manner, and the unlikely profession of psychiatry. In the great tradition of nationalists who do not come from their nation (Hitler, Napoleon, Stalin), Karadžić is from Montenegro, not Bosnia. I learned from experience that his outstanding characteristics were his stubbornness and deep-seated hostility to Muslims, Croats, and any other non-Serb ethnic group in his neighborhood.

I was startled to hear the extravagance of Karadžić's claims on behalf of the Serbs. He told me that "Serbs have a right to territory not only where they're now living but also where they're buried, since the earth they lie in was taken unjustly from them." When I asked whether he would accept parallel claims on behalf of Croats or Muslims, he answered, "No, because Croats are fascists and Muslims are Islamic fanatics." His disdain for the truth was absolute; he insisted that "Sarajevo is a Serbian city," which it has never been. His apartheid philosophy was as extreme as anything concocted in South Africa. He was the architect of massacres in the Muslim villages, ethnic cleansing, and artillery attacks on civilian populations. In his fanaticism, ruthlessness, and contempt for human values, he invites comparison with a monster from another generation, Heinrich Himmler.

Karadžić and Milošević both made an elaborate pretense to me of not knowing each other very well and having no operational contacts. Milošević always reacted with cherubic innocence when I accosted him over Bosnia. "But why do you come to me, Mr. Zimmermann? Serbia has nothing to do with Bosnia. It's not our problem." This fiction suited each leader—Milošević to escape respon-sibility for aggression, Karadžić to avoid the charge that he was a henchman of Milošević's rather than a Serbian folk hero in his own right.

There is no doubt, however, that the two were partners in war crimes. Copying Milošević's strategy in Croatia, Karadžić's followers—beginning a year before the Bosnian war broke out—declared three "Serb Autonomous Regions" in Bosnia, began an arms supply relationship with the JNA, and accepted jna intervention in September to define their borders. They established artillery positions around Sarajevo and other towns, created a "Bosnian Serb" army (effectively a branch of the JNA, commanded by a JNA general and using JNA-supplied heavy artillery, tanks, and air power), established their own parliament, and attempted a putsch in Sarajevo on March 2, 1992. In March 1992—before any country had recognized the independence of Bosnia—they declared a "Serbian Republic." These steps, particularly those involving the JNA, would not have been possible without Milošević's direct involvement.

In response to the evidence of Serbian collusion and the results of the Bosnian referendum, and in hopes that recognition might deter a Serbian attack, the United States and other NATO countries recognized Bosnia in early April 1992. However, a few days before, Serbs had launched an attack from Serbia across the Drina River, which forms the border between Serbia and Bosnia. Milošević, Karadžić, and their spokesmen have asserted that the Western recognition of Bosnia had forced the Serbs to move. I doubt this. The two Serbian leaders already had a joint strategy for dividing Bosnia and they were going to carry it out, regardless of what the rest of the world did.

The attack on Bosnia showed that Milošević and Karadžić are apostles of the most aggressive form of nationalism. Milošević-style nationalism has proven singularly resistant to economic inducements, penalties, or any other pressures short of force. Unfortunately, neither the Bush nor the Clinton administration was willing to step up to the challenge of using force in Bosnia, despite significant American interests in the Balkans. Moreover, the two Serbian strongmen, behind their propaganda, espouse the doctrine of the single nation-state, a deeply uncivilized concept. Nation-states have nothing to unify them but their nationalism, and power within them will naturally gravitate to the most strident nationalists. Multinational states, a majority in the world, can be deeply conflicted, as Yugoslavia proves. But they can also be schools of tolerance, since the need to take account of minority interests moderates behavior. Yugoslavia had its democrats as well as its demagogues. The attackers across the Drina, however, were barbarians, pure and simple.

The Serbian attack was directed at towns with large Muslim majorities. Gangsters from Serbia proper, including the notorious Arkan, who had left a trail of murder and pillage during the Croatian war, were displayed on Belgrade television swaggering on the debris of Bijeljina and other Muslim towns. Those Serbia-based marauders accounted for the high volume of atrocities committed in the early days of the war—the gang rapes, ethnic cleansing, and wanton murder of Muslim villagers. The presence in Bosnia of irregulars from Serbia drained all credibility from Milošević's assertion that Serbia had nothing to do with what was going on there.

During one of the meetings in which, on Washington's instructions, I accused Milošević of aggression in Bosnia, he asserted, "There isn't a single Serb from Serbia involved in the fighting in Bosnia."

"But," I said, "I saw Arkan on your own Belgrade television boasting about his capture of Bosnian villages."

"Our television is free to broadcast whatever it wants," said Milošević. "You shouldn't take it so seriously. Besides, you needn't worry about trouble in Bosnia. Serbs have no serious grievances in Bosnia;

they're not being abused there. This is a big difference with Serbs in Croatia." Via this backhanded compliment to the Izetbegović government, Milošević reduced the Serbian argument for naked aggression to the assumption that Serbs had a right to murder, torture, and expel simply because they did not want to live under an independent multiethnic government that was not abusing them.

LAST WORDS

JUST A FEW weeks before I was recalled in protest against the Serbian aggression in Bosnia, I had my last talk with Karadžić in Belgrade, where he was pretending not to see Milošević. He came to the U.S. embassy, bringing with him as usual his deputy and pilot fish, Nikola Koljević, a Bosnian Serb who had taught in the United States and was an expert on Shakespeare. Koljević's specialty was sidling up to me after my meetings with Karadžić and portraying himself as the humane influence on Bosnian Serb policy. Several months after my departure from Belgrade, I saw a photograph of Koljević directing artillery fire on the civilian population of Sarajevo from a hill above the city.

Perhaps it was fitting that I should have one of my last meetings in doomed Yugoslavia with this macabre pair, the professor of English literature and the psychiatrist. At least Shakespeare and Freud would have understood the power of the irrational that provoked these and other madmen to destroy the human fabric of Yugoslavia.

Karadžić began the conversation by running down his usual litany of criticisms of the Europeans, attacks on Izetbegović's character and ideology, and laments that the United States should be so blind as to abandon its traditional Serbian allies. He then launched into a stream-of-consciousness justification for everything he was doing. "You have to understand Serbs, Mr. Zimmermann. They have been betrayed for centuries. Today they cannot live with other nations. They must have their own separate existence. They are a warrior race and they can trust only themselves to take by force what is their due. But this doesn't mean that Serbs can hate. Serbs are incapable of hatred."

I sought to pin him down. "What sort of Bosnian Serb republic do you have in mind?" I asked. "Will it be a part of Serbia?"

"That will be for the Bosnian Serb people to decide," he said. "But our first goal is independence, so we can live separately from others."

"Where will your capital be?" I asked.

"Why, Sarajevo, of course."

"But how can a city which is nearly 50 percent Muslim and only 30 percent Serb be the capital for the Serbs alone?"

Karadžić had a ready answer. "The city will be divided into Muslim, Serbian, and Croatian sections, so that no ethnic groups will have to live or work together."

"Just how will it be divided?"

"By walls," he said matter-of-factly. "Of course people will be able to pass from one part of the city to another, as long as they have permission and go through the checkpoints."

I thought of Sarajevo, which for centuries had been a moving symbol of the civility that comes from people of different ethnicities living in harmony. Then I thought of Berlin, where the wall, which had symbolized all the hatreds and divisions of the Cold War, had been torn down just over a year before.

"Do you mean," I asked, "that Sarajevo will be like Berlin before the wall was destroyed?"

"Yes," he answered, "our vision of Sarajevo is like Berlin when the wall was still standing." ✹

America,
a European Power

Richard Holbrooke

THE NEW SECURITY ARCHITECTURE

PRESIDENT CLINTON made four trips to Europe last year. This commitment of presidential time and attention underlines an inescapable but little-realized fact: the United States has become a European power in a sense that goes beyond traditional assertions of America's "commitment" to Europe. In the 21st century, Europe will still need the active American involvement that has been a necessary component of the continental balance for half a century. Conversely, an unstable Europe would still threaten essential national security interests of the United States. This is as true after as it was during the Cold War.

I do not intend, of course, to suggest that nothing has changed. The end of the Cold War, which can best be dated to that symbolic moment at midnight on December 25, 1991, when the Soviet flag came down over the Kremlin for the last time, began an era of change of historic proportions. Local conflicts, internal political and economic instability, and the return of historical grievances have now replaced Soviet expansionism as the greatest threat to peace in Europe. Western Europe and America must jointly ensure that tolerant democracies become rooted throughout all of Europe and that the seething, angry, unresolved legacies of the past are contained and solved.

THE FOURTH ARCHITECTURAL MOMENT

ONLY THREE times since the French Revolution has Europe peacefully reshaped its basic security architecture. Today, the continent is in the

RICHARD HOLBROOKE is Assistant Secretary of State for European and Canadian Affairs.

middle of nothing less than the fourth such moment in the last two centuries. The first post-Napoleonic security architecture for Europe, designed in 1815 at the Congress of Vienna, helped prevent all-out continental war for 99 years. The young United States, having fought two wars with England in only 40 years, successfully kept its distance, but for the last time.

In the second period of redesign, at Versailles in 1919, President Woodrow Wilson played a central role, but the United States withdrew almost immediately from the very structures it had helped create, thereby weakening them and thus virtually guaranteeing the tragic resumption of total war 20 years later. When the third opportunity arose in 1945, the great powers initially built a system based on Yalta, Potsdam, and the United Nations. But starting in 1947, when the leaders of the West realized that this system would not suffice to stem Soviet expansion, they created the most successful peacetime collective security system in history, centered around the Truman Doctrine, the Marshall Plan, NATO, Atlantic partnership—and American leadership.

This creative architecture reflected the underlying goals of America's postwar engagement in Europe. Its post-Cold War engagement must focus again on structures, old and new. This time, the United States must lead in the creation of a security architecture that includes and thereby stabilizes all of Europe—the West, the former Soviet satellites of central Europe, and, most critically, Russia and the former republics of the Soviet Union.

All the key participants in the new security equation in Europe—the United States, the West and central European countries, and the other nations of the former Soviet Union—desire a peaceful, stable, and democratic Russia, integrated into the institutions of an undivided Europe. No more important political goal has existed in Europe since a newly democratic West Germany was successfully integrated into the European political and security structure after World War II. It is for this and other reasons that the crisis in Chechnya, discussed more fully below, has been so disturbing.

Fortunately, most of the great structures of the postwar period offer a usable foundation for building stability. The essential challenge is to maintain their coherence, project their influence, and adapt to new circumstances without diluting their basic functions.

Measured on the post-World War II calendar, the United States is now slightly past the point in the late spring of 1947 when Secretary of State George C. Marshall made his historic speech at Harvard University. The Marshall Plan he outlined that day was not charity. Rather, it was a program of assistance and credits designed to stimulate cooperation among the European states. And it is important to remember that Marshall offered the plan not only to Western Europe but to the Soviet Union, which turned it down for itself and its satellites and instead embarked on a 45-year epoch that condemned an entire region to political and economic ruin.

Today, as after World War II, early euphoria has yielded to a more sober appreciation of the problems, new and old. The tragedy of Bosnia does not diminish the responsibility to build a new comprehensive structure of relationships to form a new security architecture. On the contrary, Bosnia, the greatest collective security failure of the West since the 1930s, only underscores the urgency of that task.

In 1947, Americans learned that those with the ability to preserve the peace have a special responsibility to assist in building stable structures in newly democratic neighbors. Then only the United States was secure and prosperous enough to offer Western Europe the assistance it needed. Today an equally prosperous Western Europe (and Japan, which has a stake in and benefits from a stable Europe) will have to put up the bulk of the actual financial assistance, but the United States must continue to play a leading part. In the words of Secretary of State Warren Christopher, the central goal of the United States is "to help extend to all of Europe the benefits and obligations of the same liberal trading and collective security order that have been pillars of strength for the West."

A final lesson of the Marshall Plan is equally important. Those receiving support must build their own futures. The new democracies must contribute to their own security through both responsible behavior toward neighbors and democracy-building from within. The United States understands, welcomes, and encourages the desire of new European democracies to join the West through membership in its key institutions. But NATO, the European Union (EU), and the other major institutions of the West are not clubs that one joins simply by filling out membership applications. Over time, each has evolved values and obligations that must be accepted by each new member.

THE CHALLENGE OF CENTRAL EUROPE

ANY BLUEPRINT for the new security architecture of Europe must focus first on central Europe, the seedbed of more turmoil and tragedy in this century than any other area on the continent. The two most destructive wars in human history began from events on its plains, and the Cold War played itself out in its ancient and storied cities, all within the last 80 years.

Other historic watersheds also have not treated this area well. First the treaties of Versailles and Trianon, then the agreements of Yalta and Potsdam, and finally the collapse of the Soviet empire—those three benchmark events left throughout central Europe a legacy of unresolved and often conflicting historical resentments, ambitions, and, most dangerous, territorial and ethnic disputes. Without democracy, stability, and free-market economies, these lands remain vulnerable to the same problems, often exacerbated by an obsession with righting historical wrongs, real or mythical. If any of these malignancies spread—as they have already in parts of the Balkans and Transcaucasus—general European stability is again at risk. And for Germany and Russia, the two large nations on the flanks of central Europe, insecurity has historically been a major contributor to aggressive behavior.

But if there are great problems there are also great possibilities. For the first time in history, the nations of this region have the chance simultaneously to enjoy stability, freedom, and independence based on another first: the adoption of Western democratic ideals as a common foundation for all of Europe. The emotional but also practical lure of the West can be the strongest unifying force Europe has seen in generations, but only if unnecessary delay does not squander the opportunity.

The West owes much of its success to the great institutions created in the 1940s and 1950s. They serve an important internal function for their members, and they also project a sense of stability and security to others. If those institutions were to remain closed to new members, they would become progressively more isolated from new challenges and less relevant to the problems of the post-Cold War world. It would be a tragedy if, through delay or indecision, the West helped create conditions that brought about the very problems it fears the most. The West must expand to central Europe as fast as possible in fact as well as in spirit, and the United States is ready to lead the way. Stability in central Europe is essential to general European security, and it is still far from assured.

Richard Holbrooke

THE BUILDING BLOCKS

THE CENTRAL security pillar of the new architecture is a venerable organization: NATO. To some, the 45-year-old Atlantic alliance may seem irrelevant or poorly designed for the challenges of the new Europe. To others, NATO's extraordinary record of success may suggest that nothing needs to be changed. Both views are equally wrong. Expansion of NATO is a logical and essential consequence of the disappearance of the Iron Curtain and the need to widen European unity based on shared democratic values. But even before NATO expands, its strength and know-how are already playing an important role in building a new sense of security throughout Europe.

Designed decades ago to counter a single, clearly defined threat, NATO is only just beginning a historic transformation. NATO's core purpose of collective defense remains, but new goals and programs have been added. Collective crisis management, out-of-area force projection, and the encouragement of stability to the east through the Partnership for Peace (PFP) and other programs have been undertaken. Command structures have been streamlined. Static forces formerly concentrated to meet a possible Soviet attack across central Europe have been turned into more lightly armed, mobile, and flexible multinational corps designed to respond to a different, less stable world.

Two new structures—the North Atlantic Cooperation Council and the PFP—are specifically designed to reach out to countries that are not NATO members. They deserve closer attention, especially the creative new concept so appropriately named the Partnership for Peace. In just one year, this innovative idea has become an integral part of the European security scene, but it remains somewhat misunderstood and underestimated. Contrary to a fairly widespread impression, PFP is not a single organization; rather, it is a series of individual agreements between NATO and, at last count, 24 other countries ranging from Poland to Armenia, including Russia. Each "partner" country creates an individual program to meet its own needs.

PFP is an invaluable tool that encourages NATO and individual partners to work together. It helps newly democratic states restructure and establish democratic control of their military forces and learn new forms of military doctrine, environmental control, and disaster relief. In the future, it will provide a framework in which NATO and individual partners can cooperate in crisis management or out-of-area peacekeeping.

PFP proved its value immediately. In its first year of existence, allies and partners held joint military exercises in Poland, the Netherlands, and the north Atlantic. Ten partners have already established liaison offices with the NATO military command. Sixteen partners have begun joint activities with NATO, and others will follow. A defense planning and review process has been established within the partnership to advance compatibility and transparency between allies and partners. PFP is also a vehicle for partners to learn about NATO procedures and standards, thus helping each partner make an informed decision as to whether it wishes to be considered for membership in the alliance.

From the alliance perspective, PFP will provide a valuable framework for judging the ability of each partner to assume the obligations and commitments of NATO membership—a testing ground for their capabilities. And for those partners that do not become NATO members the PFP will provide a structure for increasingly close cooperation with NATO—in itself an important building block for European security. If U.S. hopes are realized, and the first year gives every reason to be optimistic, the PFP will be a permanent part of the European security scene even as NATO expands to take in some, but not all, PFP members.

EXPANDING NATO

No ISSUE has been more important, controversial, or misunderstood than whether NATO should remain an alliance of its 16 current members or expand, and if it expands, why, where, when, and how. At the beginning of an important year on this issue, it is useful to clarify where the United States stands, and where it is going.

In essence, 1994 was the year in which, led by the United States, NATO decided it would eventually expand. This decision was reached during the January NATO summit in Brussels and reaffirmed by President Clinton during his return to Europe last June, when he stated that the question was no longer whether NATO would expand but how and when.

Last December, the NATO foreign ministers met again in Brussels, and, again led by the United States, they committed themselves to a two-phase program for 1995. During the first part of this year, NATO will determine through an internal discussion that is already under way the rationale and process for expanding the new, post-Cold War NATO. Then, in the months prior to the December 1995 ministerial meeting, NATO's views on these two issues—"why" and "how"—will be presented individually to PFP members who have expressed an interest in such discussions. This critical step will mark the first time detailed discussions on this subject have taken place outside the alliance. Then the ministers will meet again in Brussels in December and review the results of the discussions with the partners before deciding how to proceed.

This process, which at every stage requires the agreement of all 16 NATO members, is still in its initial stages. It is not yet widely understood. Given the importance of NATO, it is not surprising that some outside observers wish to accelerate the process while others do not want it to commence at all. The Clinton administration and its NATO allies, after some initial disagreements, have chosen a gradual and deliberate middle course—and have begun the process.

Several key points should be stressed:

•First, the goal remains the defense of the alliance's vital interests and the promotion of European stability. NATO expansion must strengthen security in the entire region, including nations that are not members. The goal is to promote security in central Europe by integrating countries that qualify into the stabilizing framework of NATO.

•Second, the rationale and process for NATO's expansion, once decided, will be transparent, not secret. Both Warsaw and Moscow, for example, will have the opportunity to hear exactly the same presentation from NATO later this year, and both should have access to all aspects of the alliance's thinking in order to understand that NATO should no longer be considered an anti-Russian alliance. As former National Security Adviser Zbigniew Brzezinski, an advocate of rapid expansion, wrote in the January/February 1995 issue of *Foreign Affairs*, "Neither the alliance nor its prospective new members are facing any imminent threat. Talk of a 'new Yalta' or of a Russian military threat is not justified, either by actual circumstances or even by worst-case scenarios for the near future. The expansion of NATO should, therefore, not be driven by whipping up anti-Russian hysteria that could eventually become a self-fulfilling prophecy."

•Third, there is no timetable or list of nations that will be invited to join NATO. The answers to the critical questions of who and when will emerge after completion of this phase of the process.

•Fourth, each nation will be considered individually, not as part of some grouping.

•Fifth, the decisions as to who joins NATO and when will be made exclusively by the alliance. No outside nation will exercise a veto.

•Sixth, although criteria for membership have not been determined, certain fundamental precepts reflected in the original Washington treaty remain as valid as they were in 1949: new members must be democratic, have market economies, be committed to responsible security policies, and be able to contribute to the alliance. As President Clinton has stated, "Countries with repressive political systems, countries with designs on their neighbors, countries with militaries unchecked by civilian control or with closed economic systems need not apply."

•Lastly, it should be remembered that each new NATO member constitutes for the United States the most solemn of all commitments: a bilateral defense treaty that extends the U.S. security umbrella to a new nation. This requires ratification by two-thirds of the U.S. Senate, a point that advocates of immediate expansion often overlook.

A BROAD CONCEPT OF SECURITY

NATO EXPANSION cannot occur in a vacuum. If it did, it would encourage the very imbalances and instabilities it was seeking to avoid. In addition to NATO, a variety of organizations and institutions must contribute to the new structure of peace. The new architecture should involve both such institutions as NATO and the EU, which strive for true integration among members, and others such as the Organization for Security and Cooperation in Europe (OSCE), which provide a wide, inclusive framework for looser forms of cooperation.

Although the EU is primarily a political and economic entity, it also makes an important contribution to European security. The integration of West European nations has virtually transcended the territorial disputes, irredentist claims, social cleavages, and ethnic grievances that tore apart European societies in earlier eras.

The extension of the EU eastward (and southward, if Cyprus and Malta join) will therefore be immensely important. It will integrate and stabilize the two halves of Europe. This process began with the entry of Austria, Finland, and Sweden at the beginning of this year. Europe agreements committed the EU and six central European nations to industrial free trade on January 1, 1995, except in steel and textiles, which will follow in 1996 and 1998. Slovenia and the Baltic states are expected to sign similar agreements soon. In December, the EU heads of state and government agreed on a "pre-accession" strategy for eventual entry, presumably sometime early in the next century, of the central European states, Cyprus, and Malta. For Germany, which, in Chancellor Helmut Kohl's powerful phrase, "cannot remain indefinitely Europe's eastern boundary," the extension of the EU is especially important, which is why Germany led this move during its term in the EU presidency.

Expansion of NATO and the EU will not proceed at exactly the same pace. Their memberships will never be identical. But the two organizations are clearly mutually supportive. Although the relationship between nato and the EU is complex, particularly as the EU seeks to define its relationship with the WEU to create a European defense identity, it is clearly mutually supportive; the expansion of both are equally necessary for an undivided and stable Europe.

It would be self-defeating for the WEU to create military structures to duplicate the successful European integration already achieved in NATO. But a stronger European pillar of the alliance can be an important contribution to European stability and transatlantic burden-sharing, provided it does not dilute NATO. The WEU establishes a new premise of collective defense: the United States should not be the only NATO member that can protect vital common interests outside Europe.

STRENGTHENING THE OSCE

NEITHER NATO nor the eu can be everything to everyone, and the other organizations above are focused on narrower issues. There is, therefore, a need in the new European architectural concept for a larger, looser region-wide security organization—smaller, of course, than the United Nations—that offers a framework for dealing with a variety of challenges that neither NATO nor the EU is designed to address, one that includes both NATO members and other countries on an equal basis.

Fortunately, the core for such a structure has existed for some years—the Conference on Security and Cooperation in Europe. Its 53-nation structure of human rights commitments, consultations, and efforts at cooperative or preventive diplomacy was intended to fill a niche in the new Europe. Born out of the 1975 Helsinki Accords, the CSCE unexpectedly provided, through its famous Basket III, a lever on human rights and democratic values that played a major role in undermining communism.

But it was clear by the middle of last year that the CSCE, while offering intriguing possibilities, had neither the internal coherence nor the political mandate to meet the challenges facing it.

Moscow and the major NATO allies shared this view. By the fall of last year, all had agreed that as NATO began to look at expansion, the CSCE should be strengthened and upgraded. A significant evolution of this organization, including a name change, began in December 1994 at the Budapest summit attended by President Clinton and Secretary Christopher. The result was a series of steps toward a clearer political and operational mandate, a strengthened consultative apparatus, and a new status. The old "conference" became a full-fledged "organization," and the OSCE was born.

The role of the new OSCE must now be more clearly established. Rather than enforcing behavior through legal or military action, it seeks to improve security by building new forms of cooperation based on consensus. With a membership that literally spans all 24 time zones and a huge array of cultures and nations, OSCE members will often disagree on how its standards are to be implemented. Taking such disagreement as a given, the OSCE must be more aggressive in the search for common ground.

Today security in Europe requires addressing potential conflicts earlier. The OSCE must prove its worth in this area, as the CSCE did in spreading democratic values and legitimizing human rights. The organization has pioneered efforts, however limited, at conflict prevention and crisis management through innovations such as establishing a high commissioner for national minorities and sending resident missions to conflict areas. More must be done.

The United States has taken the lead in pursuing innovations within the OSCE. In the future, the United States will make more vigorous use of the OSCE's consultative and conflict prevention mechanisms. The goal is to establish the OSCE as an integral element of the new security architecture. In a time of great burdens for the United Nations, the OSCE, as a regional organization under Chapter VII of the U.N. Charter, can perform many functions normally expected from the United Nations. The participation of U.N. Secretary General Boutros Boutros-Ghali in the OSCE Budapest summit underlined the importance of such cooperation.

Under no circumstances can the OSCE be a substitute for NATO or the EU. The OSCE can in no way be superior to NATO; the functions of the two organizations are and shall remain entirely different. Conversely, expansion of the role of the OSCE does not conflict with the responsibilities of NATO. Its methods occupy a totally different dimension than those of NATO.

A recent example of this function was the agreement reached at Budapest between Russia and the OSCE to merge negotiating efforts on the difficult issue of Nagorno-Karabakh and provide peacekeeping troops once a political agreement is reached—important steps on the OSCE's path to becoming a more meaningful organization. More recently, the Russians agreed to an OSCE fact-finding mission on Chechnya. The very fact that Moscow accepted OSCE involvement is significant, but this involvement came far too late and is too limited.

Without question Chechnya is part of the Russian Federation. At the same time, the United States has maintained from the outset that the Russian government should adhere to international standards, enshrined in OSCE resolutions and elsewhere, of respect for human rights. Tragically and unnecessarily, the Russian government prosecuted its military campaign against the city of Grozny in ways certain to cause large numbers of civilian casualties and hinder humanitarian assistance.

The West's overall objective in Russia and the rest of the former Soviet Union remains integration—bringing emerging democracies into the fold of Western political, economic, and security institutions. From the beginning of the battle for Grozny, Chechnya worked in exactly the opposite direction for Russia. Chechnya also has proved a deeply divisive element in Russian political life and has become a serious setback for the cause of reform, democratization, and the evolution of the Russian Federation as a stable, democratic, multiethnic state. The Chechnya conflict, terrible though it is, has not changed the nature of U.S. interests. President Clinton stated in January that, as Russia undergoes a historic transformation, reacting reflexively to each of the ups and downs that it is bound to experience, perhaps for decades to come, would be a terrible mistake. If the forces of reform are embattled, the United States must reinforce, not retreat from, its support for them.

The U.S. objective remains a healthy Russia—a democratic Russia pursuing reform and respecting the rights of its citizens, not fragmenting into ethnic conflict and civil war. America's ability to pursue and develop its partnership with Russia depends on a common pursuit of these values and objectives. The reason Russia has qualified as a friend and partner of the United States is that its people and government have embarked on a path of democratization, development of an open civil society, and respect for basic human rights. That is what the United States continues to support in Russia.

RUSSIA AND UKRAINE

To REPEAT: if the West is to create an enduring and stable security framework for Europe, it must solve the most enduring strategic problem of Europe and integrate the nations of the former Soviet Union, especially Russia, into a stable European security system. Russia is already involved in most aspects of the emerging architecture. It participates actively in the OSCE and worked closely with the United States in upgrading that organization. Russia has signed an ambitious partnership agreement with the EU. It has joined the Partnership for Peace with NATO. It is a candidate for membership in the Council of Europe. The United States supports deeper Russian participation in the Group of Seven industrialized nations and is sponsoring Russia's membership in the World Trade Organization, successor to the General Agreement on Tariffs and Trade. For the first time since 1945, Russia is participating, as a member of the Contact Group on Bosnia, in a multinational negotiating team presenting a unified position on a difficult security issue.

Enhancement of stability in central Europe is a mutual interest of Russia and the United States. NATO, which poses no threat to Russian security, seeks a direct and open relationship with Russia that both recognizes Russia's special position and stature and reinforces the integrity of the other newly independent states of the former Soviet Union. There have been proposals, including one by Russian President Boris Yeltsin in late 1993, for a special arrangement between NATO and Russia, which could take a number of forms. In urging rapid expansion of NATO, Brzezinski proposed in his *Foreign Affairs* article a "formal treaty of global security cooperation between NATO and the Russian Federation," in conjunction with an upgrade of the OSCE.

Any negotiations between NATO and Russia on this or any other arrangement would be quite complex. They would need to take into account a wide range of factors, including the pace of NATO expansion, the state of other Russian-NATO ties such as the Partnership for Peace, the degree to which the OSCE has been turned into a more useful organization, and the implications of events such as the fighting in Chechnya. Notwithstanding this array of issues, the U.S. government as well as its major allies have supported development of this important new track in the European security framework. Informal discussions of this possibility, while in a highly preliminary phase, began in January when Secretary Christopher met in Geneva with Russian Foreign Minister Andrei Kozyrev.

Any such arrangement must consider the special case of Ukraine. Its geostrategic position makes its independence and integrity a critical element of European security. In Budapest last December, President Clinton and the leaders of Belarus, Kazakhstan, Russia, and Ukraine exchanged documents of ratification for the Strategic Arms Reduction Treaty, formally bringing START I into force. At the same time, Ukraine also deposited its instrument of accession to the Nuclear Nonproliferation Treaty, and the United States, Russia, and the United Kingdom provided security assurances to Belarus, Kazakhstan, and Ukraine.

The basic goals of those seeking to take advantage of this moment in history are the expansion of democracy and prosperity, the integration of political and security institutions, and a unity that has always eluded Europe, even with American involvement. Leaders will have to lead to break through the layers of ambivalence, confusion, complacence, and history that inhibit reforms. As the great architect of European unity, Jean Monnet, observed, "Nothing is possible without men, but nothing is lasting without institutions." The efforts of Monnet, Marshall, and others produced unparalleled peace and prosperity for half a century— but for only half a continent. The task ahead is as daunting as its necessity is evident. To turn away from the challenge would only mean paying a higher price later.@

The Case Against 'Europe'

Noel Malcolm

A FLAWED IDEAL

THE CASE against "Europe" is not the same as a case against Europe. Quite the contrary. "Europe" is a project, a concept, a cause: the final goal that the European Community (EC) has been moving toward ever since its hesitant beginnings in the 1950s. It involves the creation of a united European state with its own constitution, government, parliament, currency, foreign policy, and army. Some of the machinery for this is already in place, and enough of the blueprints are in circulation for there to be little doubt about the overall design. Those who are in favor of Europe—that is, those who favor increasing the freedom and prosperity of all who live on the European continent—should view the creation of this hugely artificial political entity with a mixture of alarm and dismay.

The synthetic project of "Europe" has almost completely taken over the natural meaning of the word. In most European countries today, people talk simply about being "pro-Europe" or "anti-Europe"; anyone who questions more political integration can be dismissed as motivated by mere xenophobic hostility toward the rest of the continent. Other elements of the "European" political language reinforce this attitude. During the 1991-93 debate over the Maastricht treaty, for example, there was an almost hypnotic emphasis on clichés about transport. We were warned that we must not miss the boat or the bus, that we would be left standing on the platform when the European train went out, or that insufficient enthusiasm would cause us to suffer a bumpy ride in the rear wagon. All these images assumed a fixed itinerary and a preordained destination. Ei-

---

NOEL MALCOLM is a political columnist for London's *The Daily Telegraph*. His latest book is *Bosnia: A Short History*, published by New York University Press.

[147]

ther you were for that destination, or you were against "Europe." The possibility that people might argue in favor of rival positive goals for Europe was thus eliminated from the consciousness of European politicians.

The concept of "Europe" is accompanied, in other words, by a doctrine of historical inevitability. This can take several different forms: a utopian belief in inevitable progress, a quasi-Marxist faith in the iron laws of history (again involving the withering away of the nation-state), or a kind of cartographic mysticism that intuits that certain large areas on the map are crying out to emerge as single geopolitical units. These beliefs have received some hard knocks from twentieth-century history. Inevitability is, indeed, a word most often heard on the lips of those who have to turn the world upside down to achieve the changes they desire.

ON LITTLE CAT FEET

THE ORIGINS of the "European" political project can be traced back to a number of politicians, writers, and visionaries of the interwar period: people such as the half-Austrian, half-Japanese theorist Richard Coudenhove-Kalergi, former Italian Foreign Minister Carlo Sforza, and Jean Monnet, a French brandy salesman turned international bureaucrat. When their idea of a rationalized and unified Europe was first floated in the 1920s and 1930s, it sounded quite similar in spirit to the contemporaneous campaign to make Esperanto the world language. Who, at that stage, could confidently have declared that one of these schemes had the force of historical inevitability behind it and the other did not? Both had theoretical benefits to offer, although they were almost certainly outweighed by the practical difficulties of attaining them. It is not hard, surely, to imagine an alternative history of Europe after World War II in which the EC never came into existence and in which, therefore, the project of a united Europe would occupy a footnote almost as tiny as that devoted to the work of the International Esperanto League. Things seem inevitable only because people made them happen.

The impetus behind the "European" idea came from a handful of politicians in France and Germany who decided that a supranational enterprise might solve the problem of Franco-German rivalry, which they saw as the root cause of three great European wars since 1870. For this purpose alone, an arrangement involving just those two countries might have sufficed. But other factors coincidentally were at work, in particular the Cold War, which made the strengthening of Western Europe as a political bloc desirable, and the barely concealed resentment of French President Charles de Gaulle toward "les Anglo-Saxons," which made him look more favorably on the EC as an Anglo-Saxon-free area that could be politically dominated by France.

Even with these large-scale factors at work, however, it is doubtful whether the "European" project would have got off the ground without the ingenuity of a few individuals, notably Monnet and former French Foreign Minister Robert Schuman. The method they invented was what political theorists now call "functionalism." By meshing together the economies of participating countries bit by bit, they believed a point would eventually be reached where political unification would seem a natural expression of the way in which those countries were already interacting. As Schuman put it in 1950, "Europe will not be built all at once, or as a single whole: it will be built by concrete achievements which first create de facto solidarity."

And so the method has proceeded, from coal and steel (European Coal and Steel Community Treaty), through agriculture and commerce (Treaty of Rome), environmental regulation and research and development (Single European Act), to transport policy, training, immigration policy, and a whole battery of measures designed to bring about full economic and monetary union (the Maastricht treaty). Step by step with these developments has been the march toward political unification, with the growth of a European Court, the development of the European Parliament from a talking-shop of national appointees into a directly elected assembly with real legislative powers, the extension of majority voting at the Council of Ministers, and even the announcement, in the Maastricht treaty, of something called European citizenship, the rights and duties of which have yet to be defined. Almost every one of these political changes was justified at the time on practical grounds: just a slight adjustment to make things easier, or more effective, or to reflect new realities. The economic changes and the transfers of new areas of competence to EC institutions are likewise usually presented as mere practical adjustments. At the same time, many continental European politicians (such as German Chancellor Helmut Kohl and French President François Mitterrand) talk openly of the ultimate grand political goal: the creation of a federal European state.

There is a strange disjunction between these two types of "European" discourse, the practical and the ideal. But this is just a sign of functionalism successfully at work. The argument for "Europe" switches to and fro, from claims about practical benefits to expressions of political idealism and back again. If one disagrees with advocates of "Europe" about the practical advantages, they say, "Well, you may be right about this or that disadvantage, but surely it's a price worth paying for such a wonderful political ideal." And if one casts doubt on the political desirability of the ideal, they reply, "Never mind about that, just think of the economic advantages." The truth is that both arguments for "Europe" are fundamentally flawed.

DUNCE CAP

THE ECONOMIC project embodied in the European Economic Community (EEC) was a true reflection of its origins in a piece of Franco-German bargaining. German industry was given the opportunity to flood other member states with its exports, thanks to a set of rules designed to eliminate artificial barriers to competition and trade within the "common market." France, on the other hand, was given an elaborate system of protection for its agriculture, the so-called Common Agricultural Policy.

The general aims of the CAP, as set out in Article 39 of the Treaty of Rome, included stable markets and "a fair standard of living for the agricultural community." On that slender basis, France established one of the most complex and expensive systems of agricultural protectionism in human history. It is based on high external tariffs, high export subsidies, and internal price support by means of intervention buying (the most costly system of price support yet invented, since it involves collecting and storing tens of millions of tons of excess produce). By the time this system was fully established in 1967, EEC farm prices had been driven up to 175 percent of world prices for beef, 185 percent for wheat, 400 percent for butter, and 440 percent for sugar. The annual cost of the CAP is now $45 billion and rising; more than ten percent of this is believed to be paid to a myriad of scams. Thanks to this policy, a European family of four now pays more than $1,600 a year in additional food costs—a hidden tax greater than the poll tax that brought rioters out onto the streets of London.

Even the most hardened advocates of "Europe" are always a little embarrassed by the CAP. The massive corruption that flows from it—phantom exports picking up export subsidies, smuggled imports relabeled as EC products, nonexistent Italian olive groves receiving huge subsidies, and so on—is embarrassing enough, but it is the system itself that requires defense. Ten or twenty years ago, one used to hear its proponents arguing that at least there would be stocks of food available if Western Europe came under siege. That argument seemed thin then and sounds positively fatuous today. If pressed, they will insist that the CAP is gradually being reformed, pointing out that the beef mountains and wine lakes are getting smaller. These reforms, however, are achieved only by spending more money in such schemes as the infamous set-aside payments given to farmers as a reward for not growing anything. More commonly, though, the defenders of "Europe" will say that the CAP is just an unfortunate detail, that they are aware of its problems, and that one really should not use it to blacken "Europe's" name.

But the CAP is not just a detail. It is, by a huge margin, the largest single item of EC spending, taking up roughly 60 percent of the budget every year. It dominates the EC's external trade policy, distorting the world market and seriously undermining the ability of poorer countries elsewhere to export their own agricultural produce. It almost broke the Uruguay round of the General Agreement on Tariffs and Trade (GATT), thanks to the French government's irrational obsession with agricultural protectionism—irrational, that is, because agriculture accounts for only four percent of French GDP, and much of the other 96 percent would have benefited from lower world tariffs.

No account of the economic functioning of "Europe" can fail to begin with the CAP, and no study that examines it can fail to conclude that it is a colossal waste of money. Even the European Commission, which administers the scheme, has admitted that "farmers do not seem to have benefited from the increasing support which they have received." Enthusiasts for "Europe" often wax lyrical about European achievements such as the German highway system or the French railways—things that were built by national governments. Almost the only major achievement of the EC—the only thing it has constructed and operated itself—is the CAP. It is not an encouraging precedent.

LEVELING THE PLAYING FIELD

THE CAP SETS the tone for other areas of the EC's trading policy. Although it would be unfair to describe the EC as behaving like a "Fortress Europe" (so far), it is nevertheless true that "Europe" has evolved an elaborate system of tariffs and discriminatory trading agreements to protect its sensitive industries. Agriculture has the highest tariffs; ranging below it are such products as steel, textiles, clothing, and footwear (as Poland, Hungary, and the Czech Republic have discovered to their dismay—food, steel, textiles, clothing, and footwear being their own most important products). The EC has been at the forefront in developing so-called voluntary export restraints with countries such as Japan. In addition, "Europe" has shown extraordinary ingenuity in adapting the GATT's "antidumping" measures to block the flow of innumerable imports: electronic typewriters, hydraulic excavators, dot-matrix printers, audiocassettes, and halogen lights from Japan; compact disc players from Japan and Korea; small-screen color televisions from Korea, China, and Hong Kong, and so on.

A recent study of EC trade policy by L. A. Winters uses the phrase "managed liberalization" to describe the EC's foot-dragging progress toward freer trade. "Managed liberalization," notes Winters, "is a substitute for genuine liberalization, but a poor one, because it typically attenuates competition in precisely those sectors which are most in need of improved efficiency." Nor is this surprising, since the trade policy emerges from a system of political bargaining in which the governments of EC member states compete to protect their favorite industries. Massive state subsidies to flagship enterprises (French car manufacturers, Spanish steel mills, Belgian and Greek national airlines) are common practice. In addition, the officials at the European Commission in Brussels are strongly influenced by the French *dirigiste* tradition, which sees it as the role of the state to select and nurture special "champion" industries. This was the driving force behind the new powers granted to the EC in 1986 to "strengthen the scientific and technological basis of European industry." In practice, this means spending millions of taxpayers' dollars developing French microchips that will never compete with East Asian ones on the open market.

Inside the tariff wall, a kind of free trade area has indeed been created. Many obstacles to trade have been removed (though important barriers remain in the realm of services, as British insurance firm s are still discovering when they try to break into the German market), and industry as a whole has benefited from this process of internal liberalization. However, the long-term effects may be more harmful than beneficial. In their attempt to create a level playing field for competition on equal terms within the EC, the administrators of "Europe" have leveled up, not down. They have tried to raise both the standards and the costs of industry throughout the community to the high levels practiced in Europe's foremost industrial country, Germany. When this process is complete, industrialists inside the EC may indeed sell goods to one another on equal terms, but their goods will all be uncompetitive on the world market.

This leveling up occurs in two areas. The first is the harmonization of standards. Brussels has issued a mass of regulations laying down the most minute specifications for industrial products and processes; the dominant influence on these has been the German Institute for Norms, which has the strictest standards in Europe. Harmonization is meant to simplify matters for producers, who now have only one standard within the EC instead of various national ones. But in many cases, as the task of matching product to standard becomes relatively simpler, it is also made absolutely more expensive. In addition, the EC has powers relating to environmental protection and health and safety at work, which are increasingly used to impose German-style costs on industries and services. The costs fall especially heavily on small enterprises, which have to pay disproportionately for monitoring equipment, inspection, and certification. This distorts the market in favor of large corporations, penalizing the small enterprises that are the seed corn of any growing economy.

The second way in which the playing field is leveled up to German standards is in the social costs of labor. German employers pay heavily for the privilege of giving people jobs: there are generous pension schemes to pay for health insurance, long holidays, maternity and paternity leave, and other forms of social insurance. As a consequence, labor costs are $25 per hour in the former West Germany (the highest in the world), as opposed to $17 in Japan, $16 in the United States, and $12 in the United Kingdom. German work practices mean that a machine in a German factory operates an average of only 53 hours a week, as opposed to 69 hours in France and 76 in Britain. And the average worker in Germany spends only 1,506 hours each year actually at work, as opposed to 1,635 hours in Britain, 1,847 in the United States, and 2,165 in Japan.

Over the last five years, the European Commission has proposed a whole range of measures to increase the rights of workers and limit their working hours. When measures in this so-called social action program could not gain the required unanimous support from member states (notably Britain), they were dressed up as health and safety matters, for which only a majority vote is required. Further costs on employers were imposed by a "social protocol" added to the Maastricht treaty. Although Britain was able to gain a special exemption from this agreement, it is likely that many of the new measures adopted under the protocol eventually will filter back to Britain through other parts of the "European" administrative machine.

Some of these measures are inspired, no doubt, by concern for the plight of the poorest workers in the community's southern member states. But the general aim of the policy is clearly to protect the high-labor-cost economies (above all, Germany) from competitors employing cheaper labor. In the short or medium term, this policy will damage the economies of the poorer countries, which will have artificially high labor costs imposed on them. In the long term, it will harm Germany, too, by reducing its incentive to adapt to worldwide competition. "Europe," whose share of world trade and relative rate of economic growth are already in decline, will enter the next century stumbling under the weight of its own costs like a woolly mammoth sinking into a melting tundra.

The final expression of this leveling-up syndrome is the plan for monetary union. As outlined in the Maastricht treaty, the idea is to create a Euro-deutsche mark, operated by a body closely modeled on the Bundesbank and situated in Frankfurt. Earlier moves in this direction were not encouraging: the European Exchange Rate Mechanism, which linked the currencies of member states to the deutsche mark, fell apart spectacularly in October 1992. In the process, the British government spent nearly $6 billion in a doomed attempt to prop up the pound, and Germany is thought to have spent roughly $14 billion in an equally futile effort to support the Italian lira. The artificially high interest rates that countries such as Britain had imposed to maintain their currency's parity with the deutsche mark severely intensified the 1989-93 recession; the human costs of the unnecessary indebtedness, bankruptcies, and unemployment cannot be calculated.

The Exchange Rate Mechanism was, as Professor Sir Alan Walters, an adviser to former British Prime Minister Margaret Thatcher, famously put it, "half-baked." Currencies were neither fully fixed nor freely floating but pegged to so-called fixed rates that could be changed. This provided the world markets, at times of pressure on any particular currency, with an irresistible one-way bet. That problem, of course, will not arise once the currencies of "Europe" are merged into a single Euro-mark—though the activities of the world currency markets in the days just before the conversion terms are announced will be a wonder to behold.

Once the Euro-mark is in place, a different set of problems will arise. Whatever the "economic convergence programs" dutifully embarked on by the governments of member states, this single currency will be covering a number of national economies with widely varying characteristics. Hitherto, changes in the values of their national currencies have been one of the essential ways in which the relative strengths and weaknesses of those countries were both expressed and adjusted. With that mechanism gone, other forms of expression will operate, such as the collapse of industries or the mass migration of labor.

The European Commission understands this problem and has a ready solution: massive transfers of money to the weaker economies of "Europe." The machinery to administer this huge program of subsidies is already in place, in the form of regional funds, "structural" funds, and "cohesion payments." All that is lacking so far is the actual money, for which purpose the outgoing president of the European Commission, Jacques Delors, recently proposed increasing the European budget by more than $150 billion over the next five years.

A model for the future of an economically unified Europe can be found in modern Italy, which united the prosperous, advanced provinces of the north with the Third World poverty of the south. After more than a century of political and economic union, huge disparities still remain between the two halves of Italy—despite (or indeed partly because of) all the subsidies that are poured into the south via institutions such as the Cassa del Mezzogiorno, the independent society established by the Italian government to help develop the south. As southern Italians have had the opportunity to discover, an economy based on subsidies unites the inefficiencies of state planning with almost limitless opportunities for graft and corruption. It is a sad irony that today, just as the leaders of "Europe" are preparing for unification, the politicians of Italy are seriously considering dismantling their country into two or three separate states.

DECAFFEINATED POLITICS

SO MUCH FOR the economic benefits of European unity. At this point the advocates of "Europe" usually shift to their other line of defense. This is not just a money-grubbing enterprise, they say, to be totted up in terms of profit and loss: "Europe" is a political ideal, a spiritual adventure, a new experiment in brotherhood and cooperation. Has it not made war in Europe unthinkable? Is it not the natural next step for mankind, at a time when the old idea of national sovereignty is evidently obsolete? Does it not show the way to the abolition of old-fashioned national feeling, with all its hostilities, prejudices, and resentments?

The answer to all these questions, unfortunately, is no. The argument that the EC is responsible for the lack of war in post-1945 Europe is hard to substantiate. A far more obvious reason is the Cold War, which obliged Western Europe to adopt a common defensive posture and a system of deterrence so effective that war between Western and Eastern Europe never happened. The fact that a group of West European countries were able to cooperate in the EC was more a symptom of the lack of belligerent tensions in postwar Western Europe than a cause. Liberal democracies had been established in most West European countries after 1945; even if the EEC had not existed, it is hard to imagine a scenario in which Germany would have wanted to invade France, or France drop nuclear bombs on Germany. Even if one concedes for the sake of argument that the EEC did ensure peace for the last generation or two, this cannot be used as a reason for closer integration, since the EEC had this supposed effect at a time when it was not a unified supranational entity but a group of cooperating nation-states.

The idea of "Europe" is founded, however, on the belief that the nation-state is obsolete. This is an article of faith against which rational arguments cannot prevail. It is no use pointing out that the most successful countries in the modern world—Japan, the United States, and indeed Germany itself—are nation-states. It matters little if one says that some of the most dynamic economies today belong to small states—South Korea, Taiwan, Singapore—that feel no need to submerge themselves in large multinational entities. And it is regarded as bad taste to point out that the multinational federations most recently in the news were the U.S.S.R. and the Federal Republic of Yugoslavia. They are merely the latest in a long list of multinational states that have collapsed in modern times, from the Austro-Hungarian Empire to the various postcolonial federations set up by the British in central Africa, east Africa, and the West Indies. Nigeria, for example, kept Biafra only by warfare and starvation; India needs armed force to retain Nagaland and Kashmir. "But Europe will not be like that," say the federalists. "We have traditions of mutual tolerance and civilized behavior." Yes, we have some such traditions; they are the traditions that have evolved within fairly stable nation-states. Whether they last indefinitely under the new conditions of multinational politics remains to be seen.

The Case Against 'Europe'

What will political life be like in the sort of European federation currently proposed in Brussels and Bonn? Some of the powers of national governments will be transferred upward to the European level, while others will move down to a "Europe of the regions" (Catalonia, Bavaria, Wales, etc.). The official vision of political life at the uppermost level is essentially that of Jean Monnet, the original inventor of the community: a technocrat's ideal, a world in which large-scale solutions are devised to large-scale problems by far-sighted expert administrators. (The most common argument for abolishing nation-states is that problems nowadays are just too big for individual states to handle. In fact, there have always been issues that cross international borders, from postal services to drug enforcement to global trade. It cannot be the size of the problem that dictates that it must be dealt with by supranational authority rather than international cooperation, but some other reason that the advocates of European federation have yet to explain.)

This technocratic vision is of a decaffeinated political world, from which real politics has been carefully extracted. Things will surely turn out differently. Real politics will still operate at the European level. The one form it will not take, however, is that of federation-wide democratic politics. For that, we would need "Europe"-wide parties, operating across the whole federation in the way that the Republican and Democratic parties operate across the United States.

There are already some ghostly transnational groupings in the European Parliament: the Socialist Group, the European People's Party (the Christian Democrats), and so on. But these are just alliances formed at Strasbourg by members of the European Parliament elected on the tickets of their own national parties. No one can really envisage ordinary voters in, say, Denmark being inspired by the leader of their preferred Euro-party, who might make his or her speeches in Portuguese. The basic facts of linguistic, cultural, and geographic difference make it impossible to imagine federation-wide mass politics ever becoming the dominant form of political life in Europe. Instead, the pursuit of national interests by national politicians will continue at the highest "European" levels. Yet it will do so in a way subtly different from the way in which local representatives within a national political system press for the interests of their localities. Although a member of parliament for Yorkshire may push hard on Yorkshire's behalf, on all major issues the member votes according to what he or she thinks is in Britain's interest; the MP belongs to a national

Noel Malcolm

party that addresses those issues with national policies.

The art of "European" politics, on the other hand, will be to do nothing more than dress up national interests as if they were Europe-wide ones. With any particular nation paying only a small proportion of the European budget, each set of national politicians will seek to maximize those European spending projects that benefit their own country. The modus operandi of European politics, therefore (already visible in the Council of Ministers today), will be logrolling and back-scratching: you support my pet proposal, even though you think it is a bad one, and in return I shall back yours. This is a recipe not only for nonstop increases in spending, but also for radical incoherence in policymaking. And with politics at the highest level operating as a scramble for funds, it is hard to see how politicians at the lower level of Europe's "regions" can fail to replicate it: they will have fewer real governmental powers but more populist opportunities to woo their voters with spending.

This type of political life is accompanied by two grave dangers. In any system where democratic accountability is attenuated and the powers of politicians to make deals behind closed doors is strengthened, the likely consequence is a growth in political corruption. Corrupt practices are already common in the political life of several European countries: their exposure has led recently to the prosecution, flight into exile, or suicide of former prime ministers in Italy, Greece, and France. A federal Europe, far from correcting these vices, will offer them a wider field of action.

A more serious danger, however, lies in store for the political life of a federal "Europe": the revival of the politics of nationalist hostility and resentment. Aggressive nationalism is typically a syndrome of the dispossessed, of those who feel power has been taken from them. Foreigners are often the most convenient focus of such resentment, whatever the true causes of the powerlessness may be. But in a system where power really has been taken from national governments and transferred to European bodies in which, by definition, the majority vote will always lie in the hands of foreigners, such nationalist thinking will acquire an undeniable logic. Of course, if "Europe" moves ever onward and upward in an unprecedented increase in prosperity for all its citizens, the grounds for resentment may be slight; that is not, however, a scenario that anyone can take for granted.

In this respect, the whole "European" project furnishes a classic example of the fallacious belief that the way to remove hostility between groups, peoples, or states is to build new structures over their heads. Too often that method yields exactly the opposite result. The most commonly repeated version of this argument is that Germany needs to be "tied in" or "tied down" by a structure of European integration to prevent it from wandering off dangerously into the empty spaces of Mitteleuropa. If Germany really has different interests from the rest of "Europe," the way to deal with it, surely, is not to force it into an institutional straitjacket (which can only build up German resentment in the long run), but to devise ways of pursuing those interests that are compatible with the interests of its allies and partners. So far, Germany's involvement in "Europe" looks rather like the action of a jovial uncle at a children's party who, to show goodwill, allows his hands to be tied behind his back. It is not a posture that he will want to stay in for long, and his mood may change when he becomes aware of innumerable little fingers rifling through his pockets.

FIRST AS FARCE . . .

THE FINAL question is whether "Europe" has a valuable role to play on the world stage. The "Europe" we have at present is a product of the Cold War era. Now that the whole situation in Eastern Europe has changed, one might expect the engineers of the EC to go back to the geopolitical drawing board. Instead, they are pressing ahead with the same old set of plans at a faster pace. Some enthusiasts for "Europe," such as former EC Commissioner Ralf Dahrendorf or British Foreign Minister Douglas Hurd, have even claimed that the internal development of the EC in the 1980s played a decisive part in bringing about the fall of communism in the east. One rather doubts many East European dissidents ever said: "Have you heard about the new Brussels Directive on Permitted Levels of Lawnmower Noise? This means we really must bring down the communist regime!" The Hurd/Dahrendorf thesis bears a curious resemblance to the recent Michael Jackson music video entitled "Redeeming Eastern Europe," in which the pop star defeats the Red Army singlehandedly while adoring children chant messages of goodwill in (coincidentally) Esperanto.

Since the removal of the Iron Curtain, the new democracies of Eastern Europe have found their ostensible savior strangely reluctant to help it in the one way that matters—namely, by buying their goods. They all want to join "Europe," of course, for two simple reasons: because it is a rich man's club in which fellow members possess huge funds for investment, and because they want to be part of some kind of security grouping. The first requirement could be met by any economic club of nations, of the sort that the EC was for its first couple of decades; it does not call for European political integration. Indeed, any such development would be a strange reward for those East European countries that have only just freed themselves from the embrace of another multinational empire.

The question of European security raises a similar point. The longterm effect of the end of the Cold War will be a gradual reduction in the American defense commitment to Europe. This prospect even causes some pleasure in those parts of Europe—above all, France and Germany— where anti-Americanism has long flourished. Clearly, the Europeans will have to take more care of their own defense. But the question is whether this requires political integration, a Euro-army, a Euro–foreign policy, and a Euro-government. For more than 50 years, NATO has managed to defend Western Europe without any such political integration, and NATO is clearly the most successful international organization in modern history.

"Of course," comes the reply, "NATO was able to function as a loose intergovernmental body because its members were facing a clear common threat. The threats and challenges will be more various now, so intergovernmental agreement will be harder to obtain." But that is precisely why such matters should not be funneled into a "European" government operating by majority vote. "Europe" is indeed a collection of countries with different national interests and foreign commitments. On each separate security issue, individual states may have concerns of their own that are not shared by their fellow members (Britain over the Falklands, France over North Africa, Germany and Italy over Yugoslavia, and so on). To try to form a single "European" policy on such issues, whether by unanimity, consensus, or majority voting, is to guarantee at best ineffective compromise and at worst total self-paralysis.

This simple truth has been demonstrated twice in the last four years—the first time as farce, the second as tragedy. The farce was "Europe's" reaction to Iraq's 1990 invasion of Kuwait, when Germany agonized over sending a few trainer jets to Turkey, France sent an aircraft carrier to the Persian Gulf bearing helicopters instead of planes, and Belgium refused to sell ammunition to the British army. The tragedy is Yugoslavia. "This is the hour of Europe!" cried the egregious Jacques Poos, foreign minister of Luxembourg, when Yugoslavian President Slobodan

Milošević's army first opened fire in Slovenia and Croatia in the summer of 1991. "We do not interfere in American affairs; we trust that America will not interfere in European affairs," said Jacques Delors, voicing the only consistent and distinctive theme of "European" foreign policy: graceless anti-Americanism. The desire to produce a foreign policy by consensus was just strong enough to ensure that those countries who did understand what was happening in Yugoslavia (above all, Germany) were kept in check by those who did not (above all, Britain). As a result, the recognition of Croatia and Slovenia was delayed by six months, and when it finally came it did so unaccompanied by any measures to protect Milošević's other prospective victims from attack.

The mentality behind the drive for a "European" foreign policy displays a childlike logic. "Think how strong and effective our foreign policies will be if we add them all together!" it says. Similarly, one might say: think what a beautiful color we can make if we mix all the colors of the paint box! The result, inevitably, is a muddy shade of brown.☯

The U.N. Idea Revisited

Abba Eban

THE SLOW DEATH OF COLLECTIVE SECURITY

THE UNITED NATIONS was born 50 years ago amid such euphoria that a fall from grace was inevitable. Its founding conference at San Francisco in April 1945 resounded with slogans of redemption and hope. Many who attended the sessions may have felt that expectations were being set exaggeratedly high, but few would have predicted that after five decades the peace organization would resemble the chorus in a Greek drama, expressing consternation at events it has no power to control.

Disappointment would be less sharp if the U.N. founders had been content to claim that they were contributing an additional technique to the repertoire of diplomacy. But they were not in a mood to accept such a modest role. They were inspired by a utopian vision. "Inexorable tides of history," one delegate proclaimed, "are carrying us toward a golden age of freedom, justice, peace, and social well-being." Another 1945 orator soared to biblical heights: "The U.N. Charter has grown from the prayers and prophecies of Isaiah and Micah."

Even statesmen renowned for their pragmatic temperament were caught up in the intoxicating rhetoric. The U.S. secretary of state until 1944, Cordell Hull, a Tennessean of austere mien, had never been known to express an enthusiastic emotion. But he saw the establishment of the United Nations as a messianic transformation: "There will no longer be need for spheres of influence, for alliances, balances of power, or any other of the special arrangements through which, in the unhappy past, the na-

---

ABBA EBAN represented Israel at the United Nations from 1948 to 1959, serving concurrently as ambassador to the United States (1950-59). He was Foreign Minister from 1966 to 1974.

tions strove to safeguard their security or to promote their interests."

This must surely rank as one of the more ill-considered statements in diplomatic history. International organization, which after all is a mechanism, not a policy or principle, was portrayed as a magic spell that would render all previous politics and diplomacy obsolete.

These salvational hopes were based on the illusion that the American-Soviet-British alliance that had won the victory would command the future—a notion any serious historian could have refuted many months before. But American leaders had evidently convinced themselves that the United Nations, by the mere fact of its existence, would cause a new story, never heard or told before, to unfold across the human scene.

By contrast, the practitioners of traditional diplomacy have never spoken of themselves in the exalted tones adopted by the devotees of international organization. Professional diplomacy is dominated by a sense of limits proceeding from a somber view of human nature. It pursues relatively modest goals, like prolonged stability, rather than a new era in the governance of humankind. It accepts that conflict is endemic to human relations at all levels and that the most that can be done in the international field is to keep conflict within tolerable limits. Diplomats, schooled in their own traditions, know that war prevented is a kind of peace, perhaps the only peace that many nations will ever know. They inhabit a middle ground between excessive skepticism and inflated hope. They understand that in a world without a universally accepted law diplomats will usually have to compromise between what justice demands and what circumstances permit.

The movement for international organization was born in revolt against this unambitious view. Its devotees insisted on nothing less than world peace under law. The theme was collective security. The central premise of this doctrine is that all nations have an equal interest in opposing specific acts of aggression and are willing to incur identical risks in opposing them. This idea, however, is so contrary to all of international experience that nothing short of charismatic authority could ever have brought it to term.

Like all new religions, international organization had a prophet who was deemed to speak consecrated words, and his name was Woodrow Wilson. But Wilson was so assiduous in seeking European support for collective security and its instrument, the League of Nations, that he failed to notice the lack of endorsement for them back home.

The Europeans who thronged the streets of Paris and London in 1919 to greet Wilson as he arrived for the peace talks after the First World War responded ecstatically to the tall, grave American who doffed his top hat in salute. Presidents of the United States were an unknown species to them; none had made such a pilgrimage before. Here was a man representing the greatest power ever to exist who had pledged himself to the most ambitious moral theory any statesman had ever articulated.

But the Europeans were not sold on Wilsonianism. They observed that self-determination had not been extended in America to the red man or the black, or to the southern states. They noted that the American empire had been won with overpowering force. The Europeans thought it natural to prefer the imprecisions of their own system to the vague idealism of a new system that Americans might fail to apply even to their own continent.

The truth is that no one outside America has ever taken the theory of American exceptionalism seriously. The theory rests on the assumption that America has an anticolonialist lineage. But the difference between ravaging populations and conquering vast territories within a continent, and conquering them in colonial fashion by sending armies overseas, has never struck non-Americans as a moral distinction.

American leaders who had qualms about their own rectitude sometimes resolved them by appeal to divine judgment. When in 1897 President William McKinley wanted to annex the Philippines, he spent a whole night on his knees praying for celestial guidance. It is certain that he would not have accepted an answer in the negative. The Heavenly Will worn down by presidential persistence, the United States made war against Spain and moved into the Philippines.

Even the virtuous Wilson, after proclaiming his vision of "open covenants," went on to organize the most closed and conspiratorial peace conference in history. He closeted himself with the British, French, and Italian leaders—David Lloyd George, Georges Clemenceau, and Vittorio Orlando—and the Big Four in a vengeful mood drafted a treaty destined to prepare the ground for a new war. A contemporary writer described Wilson as "living on terms of such intimacy with his conscience that any little disagreement between them could always be arranged."

Wilson died a sad man amid the ruins of his vision, his own country having refused to join the League of Nations, but this did not deter the U.N. founders from seeking a second chance for collective security. In the aftermath of World War II, the hope that the new international organization would have more success than its predecessor seemed well founded. For one thing, the United Nations was assured of universal membership. There were no signs of the American separatism that had spelled weakness for the League of Nations. Since American reservations had been regarded as the main cause of the league's failure, it was too innocently assumed that American participation would ensure the league's successor thrived. That the world's three most powerful leaders—Franklin D. Roosevelt, Joseph Stalin, and Winston Churchill—spent long hours at Yalta discussing the U.N. blueprint in meticulous detail lent majestic strength to the internationalist cause.

The U.N. founders had an additional reason for optimism. The new peace organization, they said, would not be toothless like the League of Nations but would be able to enforce its decisions. This idea received expression in Article 43 of the U.N. Charter. A military staff committee composed of members from the five major powers (the United States, the Soviet Union, China, Britain, and France) would work out a plan for the mobilization of U.N. forces to be held ready under the command of the Security Council. For the first time in history collective security would be institutionalized. In 1945 high officers from the armies of the five great powers gathered to discuss the U.N. force.

The conventional wisdom in the West tells us that right-minded states wanted to create an enforcement mechanism but were frustrated by the persistent Soviet veto. This argument, developed at the height of the Cold War in the early 1950s, is flagrantly untrue. As Cordell Hull told the Senate, the veto provision was an absolute condition for American participation in the United Nations and the small and medium-sized countries regarded the veto as a crucial defense against irresponsible majorities. A conscious decision was taken at San Francisco to avoid any attempt to subject the major powers to collective coercion. A representative of Sweden in 1952 declared that the willingness of the small states to accept the obligations of the new security system was "dependent upon their assurance, derived from the veto provision, that there could be no U.N. call to action against a major power." The Mexican delegate at San Francisco said, cogently, that under the U.N. Charter, "the mice would be disciplined, but the lions would be free."

It is too often forgotten that the charter, signed in June 1945, was written by men unaware that nuclear weapons existed. If they had known, surely they would not have advocated bringing American and Soviet forces into proximity in areas where the two countries' interests conflicted.

In 1947 the negotiations on Article 43 collapsed, as was inevitable. The five generals and eight admirals of the military staff committee, brilliantly uniformed and bemedaled, would hold ritual meetings a few minutes long at the beginning of each month. The chairman would call them to order, announce that no speakers were scheduled, and propose adjournment. A new chairman would take office the next month according to alphabetical rotation. A talent for perpetuating defunct institutions was to bedevil the United Nations in future decades. In this case the monthly meetings were stopped before the farce became too patent.

With the demise of Article 43, the United Nations had renounced the special quality that was intended to distinguish it from its predecessor. It had become, like the League of Nations, an arena of debate, with a capacity, still untested, to promote negotiated settlements, not by coercion but by consent. Collective security as a formula for world order was dead.

EARLY BLOOM

FOR A BRIEF period the United Nations appeared to be fulfilling a central role without the illusion of coercive force. In 1946 the Security Council ordained the withdrawal of Soviet troops from Iran and of French forces from Syria and Lebanon. In 1947 it played a major part in the decolonization of Indonesia. It resolved a potentially explosive dispute over Bahrain. In 1948-49, after some failures, it instituted a durable cease-fire followed by a prolonged armistice between Israel and its Arab neighbors. Meanwhile in 1947 the General Assembly had adopted a decision for the partition of Palestine that has been fiercely debated ever since but cannot be denied to be a strong, daring act free from the obscurity and procrastination usually ascribed to the international organization.

The disposition of the former Italian colonies (Eritrea, Somalia, and Libya) was decided in 1949 by votes in the General Assembly. The Universal Declaration of Human Rights, adopted at the end of 1948, may not have directly influenced the behavior of states but is nevertheless a bold and proud document illuminated by a vision of humanity in its more compassionate and rational aspect.

Strangely, Israel turned out to be the nation that benefited most from a U.N. action, although few Israelis or Jewish leaders acknowledge this today. The Jewish people presented themselves to the world community in the aftermath of World War II at the lowest ebb of their fortunes. Six million of them, including a million children, had been slaughtered in Europe. The fame and dignity of the Jews had been dragged down in a decade of Nazi calumny. The promised homeland in Palestine was assailed by regional violence and international alienation.

The United Nations responded to the holocaust with an endorsement in 1947 of the Jewish claim to statehood in a partitioned Palestine. A year and a half later, in May 1949, the world body revolutionized the juridical status of the Jewish people by admitting Israel to membership in the United Nations.

The subsequent spate of anti-Israel assaults in General Assembly resolutions had fewer durable effects than did the United Nations' initial stimulus to the consolidation of Israel's status. No historian has ever suggested a scenario in which Israel's sovereignty could have been recognized so quickly in a world that lacked an international organization to fill the vacuum that the end of British power left in the region.

But if the years 1945 to 1950 were the United Nations' half-decade of innovation, they held a premonition of marginality. All the major powers, including the United States, were determined to ensure that their own vital interests would not be submitted to U.N. jurisdiction. The Marshall Plan and the establishment of the NATO alliance were carried through in total disregard of the world organization. The Security Council, with great pomp and circumstance, established the Atomic Commission and the Commission for Conventional Armaments, but by 1949 both bodies had become inactive; it was evident that if Washington and Moscow ever intended to discuss arms control seriously, they would seek each other out in the privacy of traditional diplomacy.

In the Korean War of 1950-53, the Security Council could pretend to be the commander of the U.N. forces under American leadership, but this fiction was sustained only because the Soviet Union, obtusely absent from its seat, could not wield its veto in the Security Council. In any case, President Harry S Truman preceded his recourse to the United Nations by a typical unilateral decision to send forces first and explain their dispatch afterward. In Europe, the Common Market and the other institutions of the European Community were born without any relationship to the United Nations.

Abba Eban

THE HOLLOW DOCTRINE

IT IS VERY unlikely that collective security will ever regain preeminence as an aim of international politics. Its reputation was based on six assumptions, none of which is valid in any contemporary context or any foreseeable future context.

The first assumption is that states will identify their own security with the existing world order to such an extent that they will be prepared to defend that order by involvement in situations seemingly remote from their particular national interests.

The second is that states will be able and willing to agree on the determination of aggression in a particular situation.

The third is that the aggressor will be so weak or lonely that it will be possible to confront him with a superior international force.

The fourth is that states, inspired by the objective principles of collective security, will be willing to punish their closest allies as severely as they would their distant adversaries. Alliance, affinity, and common culture will simply melt away.

The fifth is that nation-states will renounce their power of separate decision in the disposition of their armed forces in areas in which their national interests are not involved.

The sixth is that public debate in a permanent international conference will prove a more effective technique for reaching accords than the traditional method of discreet negotiation between the interested parties alone.

None of these six assumptions is even remotely correct. Still less do they together constitute a realistic model for international behavior.

First, the loyalties built around the nation-state are not transferable to any notion of world community.

Second, what is aggression for one is self-defense for another and national liberation for a third.

Third, many small and medium-sized countries like Egypt, Israel, Syria, Iraq, Iran, Turkey, and Ukraine now have the sort of firepower an international force would find hard to overcome. Even the Bosnian Serbs with their antiquated weaponry have been able to intimidate U.N. peacekeepers and NATO air forces.

Fourth, nations, like human beings, are not immune from the laws of human nature; they do not react with equal and objective rigor, or indulgence, toward adversaries and allies.

Fifth, statesmen will not surrender their discretionary response on such crucial issues as the use of their country's armed forces. Even the relatively innocuous use of forces for agreed peacekeeping and humanitarian purposes arouses strong resentment when casualties are incurred.

Sixth, a half-century of experience has demonstrated that traditional diplomacy, with limited participation and the occasional recourse to reticence and secrecy, offers better chances of reaching accords than does a United Nations committed to public debate with participation on a vast scale.

My conclusion is that collective security failed to take root as the central principle of international life not because its opponents were of small mind or ignoble disposition, but because it did not reflect the spirit of the age. It came on the scene in a world of nation-states, yet called on states suddenly to behave in a way that states had never behaved in the whole of human history.

International law does not give any sort of lead. One of the most tormenting aspects of collective security is that decisions of immaculate legality become harmful if isolated from the chain of consequences. The Anglo-French decision in early 1940 to resist the Soviet invasion of Finland provides an example. The action against the Soviet Union, including its expulsion from the League of Nations, was juridically correct in terms of the League covenant; Finland was entitled to receive international aid against aggression. But Britain and France nearly found themselves at war with Hitler's Germany and the Soviet Union simultaneously! Thus the Anglo-French action, while exemplary in legal terms, would, if maintained, have prevented the eventual defeat of Hitler.

Once it became evident in 1947 that the United Nations lacked the enforcement powers envisaged in Article 43 of the charter, that body should logically have considered its future course. No such deliberations took place. Today it is still not clear what the United Nations wishes to be: an instrument for solving conflicts or an arena for waging them. The choice is between the parliamentary and the diplomatic principle. The diplomatic principle tells me I need my adversary's agreement. The parliamentary principle tells me I don't need his agreement, since I can defeat and humiliate him by a majority vote. The two techniques call for totally different psychologies and procedures. The unhappy choice of the parliamentary principle ensured that the General Assembly would have a virulently polemical character.

Abba Eban

The Wilsonian tradition praised collective security for its emphasis on publicity ("open covenants openly arrived at") and its rejection of secrecy ("everything shall proceed always frankly and in the public view"). But these are not aids to agreement; they are prescriptions for deadlock. Without phases of secrecy and avoidance of publicity, agreements are virtually impossible. The role of secrecy in negotiation is not a mere relic of tradition. It is crucial. If a nation hears of a concession its representatives have offered without hearing of a corresponding concession from the other party, indignation will erupt at the wrong time, with explosive results. A wiser Woodrow Wilson would have opted for "open covenants secretly arrived at," as Canadian Prime Minister Lester Pearson later suggested.

TURN OFF THE MICROPHONE

WITH THE Cold War over, the world seems to lack a strong incentive to reform its institutions. Nuclear arms have not been used in anger since World War II, the major powers have avoided confrontation, and some regional disputes have been solved. The international system, controlled by the power balance and negotiation, has not been ideal, but it has not been so intolerable as to encourage U.N. members to seek new systems and procedures. The prediction that the choice for humankind would be between international organization and world war has been discredited.

But prudent diplomacy in the traditional mold is a serious alternative, and here there has been important progress. Leaders of nations are now engaged in civil discourse with those whom they would have spurned a few years ago. De Klerk and Mandela bringing apartheid to an end; Rabin and Arafat laying foundations for a Middle East breakthrough; the British government negotiating with the Irish Republican Army; Israel in open contact with Jordan leading to a peace treaty; the Vatican overcoming theological inhibitions and sending a goodwill mission to Jerusalem—it is the era of odd couples, and humankind breathes more freely because of it.

Frustrated by the failure to construct a universal security system, international activists have sought compensations in other fields. One of the consolation prizes was alleged to be strong resonance around the globe. But the United Nations can no longer claim to be the world's most powerful microphone. Reporting on its debates is scanty and few news media maintain the U.N. press bureaus they once did. The addresses of foreign ministers in General Assembly debate pass from the orators' lips to oblivion without so much as a temporary resting place in *The New York Times*.

The relatively meager results for conciliation under U.N. auspices must be considered against the more impressive achievements of conventional diplomacy. The years since the end of World War II have been fruitful for international conciliation, and most of the successes have been scored outside the United Nations. The Austrian State Treaty, which prohibits Austria from possessing nuclear weapons; the termination of the Berlin blockades; the Treaty of Rome establishing the European Union; the end of Algeria's war for independence from France; the American opening to China; the conclusion of the SALT I arms limitation agreement; the Panama Canal settlement; the Ostpolitik agreements orchestrated by German Chancellor Willy Brandt, leading to the recognition of the European frontiers; the Rhodesia-Zimbabwe settlement; the establishment of the Conference on Security and Cooperation in Europe at Helsinki; the Egyptian-Israeli peace treaty; the Israeli-Jordanian peace treaty; the Declaration of Principles signed by Israel and the Palestine Liberation Organization; the British-Irish dialogue; the Israeli-Vatican reconciliation; the new agreements between the republics of the former Soviet Union and the Western states—these make an imposing list. They offer empirical evidence for a judgment that the public multilateral approach has been much less effective in conflict resolution than traditional negotiating techniques.

One of the main weaknesses of the United Nations is its predilection for public debate in vast audiences with massive participation. Wilson eulogized the idea that "the great things remaining to be done can only be done with the whole world as a stage and in cooperation with the universal interests of humankind." As with many Wilsonian utterances, this is a victory of eloquence over logic. The "whole world" is not really the most effective arbiter of disputes. There is more to be said for negotiation between concerned parties whose destinies will be harmed by failure and served by success. As things stand, countries in the United Nations with no crucial interests in a dispute may band together to outvote states whose very survival is at stake.

It is staggering to recall that only three years ago many expected the West's success in resisting Iraqi aggression against Kuwait to lead to a new world order in which the United Nations would preside over a tranquil globe. A cascade of events heralded the triumph of democracy and the market economy over the squalid repressions of the communist system. The collapse of communist ascendancy, symbolized by the crumbling of the Berlin Wall, encouraged the belief in a new order.

But this vision flowed from a basic misunderstanding of the previous decades. The West had considered the Soviet Union responsible for instigating all the tensions troubling the world, which led it to fatefully underestimate all other sources of tension and violence. Nationalist rivalries, religious fanaticism, unsolved territorial disputes, ancient prejudices and enmities, a sense of exclusion and discrimination afflicting underdeveloped countries that had thought their political emancipation would be followed by spectacular improvement in their daily lives—these had all been squeezed into a Pandora's box. The end of the Cold War set these tensions free; they can now explode in their own right and seek their own horizons. The Cold War, with all its perils, expressed a certain bleak stability: alignments, fidelities, and rivalries were sharply defined. But since no sane person would long for a return to those times, there is an urgent need for a serious appraisal of the new international situation.

It is tempting but unfair to blame the United Nations for the world's recent disappointments. The brain and heart of the organization are in the possession of its component parts; the power of correction lies not in the headquarters on the East River but in the capitals of the member states.

Not much time had to elapse before it became evident that the U.N. decision to protect oil-rich Kuwait did not create any commitment to uphold the rights of oil-free Bosnia or to bring sustained assistance to starving Somalia or Rwanda. All governments take their decisions in the name of national interest and then explain them in terms of self-sacrificing altruism. The central truth in diplomacy is that there are no collective solutions to individual crises.

CURSED ARE THE PEACEKEEPERS

IT WAS AT least feasible that the United Nations might transcend the eclipse of collective security by emphasizing its peacekeeping role. This dimension of the world organization was born during the crisis over the Suez Canal and Sinai in 1956-57. Secretary-General Dag Hammarskjöld, Under-Secretary-General Ralph Bunche, and Canadian leader Lester Pearson won merited honor for establishing the United Nations Emergency Force in Gaza and the Strait of Tiran.

The U.N. Idea Revisited

Peacekeeping—the use of international forces to monitor the peace between states that have already agreed to maintain peace—does not have a heroic sound. It is so much more modest than "peacemaking" or "peace enforcement" that it gives the impression of "a poor man's U.N." But in the Suez crisis and dozens of other troubled situations in the following years, peacekeeping measures have had stabilizing effects. The dozens of volunteer soldiers who sacrificed their lives nobly under the U.N. flag have left humankind in their debt. A real flowering of the peacekeeping dimension would give the United Nations a much-needed injection of prestige.

Unfortunately this prospect does not appear attainable. Since the end of the Cold War there have been useful peacekeeping missions in Namibia, El Salvador, Cambodia, Mozambique, and Haiti, but these have been overshadowed by the abject flight of the peacemakers from Somalia, and even more by the dramatic fiasco of peacekeeping in the former Yugoslavia.

Britain and France provide the bulk of the 40,000-troop peacekeeping operation in the Balkan region. These troops, despite their proud military lineage, are mocked, harassed, and humiliated by Serb warlords who block the arrival of U.N. relief convoys and impose starvation, as well as cruel bombardment and "ethnic cleansing," on Muslim populations in Bosnia. The modest aim of the peacekeepers is to ensure that food and medical aid reach Sarajevo and other urban centers, but this cannot be achieved without the United Nations occasionally fighting its way in to the aid recipients and sometimes calling on NATO for air strikes against Serb artillery.

In mid-June the United States strongly pressured its European allies to carry out an air attack on the Bosnian Serb forces. As might have been predicted, the Serb response was to take hundreds of British, French, and Canadian peacekeepers hostage. The peacekeeping commanders meekly suspended the air strikes for several weeks. The hostages were subsequently released, but the spectacle of U.N. officers and soldiers overpowered and threatened by the arrogant Serbs stripped the United Nations of the deference its flag had previously been accorded by member states, even when its power was being defied. The United States maneuvered itself into an intolerable moral position by advocating military action and then passing the consequences on without exposing itself to danger, since it is an American axiom that American lives must not be risked in non-American contexts. Sending lightly armed peacekeepers to areas where there is no peace to keep has brought international discredit to the U.N. system.

At this writing the United Nations faces grave erosion of its effectiveness and authority. Its flame is burning low. In the ruins of what was once Yugoslavia, Serb armies mount brutal assaults that have been the main cause of approximately 200,000 deaths. They carry out the policy of ethnic cleansing in Bosnia, starving and torturing their Muslim opponents and inflicting on the civilized world, represented by the U.N. peacekeepers, the worst torment and humiliation ever directed against international emissaries. Ironically, the perpetrators of these attacks on the international order are not powerful armies, to whose tyranny weaker powers have been accustomed to submit. They are from a less than medium-sized semi-nation that could have been subdued by the forces of any one of the several nations that have sent peacekeepers into action. Bosnia demonstrates not a failure of power but a paralysis of will among the European nations and the United States.

In July 1995 Britain and France, in a rare gesture of resolve, announced their intention to establish a U.N. rapid reaction force to protect the Muslim "safe areas" in Bosnia, but the Serb armies overran Srebrenica and threatened Zepa and Bihać before any U.N. action could be concerted. At a meeting in London on July 21, the United States, France, and Britain resolved to resist Serb "aggression," to reinforce the U.N. peacekeeping mission, to refuse to be intimidated by hostage-taking, and to ensure the delivery of humanitarian supplies to Bosnia "by all means." This was the most emphatic commitment yet by the Western leaders, but it remains to be seen whether they will act to rescue their governments from the credibility crisis created by similar brave declarations in the past.

THE YEAR OF THE PLANET

IF THERE is no hope for a real collective security system, and if traditional diplomacy is more effective than public rhetoric, what is left for the United Nations to do?

It is easier to diagnose the world's problems than to find a solution, and easier to formulate solutions than to get the public to accept them. I believe, however, that U.N. Secretary-General Boutros Boutros-Ghali would elicit a positive response if he proclaimed this the Year of the Planet and devoted the 1995 General Assembly to problems whose solution is beyond the capacity of individual states.

The U.N. Idea Revisited

The inhabitants of the earth now number 5.3 billion and at the present rate of increase will number 7 billion by the end of the century. More than half the globe's people suffer from malnutrition. Life expectancy, which exceeds 70 years in developed countries, is as low as 30 in parts of Asia and Africa. Hundreds of millions of people are afflicted by waterborne diseases for which remedies exist. Some 800 million adults throughout the world are illiterate. The most affluent countries are 3,000 percent more prosperous than the least affluent. Science, technology, and industrial progress are still largely confined to the advanced countries, which are home to less than a quarter of the human race. Some of the world's energy resources are nearing depletion, while the atmosphere and many water sources are suffering wholesale pollution.

Planetary interests may now be the arena most congenial to discussion in multilateral agencies. When disasters occurred in Somalia and Rwanda it would have been logical for the U.N. secretariat to have visibly led the humanitarian effort. Yet the U.N. was marginal even in those two cases. There are many issues that are everybody's business and, therefore, nobody's responsibility.

Balked in its quest for a decisive role in international security, the United Nations can be credited with one momentous triumph for its labors: it has given stalwart and audacious support to the pageant of decolonization that has swept scores of new states into the world community. Nothing does more to excite the identity of new nations than the sight of their flags and names around U.N. tables. It is impossible to narrate the story of the end of apartheid and the South African revolution without paying tribute to the U.N. role.

The United Nations must face the central political anomaly of our age—the multiplicity of nation-states in a world where sovereignty has lost a large measure of its meaning. Social history describes the expansion of the sense of community, from family to tribe, from tribe to village, from village to city, from city to nation-state. At every stage people have sought larger arenas in which to express their sense of solidarity and cohesion. For some reason the expansion of community seems to have got stuck at the nation-state level. But the idea of a world community of independent states is alive in the human imagination, though not yet in the world of action. Along with the proliferation of the nation-states in their guise as the most important actors in today's international system goes a countertendency to transcend nationhood through larger units of cooperation. Regional and multilateral bodies are multiplying. The world is integrating and fragmenting at the same time.

Yet there is little hope of a revival for international institutions without a strong impulse for change from an outside power. Under present conditions this impulse can come only from the United States. But at precisely the moment when the United States has virtual command of the U.N. system, it appears to be turning its back on the multilateral idea. The new Congress in Washington is cutting support for U.N. peace-keeping and placing strangling restraints on the use of American manpower for international service. The current administration, which came to power amid strong expressions of support for multilateral frameworks, has accepted limitations beyond anything that previous administrations were prepared to envisage. An esteemed liberal voice, Arthur Schlesinger, Jr., in the July/August 1995 *Foreign Affairs*, reminded us that the United States stands twentieth on the list of nations contributing troops to U.N. operations—"well behind such world powers as Bangladesh, Ghana, and Nepal." America has cut back its budget allocation for the United Nations to a mere 0.15 percent of GDP, putting it last among the 21 wealthiest industrial nations. Congress' retreat from its previous devotion to world community is by far the greatest threat to the hope of a revived United Nations.

The world organization had the misfortune to be born with a grossly inflated vision of its interventionist power. Yet if expectations are reduced it might still be possible to reach a positive balance between vision and reality. It would be ridiculous if the first era of planetary interdependence were to find the world without a unitary framework of international relations. With all its imperfections, the United Nations is still the main incarnation of the global spirit. It alone seeks to present a vision of humankind in its organic unity.

At no other time have so many people crossed frontiers and come into contact with people of other faiths and nationalities; the new accessibility is steadily eroding parochialism. In light of these slow but deep currents of human evolution, the idea of an international organization playing an assertive role in the pacification of this turbulent world may have to bide its time, but it will never disappear from view. History and the future are on its side.◉

A New China Strategy

Kenneth Lieberthal

THE CHALLENGE

THE PEOPLE's Republic of China has been in the news this year for a number of disturbing reasons. It has mounted muscular military actions to back its diplomacy regarding Taiwan and the South China Sea, allegedly transferred M-11 missile technology to Pakistan, sold nuclear technology to Iran, conducted nuclear weapons tests, and augmented its military budget when most other countries have been cutting back in the wake of the Cold War. It has continued the repression of political dissidents, displayed gross insensitivity in its handling of the U.N.-sponsored Fourth World Conference on Women and Nongovernmental Organization Forum, and become a prickly interlocutor at many international negotiations. One of the most important issues now confronting Asia is how an increasingly strong China will act in the region.

Beijing recognizes the importance of expanding its economic links with the rest of the world. The People's Republic of China (P.R.C.) has sustained very rapid economic growth: since 1978, the per capita GDP of more than one-fifth of the globe's population has roughly quadrupled. China's foreign trade grew more than 16 percent per year from 1978 to 1994, with imports exceeding exports for all but six of those years. Concurrently, it has overseen huge changes in its economy, social development, and political dynamics.

These domestic changes, generally welcomed abroad, have nurtured

KENNETH LIEBERTHAL is Arthur F. Thurnau Professor of Political Science and William R. Davidson Professor of Business Administration at the University of Michigan. His most recent book is *Governing China: From Revolution through Reform* (W.W. Norton, 1995).

many of the problems that now cause concern. They have vastly reduced the compliance of the country's officials with Beijing's directives, making it difficult for China's leaders to implement international agreements they have signed on such issues as intellectual property rights, and they have made the military a far stronger domestic player, with potentially worrisome consequences abroad. They have undermined faith in communism, and China's leaders have turned to nationalism to tighten discipline and maintain support. Most important, these changes have strengthened the P.R.C. to such an extent that it is becoming a major regional and global actor.

A strong China will inevitably present major challenges to the United States and the rest of the international system. In the past, the rise of a country to great power status has always forced realignment of the international system and has more than once led to war. One of America's most important diplomatic challenges, therefore, is to try to integrate China into Asia and the global political system. America's leverage, however, is modest. Given the limits on its will and resources, the United States must think through the type of China that will best serve its long-term interests in East Asian peace, stability, and open economic development, and then develop a strategy to promote those objectives. Especially during the 1990s, Washington has been sidetracked by short-term irritants and has failed to undertake this sort of analysis.

On balance, China is likely to act constructively in the future if it is secure, cohesive, reform-oriented, modernizing, stable, open to the outside world, and able to deal effectively with its problems. A secure and cohesive China will feel less need to build up its military and demonstrate its toughness, it will not confront the world with large refugee flows and internal warfare, and it will not invite external intervention because of political fragmentation. A reform-minded and modernizing China will continue to advance toward a market-driven system guided by law rather than by corrupt families and will better meet the material needs of its citizens, eventually creating a middle class with a moderating influence. An effectively governed China will be able to feed, clothe, and satisfy the basic needs of more than 1.2 billion human beings, thus relieving the international system of major potential burdens. A stable China requires a political system that is responsive enough to keep up with the rapid social change engendered by reform and modernization. An open China will be more prosperous, expose its citizens to international thinking and practices, and have strong incentives to participate constructively in the international system.

Many in the United States disagree with this vision. Some hope that a Soviet-type collapse will produce a liberal democratic polity and a reduced Chinese threat. Far more likely, however, is that political disintegration would result in large-scale bloodshed, famine, and substantial migration. The remnants of this nuclear power could become rogue proliferators of nuclear and other military technologies and weapons. In short, although a strong, dynamic China will challenge American patience, skill, and interests, a failed China would produce even less welcome problems.

The United States has pressing interests in a cooperative relationship with China that would inhibit Asia's division into competing camps. Co-operative Sino-American relations ought, indeed, to permit America to maintain a robust, effective military force in Asia at relatively low cost and reduce the chances of North Korean nuclear development and destabilization of the Korean peninsula. Such a relationship would also enhance stability and prosperity across the Taiwan Strait and enable American businesses to participate in the modernization of the huge continental Chinese economy. Finally, cooperation would facilitate U.N. security operations in areas as diverse as Iraq and Bosnia and strengthen international agreements in such areas as trade, nuclear proliferation, and the environment.

Of course, should the People's Republic hold together and continue its economic development, yet still perceive major threats to its security and internal stability, it will more likely become a nationalistic bully on the regional level and an obstructionist on global issues. Some in the United States anticipate these developments and are calling for America to prepare the ground for a policy of containment. But a containment strategy would represent a major policy failure. It would divide Asia (with few countries other than Vietnam likely to commit wholly to the U.S. position), strengthen narrow nationalisms, and reduce prosperity, security, and the prospects for peace throughout the region. It would be a costly strategy, all the more so because it could easily become the catchall justification for otherwise disparate decisions such as normalizing relations with Vietnam and selling F-16s to Indonesia. Worse, containment would likely enhance the positions of the most nationalistic, militaristic elements in China. It is in America's interest, therefore, for the Clinton administration to reduce the emotionalism of the United States' China policy, develop a strategic approach that focuses on the essentials of a mutually beneficial relationship, and build both public and congressional support to implement such a strategy.

DIFFICULT PARTNER I: CHINA

THE NATURE and extent of the reforms under way in China almost assure continuing problems in Sino-American relations. The loosening of the monolithic structure that existed before the ascendancy of paramount leader Deng Xiaoping makes the P.R.C. attractive to investors and reformers and also explains many of the problems facing American policymakers.

Aspects of China's current political and economic system complicate relations between the two countries. China's economy is far from a free market; in addition, its legal framework is weak, its regulatory environment opaque, its military secretive, and its politics authoritarian. In virtually every one of these dimensions, although long-term trends appear headed in the right direction, in the short term China wants the world to accept its "Chinese characteristics" as part of the price of having the country join international councils. Though a new player, China wants to be a rule setter and not just a rule accepter.

Many Chinese intellectuals and officials, moreover, now believe that the world's willingness to bend the rules to accommodate China has noticeably diminished during the 1990s. They see that the opportunity for easy progress, exemplified by World Bank actions in the 1980s that sought to jump-start reform of China's economy and promote its growth, has shriveled, replaced by concerns about the consequences of a strong China. They maintain that China must now stand up for itself, often in prickly, narrowly nationalistic fashion, and push hard for the world to accept it on its own terms. While tactical compromises are possible, after nearly 150 years of humiliation at the hands of the great powers China must act in accordance with its new sense of strength, resolve, and self-confidence. Because the United States often takes the lead in arguing against accepting China's violations of international standards, these intellectuals feel it is especially important to resist Washington's zeal in defining the terms on which China interacts with the major powers. Significantly, Beijing is allowing intellectuals to express such sentiments, even as it prohibits open discussion of the popular demand for Japan to pay war reparations.

A New China Strategy

The political succession now under way poses additional risks to Sino-American relations. Deng's imminent demise marks a material change, as he has personally played a key role since the 1970s in protecting this bilateral tie from attack. Time and again, frustration over American positions and actions has driven some Chinese, especially in the military, to advocate a hard line. In each such instance, Deng has intervened to set China's strategic sights on a basically cooperative relationship that would serve China's long-term goals of rapid economic development and closer integration into the community of nations.

Now it appears that no contender among China's leaders has the courage to dismiss the military's strongly held views and demand that China keep to a cooperative course with the United States. The resulting dynamic was fully evident in the aftermath of the United States' recent decision to grant a visa to Taiwanese President Lee Teng-hui. Chinese President Jiang Zemin initially fashioned a relatively mild response, consisting of the postponement of U.S.-China talks on the production of fissile material and on missile technology control, but little else. The military leadership quickly weighed in with a recommendation for a tougher line, though, arguing that the United States was effectively supporting the division of China.

After several hastily called Politburo meetings, Jiang adopted the approach advocated by the People's Liberation Army—harsh rhetoric directed at the United States, cancellation of many bilateral meetings, recall of the Chinese ambassador to Washington for consultation, demands that Washington abjure all future visas for Lee, tougher language concerning Lee personally, and missile tests and other military exercises in the Taiwan Strait. Other measures, such as the arrest of American human rights activist Harry Wu and the publicized expulsion of two American military observers taken into custody near the Taiwan Strait in August, also quite possibly formed part of the Chinese response.

As they contend for the succession, moreover, China's leaders realize that they govern a society wracked by the tensions that accompany rapid change and unresponsive to socialist ideological appeals. With socialism no longer credible, politicians are anxious to burnish their nationalist credentials. This shift has in turn heightened sensitivity to issues like Taiwan, to territorial claims such as those in the South China Sea, and to military views on national sovereignty and integrity. The strains that have made nationalism politically attractive also stoke worries in Beijing about potential domestic instability. America's efforts to foster dissent via such activities as Radio Free Asia are therefore viewed as particularly threatening and pernicious.

Against this background, Beijing has furiously debated America's true intentions toward China. Coloring this debate is the deep resentment of Chinese leaders over what they consider hypocritical, arrogant, and ignorant moral posturing by American officials and media on such internal matters as human rights. The debate in Beijing is not fully resolved, but most of the positions being advanced would make things difficult for Washington, even though not all are mutually compatible. Some argue that the United States is a declining power that will try desperately to prevent the rise of a major new power like China; others maintain that the United States is so accustomed to dictating principles and policies that it will insensitively and insultingly intervene in China's domestic affairs. Some assert that the American government is sufficiently responsive to business entreaties that China can protect its interests by holding out the lure of a potentially huge market, while others claim that President Clinton is not willing to protect the U.S.-China relationship from those who would destroy it and that he might in fact be anti-Chinese himself. Still others believe that the president and Congress collude in a good cop–bad cop duet to squeeze concessions out of Beijing through periodic requests that it help the White House protect Sino-American ties from congressional wrath.

Spinoffs of the decentralization and market-oriented reforms that the United States has long desired are also making the P.R.C. more difficult to deal with. Chinese officials at all levels now focus on making money, often displaying questionable business ethics. Beijing has given provincial and local leaders considerable leeway to enrich their localities and has even called on national ministries (including the defense forces) to pursue commercial deals to cover part of their budgets. Not surprisingly, officials outside the top leadership are violating Sino-American agreements on intellectual property rights and market access. This phenomenon may explain some of the weapons sales that the United States finds objectionable.

DIFFICULT PARTNER II: AMERICA

A MAJOR portion of the difficulties in Sino-American relations stems from dynamics within Washington. The 1989 Tiananmen Square incident jaundiced American views of China and made China policy a political tool for many groups in the United States. America's seeming inability to set Tiananmen aside, even when all other Group of Seven (G-7) industrialized nations had done so, and its related insistence on treating China's political leaders as morally unfit have made most of those leaders deeply resentful.

The contradiction between fundamental values and concrete national interests has troubled American foreign policy since the beginning of the republic. The Cold War enabled the United States to sidestep the issue; anticommunism was perceived as having sufficient moral weight to permit America to engage in almost any form of realpolitik to combat the Soviet empire. It is not surprising that this underlying tension has resurfaced with the end of the Cold War. Beijing now seeks realpolitik with the United States, the kind of relationship it feels it enjoyed from 1971 to early 1989 under five American presidents of both political parties. China's leaders are baffled and alarmed by Washington's unwillingness to play that game.

The Clinton administration's foreign policy process and the politics of China policy inside the Beltway contribute to tensions. The administration has what it considers to be a friendly, constructive policy toward China, which it terms "comprehensive engagement." The policy acknowledges China's increasing strength and seeks to nurture the P.R.C.'s admission into the international community—on the condition that Beijing obeys the norms that currently prevail in that arena. The administration is willing to engage China virtually across the board to promote Beijing's acceptance of these norms. In this way, Washington hopes to facilitate Beijing's entrance into global leadership forums without upsetting the current system.

Although the Clinton administration adopted these goals in 1994, it never worked out a set of priorities to achieve them. As a result, each government agency is pursuing its own China policy, with little coordination among them. While the Office of the U.S. Trade Representative threatens sanctions over market access and intellectual property rights, the Department of Commerce goes all out to increase U.S. investment in China; while the Department of State thrashes China for human rights violations and nuclear proliferation, the Department of Defense works hard to develop military-to-military ties. The Chinese search in vain for an underlying rationale to explain this welter of conflicting efforts.

Failure to set priorities has led an approach that was intended to be friendly to produce the threat or application of sanctions during the past two years in every major sphere of the relationship—trade, military, and human rights. Even if China's actions have fallen short in all of these areas, the United States' threat of sanctions in all areas nearly simultaneously has simply overwhelmed the relationship . The fact that in almost every instance the other G-7 countries have not supported America's threats has made Washington's claim that it is acting on behalf of widely accepted international norms ring hollow.

The president's performance has worsened the problem. Clinton does not have strong beliefs about China policy, and his White House has not imposed discipline on American foreign policy officials. The president's own public vacillation and about-faces on China, often in response to popular and congressional pressure, have sharply reduced his credibility and increased the collateral damage from some of his most important actions. For example, Clinton's May 1994 decision not to link most-favored nation trade status renewal to human rights demands abruptly reversed months of presidentially sanctioned efforts to highlight that linkage and his own commitment to the human rights issue. He could have managed this policy differently during these critical months, placing human rights in the context of a broader strategic relationship. The substance of the final decision was right, but by dropping the linkage as a "bad idea" after advocating it, the president undermined his credibility.

Clinton added to the damage with his handling of the decision to issue a visa to Lee Teng-hui and allow him to visit his alma mater, Cornell University, this past June. The visa issue straddled the line between upgrading official relations with Taiwan, which would have violated previous Sino-American agreements, and expanding America's definition of private U.S.-Taiwan ties, which are permitted by unofficial understandings with Beijing. The president probably could have played this issue successfully either way, so long as he was consistent and principled. Instead, he first allowed the State Department to declare that issuing a visa would violate past policy, then permitted Secretary of State Warren Christopher to assure Chinese Foreign Minister Qian Qichen personally that administration policy was to deny the visa, and finally bowed to a nonbinding congressional resolution, announcing that he would issue the visa after all. This course of events embarrassed Qian, who had assured his Politburo colleagues that the administration would not grant Lee a visa. The handling of the Lee case undercut those in Beijing who argue that China should take the Clinton administration at its word.

This decision also suggested to Beijing that Clinton, unlike George

A New China Strategy

Bush, is not willing to protect Sino-American relations from tampering by Congress. Some in Congress would destroy the relationship if given the opportunity to do so, and Congress has at times acted in stunning disregard of the fundamental requirements of Sino-American diplomacy: earlier this year Congress demanded that the United States accredit an ambassador to the Dalai Lama's exile government in India and recognize Tibet's independence. Evidence of White House unwillingness to expend the political capital necessary to sustain the Sino-American relationship against congressional assault has made it seem risky to Beijing's leaders to stake their personal credibility on pursuing cooperation with the United States.

Many facets of the approach to China inside the Beltway are, therefore, making the Chinese nervous, uncertain, suspicious, and obstreperous. Despite Washington's generally constructive goals, an increasing number of Beijing's leaders believe that America wants to isolate China by excluding it from such international groups as the World Trade Organization. They think that the United States wants to weaken China by denying it the right to purchase sophisticated American technologies, by threatening sanctions, and by supporting antigovernment forces within the country. Some even interpret American policy as seeking to divide China by promoting gradual independence for Taiwan and Tibet and intruding into China's resumption of active sovereignty over Hong Kong.

WORRISOME CONTINGENCIES

LARGE-SCALE political unrest in China is a possibility. Despite enormous success in achieving rapid economic growth, there are fundamental strains in the society. Inflation, over 20 percent in recent years, is dangerously high, and corruption is widely resented among the populace. Tens of millions of "floaters" have flocked to the major cities, differentiation of wealth is growing, many state enterprise workers fear the effects of further development of the market economy, control over individuals through their work units has eroded, and massive urban construction projects are displacing hundreds of thousands, causing tensions. If the political succession to Deng Xiaoping does not go smoothly, these underlying pressures may erupt into enormous street demonstrations and protests.

Such an eventuality is unlikely to produce a Soviet-type disintegration of the Chinese political system. But the ensuing measures to restore order would almost certainly include the extensive use of armed police and military units, with substantial loss of life. That sequence of events in China might well galvanize Congress to demand major economic sanctions, and these demands could prove politically impossible for the White House to set aside, especially during a presidential election campaign. Sanctions would have a series of deleterious long-term effects: they would make China a far less attractive place for American business and cause a great deal of American capital to flee the country, disrupt all contact between the American and Chinese militaries and increase the perception of threats on both sides, and convince China's leaders that the United States really does wish to encourage the overthrow of the government in Beijing.

Creeping Taiwanese independence poses a second potential danger. China feels that Taiwan is moving toward independence in small steps and has decided that it must demonstrate its resolve to prevent Taiwan from going too far. The resulting P.R.C. military exercises in the Taiwan Strait this past summer may backfire by increasing the vote for the Democratic Progressive Party in Taiwan in the March 1996 elections and by adding pressure on Congress to sell Taiwan a theater missile defense system. Although a formal Taiwanese declaration of independence and request for diplomatic recognition from the United States and other countries is unlikely, Taiwan's leaders have pursued intermediate forms of international recognition vigorously.

Miscommunication between Taipei and Beijing may produce initiatives by Taiwan that would trigger a military response from China. While America is not rigidly bound by the Taiwan Relations Act to protect Taiwan at all costs, political pressure in Washington to move in that direction would be strong, especially if this occurred in the context of political crisis and resulting repression on the mainland.

The third explosive contingency would be a major destabilization of Hong Kong. That would transpire only if political instability on the mainland drew Hong Kong into the fray. The scenario would entail active support of some mainland elements by Hong Kong's citizens, followed by flows of political refugees across the Chinese border and repression in Hong Kong by Chinese security forces. Given the amount of American investment in Hong Kong and the generally high regard in which Americans hold its citizens and society, such developments would intensify the calls in Washington to act against the victorious political forces in Beijing.

A New China Strategy

SINO-AMERICAN relations are in danger. Without sacrificing its fundamental interests, the United States must revamp its bilateral and multilateral approaches to create a more stable relationship with China.

The United States should engage other countries in Asia (particularly Japan) and Europe in the effort to articulate and convey to China's leaders the conduct expected of major powers. It must not allow others to make Washington the sole enforcer of these norms, especially in sensitive areas such as human rights. The United States should use its influence in Asia and in international organizations to encourage others to work toward China's integration into Asian and global organizations and activities. Even though most Asian countries regard China warily and worry about the "China threat," America should play a leading role in promoting regional initiatives that seek engagement, rather than containment.

A containment strategy toward China would likely engender precisely the type of Chinese behavior that will prove most upsetting to the regional and international systems. Furthermore, the emphasis given here to constructive integration does not mean that the United States should ignore Chinese activities that threaten the international order—quite the opposite. The objective is to leave China with a clear understanding of the kinds of behavior that will produce widespread international opposition. It is the lack of such clarity in recent years—when the United States has often stood alone in threatening and applying sanctions—that may have encouraged the Chinese to test the limits of international tolerance.

America should retain its current robust military presence in East Asia. These forces may reduce regional tensions, including those that can produce regional arms races. Playing this role effectively, of course, requires that America retain basically healthy diplomatic relations with all major countries in the region. America may also have to impose some additional restrictions on its arms sales.

Bilaterally, the United States should adopt positions that move the diplomatic relationship with China in a less emotional direction. As ardently as Americans might wish to see democracy appear in China and a liberal, law-driven system develop there, America lacks the resources to impose these desires; it is worth bearing in mind that China's population is over 300 times larger than that of Haiti. America should always stand internationally for democracy and human rights, but these should become far less central elements in American bilateral policy toward China.

The United States must treat with respect whatever leaders the Chinese system produces and make domestic Chinese issues less of an object of American bilateral diplomatic priorities. Pursuing this approach, the United States would likely find it easier to discuss with China bilateral problems in trade, security, and other spheres. Regular high-level meetings between American and Chinese leaders would enhance the mutual trust and understanding that is critical to realistic negotiations and problem solving.

The top priority on the American side should be the development of a long-term, concrete strategy toward China based squarely on these guidelines. The president must be able to explain it to Congress and the public and then implement it in a coordinated, disciplined, and consistent fashion. This policy should protect America's immediate interests and promote the fundamental goal, important to America as a global power, of China's constructive integration into the international arena.

One senses that Chinese leaders, like their American counterparts, do not have a strategic approach to this bilateral relationship. This may reflect a combination of Deng Xiaoping's fading from the scene, contention among potential successors, uncertainty over how to exercise the country's rapidly increasing power, and a growing military role in defining foreign policy responses. China's failure to think about the long run also risks missteps and tragedy.

Five years from now the mid-1990s may be viewed as a historic turning point during which China's engagement in the international arena went seriously awry, despite the country's domestic reforms. Given the nature and magnitude of changes coursing through China, even a carefully considered American approach will encounter significant frustrations and disappointments—and might ultimately fail to secure its goals. But to date American policy has fallen far short of the basic requirements for success, and each side's shortcomings are affecting the other's posture. America and China may still stumble along in a troubled but manageable relationship, but in the absence of realistic strategies on either side, the chances that they will stumble into mutual hostility are growing unacceptably high.@

Is Iran's Present Algeria's Future?

Edward G. Shirley

FUNDAMENTALISM IN POWER

CAN ONE negotiate with Muslim fundamentalists? The United States is in the process of testing this crucial question, on which may hang the future of Western relations with the Muslim world. Late in 1993, U.S. diplomats began discreet discussions with Anwar Haddam, the Washington, D.C.-based representative of Algeria's Islamic Salvation Front, commonly known by its French initials, FIS. In contacting Haddam and other FIS militants, the Clinton administration began a new experiment with potentially wide-ranging implications: preemptive U.S. diplomatic contact with fundamentalists who have grass-roots strength and, potentially, the power to topple regimes.

It is too soon to tell whether the experiment will evolve into policy. The Clinton administration may lose interest in Algeria, a country with few historical ties to the United States. More importantly, the policy may be too cerebral to withstand the vicissitudes of war. The daily clashes between the Algerian military and militants are bloody. Though less culpable than the army, the FIS unquestionably has had a hand in the killing. The gruesome, indiscriminate, and intensifying violence could at any point derail an attempt at dialogue.

But there are reasons to believe Washington will stay interested. Most of those who study Algeria, including (in private) U.S. officials, echo the prediction of *The Economist*: Algeria's ruling regime will probably fall sooner rather than later. Islamic radicalism will then have gained its second Arab state—Sudan was the first in 1989—and its most impor-

EDWARD G. SHIRLEY is the pseudonym of a former Iran specialist for the Central Intelligence Agency.

tant victory since Ayatollah Ruhollah Khomeini unseated the shah of Iran in 1979. Unengaged, Algerian extremism could promote mischief throughout the Middle East.

If the Algerian regime is doomed, then the logic of encouraging co-operation between moderate Muslims, fundamentalist and otherwise, seems compelling. If U.S. officials can talk to the FIS, perhaps they can improve America's reputation among fundamentalists, diminishing the chances of the United States being portrayed again as the implacable enemy of Islam, the preferred target for martyr-driven truck bombs. Indeed, according to some observers, the United States in Algeria could experiment in dealing with fundamentalism, thereby fine-tuning a long-term approach and revamping our image in the militant Islamic world without jeopardizing much—and certainly not a strategic partner, as was the risk in prerevolutionary Iran. But is such a policy practicable and wise? Is there really sufficient common ground? In opening a dialogue with fundamentalists in Algeria, might the United States conversely aid and abet what it is trying to quarantine in Iran?

ARE THERE MODERATES?

IT IS DOUBTFUL that Paris and Washington appreciate the irony in their current approach to Islamic fundamentalism. Toward the Algerian version, the United States argues for contact with "moderate" fundamentalists who promise a more democratic Algeria. Though not rejecting the idea of dialogue, the French complain that such moderates have so far been very hard to find. Toward the Iranian version, the United States takes a hard-line position, arguing in favor of containment, belittling the existence of moderates and the achievements of Iran's Islamic democracy. The French, on the other hand, advocate continuing dialogue with clerical Iran, support its "pragmatists," and praise its nascent though troubled democracy.

Nobody is quite certain about what to do with Islamic activism except to suggest that dialogue must somehow be possible with someone. Many faithful Muslims surely share U.S. concerns about democracy and human rights. But what French Interior Minister Charles Pasqua says about Algeria and Secretary of State Warren Christopher about Iran is essentially correct: there are no moderate fundamentalists. The idea of talking to tepid Middle Eastern true believers is a comforting and typically secularized illusion.

Is Iran's Present Algeria's Future?

We should have little misunderstanding about fundamentalist doctrine, particularly in Algeria. Long before the FIS was outlawed and denied its triumph at the polls, the organization had made its theology clear: you cannot subordinate God to democracy or nullify his law through parliamentary debate and legislation.

The notion of moderate fundamentalism falls apart quickly whenever women and the holy law come into view. Always side by side, the two issues form Islamic fundamentalism's core. Point 11 in the FIS platform commands the chief of state to enforce the *sharia*, or Muslim religious law; point 12 enjoins the protection of feminine dignity, morals, and honor as guaranteed by Islam. Some Western observers of Islamic activism stress that the *sharia*, like any body of law, must be interpreted and applied, raising the possibility of gradual innovation and adaptation to the modern world. But Sunni fundamentalists are, as a general rule, strict constructionists. They believe in God's sole legislative authority. They are not impressed by Islamic modernists—Muslim Episcopalians, as it were—who want to use *ijtihad*, the practiced but unacknowledged right of a religious jurist to interpret the holy law, and *ijma*, a historical understanding that Muslims as a community can modify Islamic practice, as traditional devices to delete medieval legalism from modern-day life.

Today's Arab fundamentalists are more adroit than their predecessors: they have, like everybody else in the Middle East, imbibed Western culture. They have learned the vocabulary of modern nation-states. They have become nationalists without abandoning in their hearts Islam's borderless appeal. The FIS' popularity derives in no small part from its success in stealing the nationalist mantle from its former archrival, the National Liberation Front (FLN), the victor in the campaign against colonial France. But the FIS' political acumen, nationalist adaptability, and use of Western political vocabulary have not made it more amenable to the West. The FLN and the FIS have always shared an anti-Western faith. The FLN opposed the West both because of its left-wing, anti-imperial ideology and because its members were Muslim, however calcified. The Islamic sensibilities within the FLN have become the FIS' ideology. The FIS' war with France is not primarily political, as was that of the FLN, which wanted French settlers out of "l'Algérie française." It is cultural. The FIS wants Christian France, with its American television shows dubbed into French, out of the Algerian mind.

The military's suppressive actions in 1992 enraged the FIS but in no way altered the group's understanding of right and wrong. What the FIS thinks today about women, freedom of thought, crime and punishment, Jews, westernized Muslims, France, Israel, and America is no different from the views it held before the military crackdown.

HOW MODERATES LOSE

EVEN IF there really are moderate fundamentalists, Washington should not want to talk to them. They can do little for us. More important, we would most likely do them harm.

President Clinton has stated that he hopes the United States could have a dialogue with Muslims "who want to follow the rules of civilized people"—in other words, fundamentalists who do not take hostages. But what good did it do Mehdi Bazargan, the first prime minister of the Provisional Islamic Republic of Iran and an exquisitely civilized moderate, to meet with President Carter's national security adviser, Zbigniew Brzezinski, in Algiers in 1979? Weakened by the American contact, Bazargan soon fell victim to Iran's hard core. Bazargan and Iran's other prominent but powerless moderates would have lost control in any case, but Brzezinski's contact tarnished their "Islamic" credentials and hastened their fall. The Iranian Revolution did not go sour because the United States failed to maintain a dialogue with Islamic moderates; the revolution turned Jacobin because Islamic moderates with whom the United States was in contact failed to anticipate the strength and determination of their hard-core partners.

Thus if we are going to talk to "moderates" in Algeria, we must find them within the FIS. It seems pointless to waste our time trying to build a bridge with such moderate fringe groups as the Democratic Movement for Algerian Renewal, a powerless though pleasant party of secularized Muslims. As the Clinton administration correctly deduced, we have to talk to fundamentalists who have both ballot box and street power.

The FIS has published a great deal since its inception in March 1989. Rarely does one find in its newspapers, manifestoes, or pamphlets a strong affirmation of democracy or individual liberty. But let us, for the sake of argument, find our moderates in the faction behind Abassi Madani, the FIS' main spokesman and leader. Jailed or under house arrest since June 1991, Madani is the premier Islamic technocrat, a sophisticated pragmatist with a Ph.D. who gave the FIS its name and tried to keep the group's holy warriors in check. If we really believe Madani is a moderate—and he and his followers are unquestionably milder than some of their Koran-screaming colleagues—why do to him what we did to Bazargan? When Iraqi President Saddam Hussein invaded Kuwait in 1990, Madani was severely criticized by Ali Belhadj, the FIS' fiery number two, for not being sufficiently pro-Iraqi and anti-Western. Madani, who had been trying to protect the FIS' Saudi backing by his defense of Kuwait, quickly changed his tune when he saw the street appeal of Belhadj's pro-Saddam and anti-Western line.

Why would a "moderate" like Madani, a highly educated and clever man, be so stupid as to risk a similar compromise with us? First, U.S. contact could deliver to him the power he has so far failed to obtain through elections and guerrilla war. Even in the fervid, conspiracy-mad world of the Middle East (where the CIA is poisoning every oasis well), the FIS probably does not believe the United States has such power in Algeria. Nevertheless, it gives Washington the conspiratorial benefit of the doubt, which probably explains why no American citizen has been among the around 90 foreigners so far murdered by Islamic militants. Second, if the United States cannot help the FIS win in Algeria, it also cannot deny them power—another reason for Madani to negotiate.

In any dialogue with the United States, however, the FIS will be at an advantage. Its objectives are concrete and easy: nourish Washington's fears of militant Islam and emphasize the inevitability of an FIS victory, the need for compromise, and the misguided stubbornness of the French. By comparison, U.S. policy toward the FIS is psychoanalytic quicksand: find and encourage fundamentalists who do not believe that God's word is law and that Washington is the cultural font of evil. Given this disadvantage, the United States should keep its distance from parties that promise salvation at the polls.

THE FIRST BATTLEGROUND

MUSLIM fundamentalism is a diplomatic challenge that Americans are particularly ill-equipped to handle. Many Americans do not really comprehend how others can unify church and state because they themselves no longer believe in communication between God and man. Under traditional Islam, Muslims can disagree on what God's will is, but not about the truth that God's will exists, must be ascertained, and must be followed. No right-believing Muslim would obey a man-made edict before one of God's.

In addition, both the West and Islam still conceive of themselves as universal civilizations. Both Western human rights and Islamic *sharia* are inalienable. How do you compromise when the two collide? How do you oppose Islam's extremists without offending or enraging more moderate practitioners of the faith? Muslims' moral reflexes differ in degree, not in kind. The Muslim division of the world into the *Dar al-Islam* ("House of Islam") and the *Dar al-Harb* ("House of War") is traditional *sharia*, not radical doctrine. King Fahd of Saudi Arabia—an ally—and Iran's supreme religious leader, Ali Khamenei—an enemy—would agree on this divide. So would Algeria's former ruling Arab nationalist party, the FLN, and the FIS.

Fundamentalism's greatest strength lies in the failure of secularized Muslims to create a solid, historically secure, and competitive identity. Even though Ayatollah Khomeini's death sentence on the British novelist Salman Rushdie contradicted Islamic legal theory and practice, few religious moderates or secularized Muslims defended Rushdie. When fundamentalists charge collaboration, moderates invariably wince or head directly to a mosque to deny the charge. Having ceded theology and history to the militants, the moderates had to master economics to stay alive. Given the age-old poverty of the Middle East and westernized Muslims' love affair with socialism, the militants obviously made the better choice. Poverty is a common denominator in the Middle East. So is profound faith, a sense of inferiority vis-à-vis the West, and a historical understanding that once upon a time, the positions were reversed. Millions of half-educated, unemployed young men who dream of wealth and women are targeted by militants who promise a new, more prosperous, egalitarian order. U.S. diplomacy must cope with the consequences of unsuccessful secular Muslim choices. Western political and economic theories in the Middle East have been debased by decades of nationalist, socialist, and "democratic" despotisms.

Today's Arab fundamentalists, who watched their spiritual fathers fall in murderous frontal assaults against powerful secular regimes, such as Egypt's in the 1950s and Syria's in the 1980s, now aim at constructing an Islamic society independent from the state. Culture, not politics, is the first battleground. The primary target of "neofundamentalism" is individual Muslims, their consciences, and their environments—hence the FIS' preachy manner, its explicit and long-winded discussions about Islamic ethics and behavior, and its secondary interest in the mechanics of government.

In the Middle East's dilapidated universities, better-educated students in science, philosophy, and engineering zealously embrace Islam. With passion and discipline, they dream of the future by engaging a glorious past that is both real and imagined. Western culture will retreat before resurgent Islam. Westernizing Muslims, the most despised enemy, will fall from power. The female temptation—the oldest and most dangerous challenge to a Muslim's fidelity to God—will be countered just in time by the traditional veil.

The suppression of the FIS as a legal political party worsened the violence in Algeria. But one should not overestimate the crackdown's damage to the Islamic movement's moderation. As the French scholar Olivier Roy points out, the modus operandi, if not the nature, of Islamic radicalism has changed significantly in the last 30 years. Radical Islam in most countries, including Algeria, has moved away from its more explicit political dreams: building Islamic states by confrontation, coup d'état, and assassination.

The FIS is everywhere in Algeria: in the schools, hospitals, unions, mosques, and neighborhood grocery stores. The FIS' political triumph at the polls would not be—as it was in Iran—the beginning of society's re-Islamization; it would be the final step, eliminating an irreligious leadership that no longer lawfully commanded a faithful community. But what would happen once it took power? That brings us to the case of Iran.

THE IRANIAN FAILURE

TO UNDERSTAND the likely course of fundamentalism in power, we can do no better than look at Iran, the first and most important state to be overwhelmed by militant Islam. Fifteen years after the new regime's jubilant beginnings, the verdict is clear. Iran's revolution has failed, dismaying its people and bankrupting its coffers. As a result, good and evil have been reversed in Iranian life. America—an undefined but vivid, almost mystical concept of a better life—has filled the void left by the 1979 revolution's failure. "West-toxification," the worship of things Western that was Khomeini's great fear, has become a common refuge from the clergy's junking of Islamic life. By depicting the Islamic revival as a rejection of Western culture, the leaders of Islamic militancy have set themselves up for an awful fall. They may have quite unintentionally helped trigger a post-fundamentalist tidal wave of American culture throughout the Middle East.

For every vision an Iranian Revolutionary Guardsman may have about a martyr's rendezvous with the Prophet Muhammad's nephew Ali, the spiritual father of Shiism, he has an equally vivid Western fantasy. Young FIS radicals are at least equally impregnated with Western desires. Often portrayed as a rejection of Western materialism, for most radical young men the Islamic revolution is just the opposite: a promise that the omnipresent images of Western civilization—wealth, military power, technology, sexual fulfillment—can be had without violating a Muslim's faith. Iranians now know that the promise has vanished. Iranian revolutionaries are at a loss to judge their revolution except by Western standards of material progress. The "perfect Muslim man," that special creature waiting to be born in 1979, is now 16 years old. He does not feel particularly more moral or blessed than a 16-year-old felt during the shah's regime. Despite Iran's Islamic education system, he dreams the same adolescent dreams as did his prerevolutionary older brother. Unlike his brother, he also dreams nostalgically about better times under the shah.

The decomposition of Iran's Islamic revolution is striking even among the revolutionary hard core: the politicized clerics and the faithful, unshaven young men—the Hezbollahis—who form the backbone of the Revolutionary Guard Corps and the Basij, the paramilitary mobilization force. Even politicized mullahs, who spew the party line in public, can privately damn their own kind for destroying the revolution and the public's historical faith in the clergy.

In July 1994, Ayatollah Muhammad Reza Mahdavi-Kani, the secretary-general of Tehran's preeminent political clerical fraternity, warned that the next president of Iran should not be a mullah. His statement, a rejection of revolutionary clerical political philosophy, is a confession from Iran's most honest and farsighted ayatollah that the revolution is in serious trouble. The excesses of marrying religious principle to power have exhausted and impoverished the nation. Political clerics and Islamic militancy must both start to retreat.

The August 1994 riot in Qazvin was a telling event in the Islamic Republic's meltdown. When the Iranian parliament refused to allow Qazvin, a predominantly Persian-speaking city, to separate from predominantly Turkish-speaking Zanjan province and become a new province in order to gain more federal aid, Qazvin's principal cleric organized street demonstrations. The mullah lost control of his flock, and a riot ensued. Young men attacked government buildings, overturned cars, and screamed, "Death to the mullahs." After two days of violence, a special anti-riot force from Tehran restored order.

The Islamic Republic had known riots before. The squatter riots in 1992 in Mashhad and other cities shocked the regime, as did a soccer-related riot in Tehran in 1990. After Mashhad, anti-riot urban security forces were expanded and revamped. In particular, the regime enlarged the Basij, creating an urban-control force commanded by the interior ministry, and developed a rapid-reaction, anti-riot Revolutionary Guards Corps (RGC) unit, the Ashura Brigade.

The Qazvin riot haunts the regime. The mullahs live in fear that unexpected demonstrations could start a chain reaction that could show they are no longer in command. Two subsequent riots in Tabriz in August and September, both squelched, reinforced that fear. And the army has made its position clear: it will not shoot Iranians in the streets. Qazvin underscored the clergy's complete dependence on the Basij and the RGC. But the Basij is neither strong nor predictable, and the rgc, though stronger, is not necessarily more reliable. The poor young men who rioted, like their compatriots in Mashhad and Tehran, are little different in background and frustration from those in the guards and no different from those in the Basij. One moment they might be loyal, the next not.

Clerical-military relations are also worsening. Inspired in part by the example of the Qazvin commander who refused to shoot demonstrators, retired Brigadier General Azizollah Amir Rahimi in September called for the resignation of Iranian President Hojatolislam Hashemi Rafsanjani, the end of clerical rule, and a national salvation government. Although Rahimi, a former commander of Iran's military police, is a firebrand with a history of trouble with both the shah and the mullahs, the army widely shares his views about the inability of the clerics to govern competently and justly.

Qazvinis, Tabrizis, and soldiers are not the only ones becoming more publicly disgruntled. Last October, 134 intellectuals, some of them quite prominent, signed an open letter protesting the regime's suppression of free speech and violation of human rights. Though individual intellectuals had taken swipes at the regime before, this was the first time since the early years of the revolution that so many banded together to attack the government. The regime has been clever in countering such criticism:

coercion for the hard core but greater freedom for the rest to criticize—so long as the Islamic revolution, Khomeini, and the Koran are not directly impugned. But the intellectuals have pressed the attack. With increasing seriousness, they have sought to distance Islam from corrupting clerical power, which means eliminating the regime's *raison d'être*.

The ruling mullahs in Tehran cannot escape from Ayatollah Khomeini's legacy. Khamenei, Khomeini's successor, leads the country as both revolutionary guide (*rahbar*) and supreme religious jurist (*faqih*). The two functions are in principle inseparable: to be a rahbar alone is to be a dictator; to be a *faqih* alone is to abandon the revolution. Though Khomeini had encountered considerable clerical opposition to his one-man theocratic rule—the traditional clergy is a consensual, not an autocratic, community—his system worked because the traditional clergy buckled before Khomeini's awe-inspiring political achievement, the overthrowing of the shah.

But the two functions have proven increasingly contradictory as the revolution has rapidly aged. Khamenei, unlike Khomeini, became an ayatollah, a *faqih*, in name alone, elevated to office for his revolutionary commitment rather than his scholastic achievement. No mullah or religious student in any of Iran's seminaries, nor any ordinary Iranian in need of religious counsel, would seek a judgment, a *fatwa*, from Khamenei. Iranians who still care about what clerics think—and they are ever fewer—now give their allegiance elsewhere, most often to senior ayatollahs not active in the government. Regardless of Khamenei's actions, the erosion of his Islamic legitimacy—and with it clerical rule and prestige in general—irreversibly continues.

As *rahbar*, Khamenei still has power: many in the clerical community, particularly younger, less accomplished religious students and mullahs who have chosen government service over study and teaching, have embraced his rule. Those who have not are guarded in their criticisms. The clergy, traditionalists and radicals alike, are haunted by memories of shahs and westernized Iranian liberals splitting and diminishing the clergy during the twentieth century. To some extent, the disgruntled mullahs are pinned by their fears that clerical criticism might ignite wider protests that could lead to the chaotic collapse of the clerical order. Most traditional mullahs want a dignified partial retreat from power, not a reversal.

But the clergy is not blind to the people's loss of faith in it and in revolutionary Islam. The contradictions of the regime—wealthy mullah-bureaucrats preaching virtue to the poor—have engendered rampant anger and cynicism. Khamenei and other politicized clerics continue to talk about the revolutionary power of Islam. Many of them probably still believe what they say, but many do not. Religion has become a cover for greed and political corruption. The clerics and their Hezbollahi cohorts divide in their support for privatization over a state-run economy. Support for privatization grows among those who know that Iran is almost bankrupt and have figured out how to enrich themselves through selling state assets. Support for renewed centralization grows among those who fear the unsettling and possibly riot-producing effects of freer enterprise and envy their clerical and Hezbollahi peers who have more successfully cashed in on "free market" connections. Short on history and irony, the statist clerics have apparently forgotten the shah's mistake of dictating prices to the bazaar. Publicly, Iran still condemns America; privately, many Iranians would happily trade with the United States, an alluring power they no longer have the ideological purity to loathe. And the poor, for whom the clergy historically fought, grow poorer, enduring ever-more-severe shortages and longer lines. Or they riot. They have only one receding dream: to afford a family. In their hearts, the revolution and its utopian hopes are dead. For them, Islam has again become a means to survive quietly the awfulness of daily life.

ALGERIA'S TURN

A SIMILAR degeneration will surely happen in Algeria if the FIS comes to power. Indeed, the agony of fundamentalist decline will probably be worse in Algeria than in Iran. Less isolated than the Persians, less cohesive in culture and revolutionary spirit, Algerians will offer more resistance to universal "Islamic ideals." At the height of its popularity in June 1990, the FIS garnered only 54 percent of the vote in communal and district elections. By December 1991, in the general election's first round, the FIS' winning share had dropped by over a million votes. Forty-one percent of registered Algerians had abstained. Hostile regional and ethnic voting patterns further complicate the returns and the FIS' likely future.

France, of course, will still be just across the Mediterranean, with millions of expatriate Algerians communicating back home by telephone and fax. The slow but real progress of Muslims in French society will attract and reproach the stillborn Algerian Islamic order. French television, regardless of any FIS laws against satellite dishes, will continue to penetrate millions of Algerian homes, undermining Islamic rectitude in relentless color.

As the dream collapses, Algeria's Sunni radicals will remain tenaciously faithful to their past, certain that the Koran and the *sunna*—the traditions established by the prophet and his companions—will answer all their contemporary needs. Like their Iranian brethren, Algerian fundamentalists will quickly be frustrated and intellectually at a loss over how to generate attractive, durable dreams for a new Islamic community.

Moreover, the struggle between radicalism and the Algerian status quo may endure beyond 1995. Sunni governments, even rickety ones like those in Algeria or Egypt, are not easily toppled. Especially in Egypt, age-old reflexes and loyalties between the rulers and the ruled—the traditional Islamic disposition to view de facto government as de jure—will continue to offer stiff competition to militants feeding off street despair. And Arab security services can be diligent, clever, and very tough. Rather than seeing Sunni regimes fall, we are more likely to witness what Roy has aptly called a permanent militant coup d'état, a stalemate between two forces that cannot decisively outflank each other.

If this happens, the FIS might be lucky. If fundamentalism fails to seize power or force a ruling Arab regime to effectively transform itself into a more hard-core Islamic state, Sunni militancy may postpone its own inevitable demise. In opposition, fundamentalism can remain on the offensive, highlighting the undeniable injustices, weaknesses, and failures of the Arab world. Unless today's Arab rulers can create a new, competitive identity, seductively fusing Islam and the West, fundamentalists will only need to cite the Koran to survive.

But modern militancy can also weaken in opposition. According to Princeton historian Bernard Lewis, radical Islamic movements' rage and indignation have usually withered amid the traditional conventions and conservatism of the Muslim community. We should remember that economic despair, the oft-cited source of political Islam's power, is familiar to the Middle East. Myth-building, envy-inducing television is new, but ruling regimes that are stingy in the hope they dispense can often survive. Like Jordan's King Hussein, they may also intelligently and cautiously liberalize, attempting to build a society that allows fundamentalists a forum yet forces them to compromise.

The common Sunni faithful are not blind to the outside world. The continuing meltdown of Iran may have repercussions throughout the Muslim world. No doubt the Sunni hard core will do their best to ignore the Shiite crackup. Revolutionary Iran's missionary zeal and hubris have heightened, not lessened, the differences between the two great branches of Islam. Fundamentalist Sunnis will depict their fallen Shiite brethren as hard-core Sunni theologians always have, as flawed and destined to fail their faith. But the average Sunni may think differently. If Iran implodes, Muslims in Algeria and throughout the Middle East may come to appreciate that Lord Acton's famous dictum about power corrupting applies to mullahs as well.

Even if the fundamentalists succeed in Algiers, their cause may not efficaciously inspire others. Western officials worry about a domino effect whereby a militantly Islamic Algeria might advance struggling radical causes in such U.S. allies as Egypt, Saudi Arabia, Jordan, and Morocco. Since Algeria is both Sunni (the majority branch within Islam) and predominantly Arab, an Algerian revolution might jolt the Arab Sunni world more forcefully than did Khomeini's Shiite revolution in non-Arab Iran. If Egypt alone were to follow Algeria into fundamentalist revolution or coup d'état, the Arab-Israeli peace process would end. The demilitarization of the Sinai, the key to Israeli national security, would once again be in question.

But the universalist aspirations of militant Islam can founder on Middle Eastern differences. Algeria is neither Tunisia, nor Morocco, nor Saudi Arabia, nor Egypt. The international networks of Islamic militancy cause considerable concern, but they do not easily overcome the limitations imposed by geography, nationalism, ethnicity, cultural peculiarity, and religious factionalism. Algerian militants can distrust Egypt's Muslim Brothers, who can loathe Shiite Iranian revolutionaries. This is hardly new. The Crusaders lasted so long in the Middle East because Muslims displayed more animosity toward each other than toward European infidels. United, Muslims should have made quick work of the Jewish state when Israel declared its independence in 1948. Algerian Islamic revolutionaries will no doubt try, as good revolutionaries should, to spread their faith and undermine their neighbors. But a fundamentalist triumph in Algiers, like the triumph 15 years ago in Tehran, will probably not upend the Arab Middle East.

Edward G. Shirley

RULES OF ENGAGEMENT

WITH THE end of the Cold War, the United States can distance itself somewhat from the Middle East. The Soviet Union is no longer offering guns and butter at minimal charge to Syrians, Libyans, Iraqis, Algerians, Yemenites, and Palestinians. Washington still must pay attention—the Persian Gulf War shows clearly what can happen when the U.S. government goes to sleep at the wheel—but there are now few instances where the United States should intervene or demonstrably take sides in internal Middle Eastern debates.

Commendably, the United States has tried to downplay the confrontation of Islam with the West and to tone down the religious content in the quarrel. This is all for the best, even if the other side does not reciprocate. We have, however, an obvious interest in the outcome of today's Islamic civil wars between militants, traditionalists, and secularists. Though there is much to dislike about the ruling regimes in Algeria, Tunisia, Morocco, Egypt, and Saudi Arabia, they all possess one quality that should incline us strongly in their favor: they can evolve. It is easier to imagine the Algerian generals or Egyptian President Hosni Mubarak one day liberalizing their governments, however reluctantly and slowly, than it is to imagine similar reforms from Iran's Khamenei or Sudanese ruler Hassan al-Turabi. Though the Saudi rulers may be guilty of ugly authoritarian behavior at home and consistent stupidity in foreign affairs, including godfathering Islamic fundamentalism throughout the world in the naive hope of controlling and "deradicalizing" it, they are at least fervent hypocrites. A good deal of humanity exists in their outrageous personal foibles and split personalities, which combine American educations and Wahhabi puritanism. In Middle Eastern affairs, a fervent hypocrite is always safer than a fervent puritan.

As a general rule, if Washington likes someone who is engaged in a life-and-death struggle with Islamic fundamentalists, it should not dote on him, at least publicly. The United States should send covert support if necessary, forgive his country's public indebtedness, and state clearly and with confidence our cherished principles of free expression, liberal democracy, and the separation of church and state. Our allies should be identified with measured words, not in the bombastic way we described the shah and now describe the Saudi royal family. Washington should not ostentatiously embrace its favorites. Even the most secularized Muslims, who may adore the United States privately, grow uneasy when U.S. officials linger too long in their company. The Middle East's love-hate relationship with the United States can alternate unexpectedly. The West—or, as it is still understood reflexively even in the secular Muslim mind, Christendom—remains unalterably "other." Association even in the friendliest settings can be seen as betrayal.

The United States should not help fundamentalists achieve what they have so far been unable to gain themselves. Although U.S. influence in Algeria is far less than the paranoid French believe, U.S. diplomatic contacts with fundamentalists can suggest approval. And U.S. disapproval can be exceptionally dispiriting to domestically besieged Middle Eastern rulers. Since the end of the Persian Gulf War and the collapse of the U.S.S.R., the illusion of U.S. power in the Middle East has never been higher.

The ruling Algerian regime, distasteful as it may be, should be allowed to fight or compromise on its own terms without wondering whether the United States is encouraging a deal behind its back. If the United States wants the FIS and the army to reach a "democratic" compromise, it should do nothing to undermine the military. The FIS, which currently has the upper hand, will be more likely to seriously compromise if it and the generals both believe fundamentalism will not unconditionally win.

If the motivating spirit of the Clinton administration's Algerian policy were more Machiavellian and less irenic, its present policy of beginning a dialogue with "moderate" fundamentalists would make more sense. For if the FIS wins the war, the decomposition of Algerian Islamic radicalism will begin for real. However, the U.S. government is not that devious. It is just hopeful that the fundamentalists will stop believing so aggressively. This may happen, but in the short term we need to understand that fundamentalism is a war fought primarily in Muslim imaginations. Private and collective dreams are not amenable to negotiation.

In fact, when looking at Algeria's likely future—exploding population growth, an awful economy, ethnic strife, and political mayhem—an earlier debut for Algeria's militants has a certain appeal. It might be better to sweat out the fundamentalist fever sooner rather than later. Algeria's horrendous problems will have no chance of amelioration until Algerians stop taking refuge in imagined Koranic cures. Given time, the lessons of the costs of the Algerian and Iranian revolutions could spread. Algerians might live in hell for several years, but others of greater strategic interest to us might learn and survive.

Edward G. Shirley

Conceivably, fundamentalism could even help the democratic movement in the Middle East. Burned by firsthand experience or terrified by
the fundamentalist alternative, Middle Eastern Muslims may finally set
aside the literalist interpretation of the Koran and Islam's traditions just
enough to allow the foundations of a viable democracy to form. In general, the United States and its Muslim allies would be better off if the
United States distanced itself from Muslim civil conflicts and developed
a quieter, more patient policy against anti-Western radicalism in the
Middle East. The United States should allow time, the oft-cited ally of
fundamentalism, to work against Islamic activism. Neither dialogue nor
containment is likely to work as well.⊛

Lessons of the Next
Nuclear War

Michael Mandelbaum

THE DANGERS OF PROLIFERATION
IT DOESN'T take a superpower to pose a nuclear threat. A small, poor country with a few nuclear explosives and the means to deliver them could wreak terrible damage on the United States. Even if never used, a handful of nuclear weapons merely in the possession of an unfriendly country could change a regional balance of power against the United States. Thus, the major military danger now facing the United States in the post-Soviet world is not a particular country but rather a trend: nuclear proliferation.

Because they enhance national power, nuclear weapons are potentially attractive to a wide variety of countries. Yet relatively few have these weapons. The five permanent members of the U.N. Security Council—the United States, Russia, Great Britain, France, and China—all do. Several others either have or are very close to having operational nuclear weapons. The number, however, is far smaller than expected in the early stages of the nuclear age. In 1963 President John F. Kennedy predicted that 15 to 20 countries would have nuclear arms by 1975. Overall, Cold War efforts to prevent the spread of nuclear weapons have been successful.

The international spotlight falls on that effort in April, when the fifth Nonproliferation Treaty review conference convenes at the United Na-

MICHAEL MANDELBAUM is Christian A. Herter Professor of American Foreign Policy at the Paul H. Nitze School of Advanced International Studies, The Johns Hopkins University, and Director of the Project on East-West Relations at the Council on Foreign Relations. This essay is adapted from a forthcoming book sponsored by the Twentieth Century Fund.

Michael Mandelbaum

tions to reconsider, revise, and extend the treaty. The NPT, which came into force in 1970, now has 168 adherents. The treaty is useful; its extension, highly desirable. The course of nuclear nonproliferation in the post-Cold War era, however, will depend less on what happens at the United Nations in 1995 than in Washington thereafter. The main obstacle to the spread of nuclear weapons is not the NPT but the United States, nor is nonproliferation a single issue: it is composed of three separate problems. Each is now more complicated and urgent than in the past because the end of the Cold War has either weakened or removed the principal restraints on both the demand for and the supply of nuclear weapons. Three different types of states are candidates for nuclear armaments, and three different American policies will be required to discourage or thwart their nuclear ambitions.

The countries in the first and most important category are not ordinarily considered part of the proliferation problem, yet their acquisition of nuclear weapons would have the most powerful impact on international policies. They are the allies. Germany and Japan forswore nuclear weapons during the Cold War because they received security guarantees from the United States. Whether they continue as nonnuclear states depends on whether those guarantees continue.

The second group of would-be nuclear states are the orphans. They feel seriously threatened but lack the nuclear protection the allies have enjoyed. None has become a full-fledged nuclear power, but each is close. The orphans, particularly Pakistan, Israel, and Ukraine, are the objects of a different American policy—diplomatic efforts to end the conflicts that have made nuclear armaments attractive to them.

The third category includes those countries at the center of concern about nuclear proliferation. The rogues—Iraq and North Korea most prominent among them—are openly hostile to the United States and are seeking or have sought nuclear weapons. Thwarting them will require strengthening the restrictions on bomb-related material, which the United States was instrumental in creating and enforcing and that the collapse of the Soviet Union has weakened. But these efforts may not suffice. The prevention of proliferation may ultimately require destroying those states' nuclear programs by force. Here again the chief responsibility will fall to the United States. If the nuclear future of the allies depends on American alliance commitments, and that of the orphans on American diplomacy, the nuclear aspirations of the rogues may become one of the chief objects of American military policy.

Lessons of the Next Nuclear War

Lessons of the Next Nuclear War

THE ALLIES

WHY ARE nuclear weapons not more widely dispersed? In part, deterrence, a guiding concept of the nuclear powers' military strategies for most of the Cold War, has kept proliferation at bay. While the two strongest powers deterred each other from using nuclear weapons, other pairs of states deterred each other from acquiring such weapons. For example, India and Pakistan each has a robust nuclear weapons program. But neither state has built a bomb, in part out of concern that the other would follow.

Despite the impact of deterrence, the NPT has not been irrelevant. The organizations and policies that monitor and attempt to restrict the worldwide supply of nuclear materials contribute to nonproliferation. The treaty clarifies and publicizes which states have the bomb and which do not. But for a number of nonnuclear signatories to the NPT, adherence to the treaty was the consequence of a decision to abjure the bomb, the cause of which lay elsewhere. What was the basis for this widespread decision?

One possible basis, which has come to be known as the "nuclear taboo," is the feelings of horror that nuclear weapons arouse. This distaste is certainly widely felt but like the NPT is a doubtful explanation for the degree to which the world has been spared the spread of nuclear weapons. In the first place, the taboo is against using, not acquiring, these weapons. Hiroshima, not the Soviet-American arms race, evokes horror. Moreover, like all taboos, this one will be violated under necessity. Individuals will eat forbidden foods, even one another, if the alternative is starvation; nations will acquire and use forbidden weapons if they deem it necessary for survival.

Another possible basis for adhering to the NPT is the two benefits nonnuclear states are supposed to receive in return: assistance in obtaining technology for the peaceful use of nuclear energy and a good-faith effort by states with nuclear weapons to reduce their own arsenals, with the implication that, at some time in the future, all nuclear armaments will be gone.

The first of these promises is hollow. The economic benefits of nuclear technology are at best modest; its diffusion has complicated the effort to prevent nuclear proliferation; and whatever the advantages of nuclear power plants, they are irrelevant to security, the central purpose that nuclear weapons serve. The second promise is false. Steep reductions in and the ultimate abolition of the arsenals of the nuclear "haves" would promote rather than discourage nuclear proliferation. These reductions would undercut the very thing that has kept the spread of nuclear weapons in check: the guarantees of nuclear protection extended by the great powers, above all the United States.

During the Cold War those guarantees were credible in part because the United States had a large number of nuclear armaments, many of them deployed on territories distant from North America. If American nuclear weapons disappeared altogether, the guarantees that rest on them would be worthless. Those guarantees persuaded a class of countries with genuine security concerns and the capacity to equip themselves with nuclear weapons to forgo them. U.S. treaties and the local deployment of American forces kept the German Federal Republic and Japan from acquiring nuclear weapons. Both had the technical capacity. Both had a territorial dispute with the great nuclear rival of the United States, involving the Soviet occupation of the eastern part of Germany and the southern islands of the Kuril chain.

The protective American nuclear umbrella extended beyond West Germany to all NATO members. It even extended after a fashion to countries, such as Switzerland, Sweden, and Finland, that were not formally part of the North Atlantic alliance. These countries could reckon that American guarantees to their neighbors made Europe safe enough that they, too, could dispense with nuclear weapons.

In his 1872 book, *The English Constitution*, Walter Bagehot distinguished between the "dignified" parts of the British system of government, "which excite and preserve the reverence of the public" and the "efficient" parts, "those by which it, in fact, works and rules." For the global constitution of nonproliferation during the Cold War, the NPT constituted the dignified part, but its "efficiency" in limiting the spread of nuclear weapons stemmed principally from the American system of alliances and guarantees.

However urgent Germany's and Japan's perceived need for nuclear protection during East-West confrontation, that need has become far less pressing. It has not, however, disappeared completely. Russia and China still have nuclear weapons. Without some means of offsetting those armaments, the allies would have to consider that, at some point, a disagreement with one or the other of the two nuclear-armed giants could arise in which the possession of a nuclear arsenal would confer a decisive advantage. For the entirely legitimate and wholly defensive purpose of short-circuiting this situation, the German and Japanese governments would be moved to seek a substitute for the American nuclear guarantee. The plausible substitutes are nuclear arsenals of their own.

During the Cold War, the United States made elaborate efforts to sustain German and Japanese confidence in its security guarantee, both pledging to defend them and deploying troops and weapons on German and Japanese soil. These measures testify to the importance for the United States of thwarting proliferation, even among its closest and most important allies. Yet what Washington has worked so hard to prevent would not be a self-evidently damaging development. Japan and Germany are not only close allies, but they are democracies, with records over the last four decades—admittedly in contrast with the previous four—of spotlessly peaceful foreign policies.

The United States has at least one reason to welcome German and Japanese nuclear weapons. They would relieve Americans of defending two countries sufficiently wealthy and powerful to defend themselves and separated from North America by large oceans. The dangers of German and Japanese nuclear weapons, however, outweigh the advantages. Germany and Japan are large, powerful states. Their acquisition of nuclear weapons would cause more than a ripple in international politics: it would make waves. The change would usher in a multipolar nuclear order, which would supplant the more or less bipolar arrangement of the Cold War. A multipolar order would by some reckonings make the world more dangerous—less stable, less certain, and less easily managed. In multipolar systems, none of the great powers can ever be certain who will side with whom.[1]

The emergence of Germany and Japan as major nuclear powers would likely set off a chain reaction. This emergence would signal the end of the American system of nuclear guarantees; if Germany and Japan gave up their American protection no country could count on the American

---

[1] The argument is John Mearsheimer's. See his "Back to the Future: Realism and the Realities of European Security," *International Security*, Winter 1990/1991. The argument follows Kenneth N. Waltz, *Theory of International Relations,* Reading: Addison-Wesley, 1979, chapter 8. But Waltz elsewhere makes a contrary argument that the spread of nuclear weapons will be a force for political stability for the same reasons that they imposed a standoff on the United States and the Soviet Union. See *The Spread of Nuclear Weapons: More May Be Better,* Adelphi Paper 171, London: International Institute for Strategic Studies, 1981.

shield. This development would trigger a wholesale recalculation of security requirements throughout Europe and Asia, which would have to take into account not only the retreat of American military power but also a sharp rise in the military status of Germany and Japan.

No country, least of all Germany and Japan themselves, wishes to see these countries become nuclear powers. Avoiding this eventuality will require keeping the American nuclear commitment in good working order, which in turn means perpetuating in some form nato and the Japanese-American Treaty of Mutual Cooperation and Security. Because Germany and Japan are, at least for the moment, less threatened than during the Cold War, this commitment should require less imposing American military forces; to ward off uncertainty ought to be less expensive than to deter the Soviet Union. For this purpose, perhaps no American forces will have to be stationed on the European continent or the Japanese archipelago.

But precisely because Germany and Japan as well as the United States are less threatened, even a modest American commitment may prove difficult. The American public may be unwilling to support the deployment of major military forces to reassure prosperous democratic allies that they do not need nuclear weapons. The American people were willing, for four decades, to spend trillions for defense and deterrence; what they will be willing to spend for reassurance, and for how long, remains to be seen.

THE ORPHANS

THE SECOND cluster of nuclear aspirants were also aligned with the United States during Soviet-American confrontation but felt more threatened and less protected than the allies. These countries feared for their lives, having neighbors that they felt did not accept the legitimacy of their existence as sovereign states.

International orphans lacked as firm an American security commitment as the North Atlantic pact and the Japanese-American security treaty but were not entirely alone. They had the benefit of military assistance from and diplomatic cooperation with the United States. But they were orphaned in that they had neither formal treaties of alliance nor American troops on their territories.

Absent an American nuclear umbrella, these orphans mounted substantial nuclear weapons programs and refused to sign the NPT. While they neither formally declared themselves nuclear weapons states nor conducted official nuclear tests, by the end of the Cold War they were capable of assembling working bombs on short notice. They engaged in what might be called partial proliferation, stopping just short of full nuclear status out of deference to the nonproliferation sensibilities of the United States as well as a desire not to provoke their neighbors. While the United States disapproved of their programs, the interests it shared with these countries were such that Washington took no effective action against them.

The two prototypical orphans are Pakistan and Israel. India and Taiwan have some features in common with them. The end of the Cold War has had only a modest effect on their military policies. For another group of countries with important features in common with Israel and Pakistan, however, the end of the Cold War has had a transforming effect.

This group consists of the countries of central and Eastern Europe once dominated by the Soviet Union, as well as the former republics of the Soviet Union other than Russia. The end of the Soviet Union has, if not created, then brought into the open a demand for nuclear weapons. Former provinces of the Soviet empire have either recovered or achieved independence. They can now choose which military forces to have, and for some, nuclear weapons are a plausible choice. Their memories of Soviet and pre-Soviet Russian subjugation are fresh. The politics of the new Russia are not yet reliably democratic or respectful of its neighbors' sovereignty. To some of these new states, their recently achieved independence is bound to seem precarious, and nuclear weapons, as guarantors of independence, therefore attractive.

One such former province, Ukraine, resembles Israel and Pakistan. In Russia, Ukraine has a large, powerful nuclear-armed neighbor, some of whose leading political figures do not fully accept Ukrainian independence. Also, like Israel and Pakistan, while Ukraine is not a full-fledged nuclear weapons state it has engaged in partial proliferation. Israel and Pakistan each has something short of a fully assembled (or at least publicly acknowledged and tested) bomb. Ukraine already possesses fully assembled nuclear weapons on its territory but has at best only partial control of them; it has physical custody, but presumably lacks the actual means to launch the nuclear-tipped missiles it inherited from the Soviet period. Finally, Ukraine, like Israel and Pakistan, has looked to the United States to reinforce its security. Washington pressed Kiev to send all nuclear weapons to Russia. In return, Ukraine asked for security assurances. These Kiev has received but in the most general possible form, as a repackaging of those extended in connection with the NPT and the Final Act of the Conference on Security and Cooperation in Europe, the largely symbolic set of agreements signed by the United States and all European countries, including the Soviet Union, at Helsinki in 1975. The government of Ukraine has promised to give up all its nuclear weapons and ratify the NPT. But the process of doing so is likely to be protracted, and depending on the course of events in Russia the nuclear option may prove tempting.

Nuclear weapons would be less consequential in the hands of an orphan than in those of Germany or Japan and less dangerous than in the case of a rogue state. The United States has done less to keep nuclear weapons out of the hands of this second group of potential proliferators than the other two categories, but Washington has not resigned itself to inaction. Pakistani, Israeli, and Ukrainian nuclear weapons pose hazards that the American government has sought to avoid.

The nuclear weapons programs in South Asia raise the specter of nuclear war between India and Pakistan. The Israeli bomb makes it difficult to rally support for curbing the nuclear ambitions of other Middle Eastern countries dangerous to the West. Ukrainian nuclear weapons are undesirable because they may reestablish nuclear-armed political rivalries in Europe, where the end of the Cold War has brought a welcome end to the 40-year nuclear standoff between the United States and the Soviet Union. A Ukrainian nuclear arsenal, moreover, may trigger a decision by nearby Germany to acquire nuclear weapons.

Washington has therefore sought during the Cold War and afterward to limit and perhaps reverse these nuclear weapons programs through diplomatic efforts to reconcile the threatened countries with their adversaries. The United States has been a party to almost continuous negotiations between Israel and its Arab neighbors for two decades beginning in 1974. Peace was clearly the necessary condition for nonproliferation. Nuclear programs could be eliminated in the region only in the wake of an end to the conflict that had driven Israel down the path to an independent nuclear arsenal.

The United States adopted a similar pattern with Russia and Ukraine, serving as a mediator and broker. On January 14, 1994, the presidents of the three countries signed a tripartite accord under the terms of which Ukrainian nuclear weapons were to be moved to Russia.

Ukrainian President Leonid Kravchuk subsequently announced during a state visit to the United States in November 1994 that his country would ratify the NPT. As with Arab-Israeli peacemaking, the United States promised financial assistance to Ukraine, which was implicitly contingent on Kiev's pledge to give up the nuclear weapons it had inherited from the Soviet Union.

The United States also intervened diplomatically, albeit less frequently and forcefully, in the continuing conflict between India and Pakistan. In response to reports that the two countries were close to war, in which each would likely have targeted the nuclear facilities of the other, in 1990 the Bush administration dispatched a special envoy to prevent the outbreak of hostilities, which in the end did not take place.

Thus if the nuclear future of the allies depends on whether the United States sustains its Cold War treaty commitments, the nuclear programs of the orphans will be influenced, perhaps decisively, by the success of post-Cold War American diplomacy.

THE SUPPLY SIDE

IN ADDITION to discouraging states from seeking nuclear weapons, the nonproliferation regime erects barriers to acquiring them. It addresses the supply of as well as the demand for weapons and the materials to make them.

By the terms of the NPT, the nuclear weapons states promise not to transfer the bomb to any nonnuclear states. The NPT also created the International Atomic Energy Agency (IAEA), which has a mandate to monitor nuclear power-generating facilities as well as fuel and waste storage sites of nonnuclear signatories. The purpose is to ensure these materials are not used to produce materials for nuclear weapons.

The work of the IAEA is supplemented by the efforts of an informal group of countries that manufacture the complicated and expensive machinery for uranium enrichment and plutonium reprocessing. Known as the Nuclear Suppliers Group, its aim is to restrict the commerce in nuclear fuel fabricating facilities that can also be used to make the core of a bomb. Another association outside the formal bounds of the NPT but whose purpose is consistent with the spirit of the treaty was created in 1987, the Missile Technology Control Regime. The aim of the MTCR is to restrict the diffusion of ballistic missiles, the most dangerous vehicles for the delivery of nuclear weapons.

Although the restraints on supply are necessarily multilateral, as are the measures to suppress demand, the United States has assumed the leading role in implementing them. The American government has been far more active than any other in setting the supply-side rules, trying to enforce them, and monitoring compliance.

The different parts of the supply-side regime, like all international agreements, share a common weakness: none includes any power of enforcement. If a sovereign state violates any of its norms, no international mechanism can compel compliance or mete out punishment. Nor does the regime have a perfect record in detecting violations. Iraq mounted a substantial clandestine nuclear weapons program even after signing the NPT and submitting its declared nuclear power-generating plants to IAEA inspections. Moreover, imperfect as the system of supply restraints was during the Cold War, it has come under increased pressure from two post-Cold War developments.

The first of these developments is the improvement and diffusion of technology of all kinds, including what is required to make nuclear weapons and ballistic missiles. By some estimates, 15 to 20 countries—not all of them allies or orphans—will have or be able to have such missiles by the end of the century.[2] The second development is the surge in the availability of nuclear materials brought about by the end of the Soviet Union. Its disintegration led to the weakening or collapse of controls on tens of thousands of weapons, many of them portable, scattered throughout the former Soviet Union; thousands of scientists and engineers, the mainstays of the Soviet military-industrial complex; and hundreds of tons of fissile material from laboratories, reactors, submarines, and weapons to be dismantled under the terms of one or another international agreement. Where the materials necessary for bomb-making were concerned, the Soviet Union was, in effect, an impregnable bank vault. When the U.S.S.R. collapsed, the vast territory on which it had stood turned into a massive bazaar.

---

[2] See for example, Peter van Ham, *Managing Non-proliferation Regimes in the 1990s: Power, Politics and Policies,* New York: Council on Foreign Relations Press, 1994, p. 24 and Seth Cropsey, "The Only Credible Deterrent," *Foreign Affairs,* March/April 1994, p. 17.

THE ROGUES

THE POST-COLD War pressure on supply restraints raises the increased likelihood that a select group of countries whose possession of nuclear weapons would run radically counter to the interests of the United States will manage to get them. Most current discussion of proliferation refers to this third category of nations, the rogues, and most of the nonproliferation efforts of the American government are devoted to them. This is so because the political goals that underlie the rogues' desire for nuclear weapons are incompatible with American interests.

In some cases those goals are aggressive. Iraq and Iran want to expand their influence, which would almost certainly not be exercised in ways compatible with American interests. In other cases nuclear weapons may be sought for ostensibly defensive purposes but are unacceptable from the American point of view. North Korea is concerned with its own survival, which at least partly motivated its nuclear weapons program. But a nuclear-armed North Korea would be better able to pursue its commitment to unifying the Korean peninsula, by force if necessary, under communist control. Even if it did not try to attack, subvert, or coerce the South, a North Korea with nuclear weapons would be tempted to sell weapons-related material and equipment, perhaps even bombs, to other countries.

The number of rogue states is relatively small. The list of them invariably includes North Korea, Iran, Iraq, and sometimes Syria, Libya, and Algeria. Each is influenced by an ideology—Marxism-Leninism, Islamic fundamentalism, or Arab socialism—with anti-Western and anti-American features. All suffered politically and militarily from the collapse of the Soviet Union, which, by depriving them of a patron and protector, or at least a reliable supplier of weapons, gave added impetus to their nuclear ambitions. None is a full-fledged democracy.

The United States is at the forefront of efforts to prevent the rogues from acquiring nuclear weapons. The American role is based not only on a general aversion to nuclear proliferation but also on commitments, carried over from the Cold War, to the protection of South Korea and the security of Middle Eastern allies.

At least three methods of coping with the prospect of nuclear weapons in the hands of rogues are available. One is to provide countries that might become targets with the means to defend themselves. This approach, however, is technically problematic. Defending against a few missiles fired by a rogue is less taxing than the task President Ronald Reagan set for the United States in 1983—the protection of the continental United States against massive missile barrages that the Soviet Union was (and its Russian successor continues to be) capable of launching. Still, the capacity of current technology to produce even more modest defenses is questionable.

The second method is to offer the rogue generous inducements to give up its nuclear aspirations, the approach the United States has taken with North Korea. American policy has been to buy the North's nuclear program. Even if successful, this approach encourages blackmail. The policy is all too likely to make nuclear weapons programs seem like useful bargaining chips to be cashed for a bonanza of economic assistance from wealthy countries.[3]

Because the number of rogue states is limited, it may be possible to concentrate anti-proliferation resources on them, such as surveillance, diplomacy, and economic assistance. But because supply restraints can, sooner or later, be defeated by time, money, and determination, and because even if the world is willing to buy nuclear programs not every rogue will be willing to sell, more forceful methods may be required in order to keep nuclear weapons out of their hands.

More forceful methods have been used twice against the most determined and wealthiest of the rogues, Iraq. Both the raid on the Osiraq reactor by Israel in 1981 and Operation Desert Storm, the military campaign to evict Iraq from Kuwait a decade later, count as successful anti-proliferation measures. Each set back Iraqi President Saddam Hussein's quest for nuclear weapons. Neither, however, is an altogether promising precedent.

Would-be proliferators can insure themselves against a single crippling strike, such as that Israeli warplanes delivered, in the same way that the United States and the Soviet Union during the Cold War protected their nuclear programs from a disarming first strike. They can multiply, disperse, conceal, and shield the component parts of the program so that a single raid could not entirely destroy it. This is exactly what Iraq proceeded to do after 1981.

As for Operation Desert Storm, the anti-Saddam coalition fielded a large, sophisticated army that only the United States could provide. In

---

[3] In the case of North Korea this course has seemed to the American (and South Korean and Japanese) governments preferable to the alternative: a confrontation that would run the risk of war.

future wars of nonproliferation, the United States will again be obliged to assume the leading role. The American military has the capacity to conduct such operations, but military operations require political support, and here Desert Storm may prove a weak precedent.

The crippling of Iraq's nuclear program was a byproduct of the war. The official purpose was to evict Iraq from Kuwait. Restoring Kuwait's sovereignty was, in fact, a less important American interest than keeping Saddam Hussein from controlling a large part of the Persian Gulf's oil reserves. A sovereign Kuwait was also less important than a nonnuclear Iraq. But because it constituted an unambiguous violation of international law, the invasion and occupation of Kuwait provided the basis for the political support the war attracted.

The Bush administration probably could not have rallied such extensive domestic and international support exclusively to eliminate Iraq's nuclear weapons program. A military campaign waged solely for that purpose would have been a preventive war, which has neither a basis in international law nor a well-established historical precedent.

Under present circumstances, it is difficult to envision 168 countries supporting an arrangement for preventive war as they do the NPT. The one clear instance of nuclear preemption, the Israeli raid on Osiraq, met with general condemnation. Moreover, such an arrangement would have to sanction preventive war against some countries but not others. Its targets would be Iraq and Iran but not Israel, India, Pakistan, Germany, or Japan. To compound the difficulty, such an international convention would also require defining a point in the development of nuclear weapons when a preemptive attack would be justified.

Even if the major powers could agree on the propriety of a preventive war against a dangerous nuclear weapons aspirant, one of them would have to take the lead. The logical candidate would be the United States, which would mean the American public would have to embrace preventive war as a norm, something it was never asked to do during the Cold War.

LESSONS OF THE LAST WAR

A PRESUMPTION in favor of fighting when not directly attacked has historically emerged from a traumatic experience of armed conflict. Such a presumption represents the lesson of the last war, learned at great cost. The policies that could in retrospect have prevented or won that war become the axiomatic approach to the next one. American foreign policy during the Cold War was based on the lessons of World War II. The commitment to containing the Soviet Union and communism stemmed from the conviction that the failure to check Hitler's ambitions before 1939 led to a terrible and avoidable war.

The Cold War was not a comparably wrenching experience. The next nuclear war, however, the next nuclear shot fired in anger, almost surely would be. It would shock and horrify the world. To be sure, the post-Cold War era has already occasioned horror at the starvation in Somalia, the "ethnic cleansing" in Bosnia, and the slaughter followed by epidemic in Rwanda. But a nuclear explosion would have a more powerful psychological impact on Americans because they will be able to imagine this horror happening to them.

The next nuclear war is likely to reshape the nonproliferation policies as well as attitudes and policies well beyond nuclear proliferation of the international community and the United States. Just how it will do so, however, cannot be foreseen.

The next nuclear war could, like World War II, give rise to a powerful bias in favor of preemptive intervention. Once one nuclear weapons program led to nuclear war, the United States might decide to take whatever steps necessary to put a stop to similar programs in other countries. The next Hiroshima could create in American public opinion a consensus in favor of preventive war to keep the bomb out of the hands of rogue states.

The next war could, however, have the opposite effect. Its legacy could be more like that of World War I, which reinforced the historical American determination to remain aloof from the political and military quarrels of Europe. It could revive a foreign policy of isolation, although the geographic scope might differ from the past. Traditional isolation applied to Europe but not Latin America or East Asia. From the next nuclear war Americans might learn to eschew political engagement in any part of the world where nuclear weapons are located or might be used.

Either lesson if translated into policy would mark a basic shift in the American role in the world. In this sense, for American foreign policy, the most important event of the post-Cold War era has not yet taken place.❷

Dutch Tulips and Emerging Markets

Paul Krugman

ANOTHER BUBBLE BURSTS

DURING THE first half of the 1990s, both economic and political events in developing countries defied all expectations. Nations that most thought would not regain access to world financial markets for a generation abruptly became favorites of private investors, who plied them with capital inflows on a scale not seen since before World War I. Governments that had spent half a century pursuing statist, protectionist policies suddenly got free market religion. It was, it seemed to many observers, the dawn of a new golden age for global capitalism.

To some extent the simultaneous reversals in government policies and investor sentiment were the result of external factors. Low interest rates in the advanced countries encouraged investors to look again at opportunities in the Third World; the fall of communism not only helped to discredit statist policies everywhere but reassured investors that their assets in the developing world were unlikely to be seized by leftist governments. Still, probably the most important factor in the new look of developing countries was a sea change in the intellectual zeitgeist: the almost universal acceptance, by governments and markets alike, of a new view about what it takes to develop.

This new view has come to be widely known as the "Washington consensus," a phrase coined by John Williamson of the Institute for International Economics. By "Washington" Williamson meant not only the U.S. government, but all those institutions and networks of opinion leaders centered in the world's de facto capital—the International Monetary Fund, World Bank, think tanks, politically sophisticated in-

---

PAUL KRUGMAN is Professor of Economics at Stanford University.

vestment bankers, and worldly finance ministers, all those who meet each other in Washington and collectively define the conventional wisdom of the moment.

Williamson's original definition of the Washington consensus involved ten different aspects of economic policy. One may, however, roughly summarize this consensus, at least as it influenced the beliefs of markets and governments, more simply. It is the belief that Victorian virtue in economic policy—free markets and sound money—is the key to economic development. Liberalize trade, privatize state enterprises, balance the budget, peg the exchange rate, and one will have laid the foundations for an economic takeoff; find a country that has done these things, and there one may confidently expect to realize high returns on investments.

To many people the rise of the Washington consensus seemed to mark a fundamental turning point in world economic affairs. Now that the dead hand of the state was being lifted from Third World economies, now that investors were becoming aware of the huge possibilities for profit in these economies, the world was set for a prolonged period of rapid growth in hitherto poor countries and massive capital flows from North to South. The question was not whether optimistic expectations about growth in the big emerging markets would be fulfilled; it was whether advanced countries would be able to cope with the new competition and take advantage of the opportunities this growth now offered.[1]

And then came the Mexican crisis. The country that was widely regarded as a model for the new regime—a once-protectionist nation that had not only greatly lowered its trade barriers but actually signed a free trade pact with the United States, whose economic policy was run by articulate American-trained technocrats, and which had emerged from seven lean years of debt crisis to attract capital inflows on a scale unimaginable a few years earlier—was once again appealing for emergency loans. But what is the meaning of Mexico's tailspin? Is it merely the product of specific Mexican blunders and political events,

---

[1] The strategy of promoting U.S. exports and investment in emerging markets remains central to the Clinton administration's economic strategy. In a March 1995 speech, Undersecretary of Commerce Jeffrey Garten declared that "our exports and jobs are dependent on gaining a larger market share in the big emerging markets. No U.S. firm will be a world-class company without substantial involvement in the big emerging markets."

or does it signal the unsoundness of the whole emerging market boom of the previous five years?

Many claim that Mexico's problems carry few wider implications. On one side, they argue that a currency crisis says more about short-term monetary management than about long-run development prospects. And to some extent they are clearly right. Currency crises are so similar to one another that they are a favorite topic for economic theorists, who lovingly detail the unchanging logic by which the collision between domestic goals and an unsustainable exchange rate generates a sudden, massive speculative attack. The December 1994 attack on the peso looked a lot like the September 1992 attack on the pound sterling, which looked quite similar to the 1973 and 1971 attacks on the dollar and the 1969 run on gold. So perhaps one should not draw broad conclusions from the fact that a developing country has managed to make the same mistakes that nearly every advanced country has made at some time in the past.

On the other side, defenders of the Washington consensus point to the many uniquely Mexican aspects of the current crisis. Certainly the combination of peasant uprisings, mysterious assassinations, and bizarre fraternal intrigue has no close counterpart anywhere else in the world.

And yet Mexico's crisis is neither a temporary setback nor a purely Mexican affair. Something like that crisis was an accident waiting to happen because the stunning initial success of the Washington consensus was based not on solid achievements, but on excessively optimistic expectations. The point is not that the policy recommendations that Williamson outlined are wrong, but that their efficacy—their ability to turn Argentina into Taiwan overnight—was greatly oversold. Indeed, the five-year reign of the Washington consensus may usefully be thought of as a sort of speculative bubble—one that involved not only the usual economic process by which excessive market optimism can be a temporarily self-fulfilling prophecy, but a more subtle political process through which the common beliefs of policymakers and investors proved mutually reinforcing. Unfortunately, any such self-reinforcing process unfortunately must eventually be faced with a reality check, and if the reality is not as good as the myth, the bubble bursts. For all its special features, the Mexican crisis marks the beginning of the deflation of the Washington consensus. That deflation ensures that the second half of the 1990s will be a far more problematic period for global capitalism than the first.

THE REAL PAYOFF TO REFORM

ECONOMISTS have, of course, long preached the virtues of free markets. The economic case for free trade in particular, while not completely watertight, is far stronger than most people imagine. The logic that says that tariffs and import quotas almost always reduce real income is deep and has survived a century and a half of often vitriolic criticism nearly intact. And experience teaches that governments that imagine or pretend that their interventionist strategies are a sophisticated improvement on free trade nearly always turn out, on closer examination, to be engaged in largely irrational policies—or worse, in policies that are rational only in the sense that they benefit key interest groups at the expense of everyone else.

Yet there is a dirty little secret in international trade analysis. The measurable costs of protectionist policies—the reductions in real income that can be attributed to tariffs and import quotas—are not all that large. The costs of protection, according to the textbook models, come from the misallocation of resources: protectionist economies deploy their capital and labor in industries in which they are relatively inefficient, instead of concentrating on those industries in which they are relatively efficient, exporting those products in exchange for the rest. These costs are very real, but when you try to add them up, they are usually smaller than the rhetoric of free trade would suggest. For example, most estimates of the cost of protection in the United States put it well under one percent of GDP. Even that cost is largely due to the United States' preference for policies, like its sugar import quota, that generate high profits for those foreign suppliers granted access to the U.S. market. Highly protected economies, like most developing countries before the rise of the Washington consensus, suffer more. Still, conventional estimates of the costs of protection have rarely exceeded five percent of GDP. That is, the standard estimates suggest that a highly protectionist developing country, by moving to completely free trade, would get a one-time economic boost equal to the growth China achieves every five or six months.

Admittedly, many economists argue that the adverse effects of protection are larger, and thus the growth boost from trade liberalization is greater, than such conventional estimates suggest. Roughly speaking, they have suggested three mechanisms. First, protection reduces competition in the domestic market. The monopoly power that is created for domestic firms that no longer face foreign competition may be reflected either in slack management or, if a small number of firms are trying to secure monopoly positions, in wasteful duplication. Second, protectionist policies—and other policies like interest rate controls—create profits that accrue to whoever is influential enough to receive the appropriate government licenses. In a well-known paper, Anne Krueger, who later became the chief economist at the World Bank, argued that in many developing countries, the resources squandered in pursuit of these profits represent a larger net cost to the economy than the distortion that protectionism causes in the industrial mix.[2] Finally, many people have argued that protectionism discourages innovation and the introduction of new products, thereby having sustained effects on growth that a static estimate misses. The important point about these arguments for large gains from trade liberalization, however, is that they are all fairly speculative; one cannot say as a matter of principle that these effects of protection discourage growth. It is an empirical question.

And the empirical evidence for huge gains from free market policies is, at best, fuzzy. There have been a number of attempts to measure the benefits of free trade by comparing countries. An influential 1987 study by the World Bank classified 41 developing countries as "closed" (protectionist) or "open" and concluded that openness was associated with substantially stronger growth. But such studies have often been critiqued for using subjective criteria in deciding which countries have freer trade; the decision to class South Korea as "open," for example, has raised many doubts. A survey by UCLA's Sebastian Edwards concluded that studies which purport to show that countries with liberal trade regimes systematically grow more rapidly than those with closed markets "have been plagued by empirical and conceptual shortcomings [that have] resulted, in many cases, in unconvincing results whose fragility has been exposed by subsequent work."[3]

There are surely additional gains to reforming economies from domestic liberalization, privatization, and so on. These gains have not been as thoroughly studied as those from trade liberalization. They are, however, conceptually very similar, and there is no reason to expect them

---

[2] Anne Krueger, "The Political Economy of the Rent-Seeking Society," *American Economic Review*, June 1974.

[3] Sebastian Edwards, "Openness, Trade Liberalization, and Growth in Developing Countries," *Journal of Economic Literature*, September 1993.

to be dramatically larger or to change the picture of real but limited gains from reform.

All this does not mean that trade liberalization is not a good idea. It almost certainly is. Nor does it necessarily mean that the modest conventional estimates of the gains from such liberalization tell the whole story. But it does mean that the widespread belief that moving to free trade and free markets will produce a dramatic acceleration in a developing country's growth represents a leap of faith, rather than a conclusion based on hard evidence.

What about the other half of the Washington consensus, the belief in the importance of sound money? Here the case is even weaker.

If standard estimates of the costs of protection are lower than you might expect, such estimates of the cost of inflation—defined as the overall reduction in real income—are so low that they are embarrassing. Of course very high inflation rates—the triple- or quadruple-digit inflations that have, unfortunately, been all too common in Latin American history—seriously disrupt the functioning of a market economy. But it is very difficult to pin down any large gains from a reduction in the inflation rate from, say, 20 percent to 2 percent.

Moreover, the methods used to achieve disinflation in developing countries—above all, the use of a pegged exchange rate as a way to build credibility—have serious costs. A country with an inflationary history that tries to end inflation by establishing a fixed exchange rate almost always finds that the momentum of inflation continues for a considerable time, throwing domestic costs and prices out of line with the rest of the world. Thus an exchange rate that initially seemed reasonable usually seems considerably overvalued by the time inflation finally subsides. Furthermore, an exchange rate that is tolerable when introduced may become difficult to sustain when world market conditions change, such as the price of oil, the value of the dollar, and interest rates. Textbook international economics treats the decision about whether to fix a country's exchange rate as a difficult tradeoff, which even countries committed to low inflation often end up resolving on the side of exchange rate flexibility.

Nonetheless, during the first half of the 1990s a number of developing countries adopted rigid exchange rate targets. (The most extreme case was Argentina, which established a supposedly permanent one-for-one exchange rate between the peso and the U.S. dollar). In large part this was a move designed to restore credibility after the uncontrolled inflation of the 1980s. Nonetheless, both governments and markets seem to have convinced themselves that the painful tradeoffs traditionally involved in such a commitment no longer applied.

THE DISMAL CYCLE

IN SUM, then, a cool-headed analysis of the likely effects of the economic reforms undertaken in developing countries in recent years did not and does not seem to justify wild enthusiasm. Trade liberalization and other moves to free up markets are almost surely good things, but the idea that they will generate a growth takeoff represents a hope rather than a well-founded expectation. Bringing down inflation is also a good thing, but doing so by fixing the exchange rate brings a mixture of benefits and costs, with the arguments against as strong as the arguments for. And yet the behavior of both governments and markets during the last five years does not suggest that they took any such measured view. On the contrary, governments eagerly adopted Washington consensus reform packages, while markets enthusiastically poured funds into reforming economies. Why?

Everyone is familiar with the way that a speculative bubble can develop in a financial market. Investors, for whatever reason, come to take a more favorable view of the prospects for some traded asset—Deutsche marks, Japanese stocks, shares in the South Sea Company, tulip futures. This leads to a rise in the asset's price. If investors then interpret this gain as a trend rather than a one-time event, they become still more anxious to buy the asset, leading to a further rise, and so on. In principle, long sighted investors are supposed to prevent such speculative bubbles by selling assets that have become overpriced or buying them when they have become obviously cheap. Sometimes, however, markets lose sight of the long run, especially when the long run is complex or obscure. Thus speculative bubbles in soybean futures tend to be limited by the common knowledge that a lot more soybeans will be grown if the price gets very high. But the chain of events that must eventually end a speculative bubble in, say, the mark— an overvalued mark reduces German exports, leading to a weak German economy, so the Bundesbank reduces interest rates, making it unattractive to hold mark-denominated assets—is often too long and abstract to seem compelling to investors when the herd is running.

It seems fairly clear that some of the enthusiasm for investing in developing countries in the first half of the 1990s was a classic speculative bubble. A modest recovery in economic prospects from the dismal 1980s led to large capital gains for those few investors who had been willing to put money into Third World stock markets. Their success led other investors to jump in, driving prices up still further. And by 1993 or so "emerging market funds" were being advertised on television and the pages of popular magazines.

At the same time that this self-reinforcing process was under way in the financial markets, a different kind of self-reinforcing process, sociological rather than economic, was taking place in the world of affairs—the endless rounds of meetings, speeches, and exchanges of communiqués that occupy much of the time of economic opinion leaders. Such interlocking social groupings tend at any given time to converge on a conventional wisdom, about economics among many other things. People believe certain stories because everyone important tells them, and people tell those stories because everyone important believes them. Indeed, when a conventional wisdom is at its fullest strength, one's agreement with that conventional wisdom becomes almost a litmus test of one's suitability to be taken seriously.

Anyone who tried, two or three years ago, to express even mild skepticism about the prospects for developing countries knows how difficult it was to make any impression on either business or political leaders. Views contrary to the immense optimism of the time were treated not so much with hostility as bemusement. How could anyone be so silly as to say these gloomy things?[4]

While both a speculative bubble in the financial markets and the standard process whereby influential people rally around a conventional wisdom surely played a role in the astonishing rise of the Washington consensus, there was, however, an additional, distinctive self-reinforcing process that arguably played an even greater role. This was a political

---

[4] Academic economists with expertise in the macroeconomics of developing countries were issuing clear warnings about excessive euphoria, which Wall Street simply shrugged off, as early as the beginning of 1993. See, in particular, Rudiger Dornbusch, *Stabilization, Debt, and Reform: Policy Analysis for Developing Countries,* Englewood Cliffs: Prentice Hall, 1993, and "Mexico: Stabilization, Reform, and No Growth," *Brookings Papers on Economic Activity,* No. 1, 1994. I gave a speech warning of a peso crisis in Mexico City on March 25, 1993.

economy cycle, in which governments were persuaded to adopt Washington consensus policies because markets so spectacularly rewarded them, and in which markets were willing to supply so much capital because they thought they saw an unstoppable move toward policy reform.

One must begin with a key insight of Dani Rodrik of Columbia University. Rodrik pointed out that economists and international organizations like the World Bank had been arguing for a long time in favor of freer trade in developing countries.[5] The intellectual case for protectionism to promote industrialization, while popular in the 1950s, has been pretty much moribund since the late 1960s. Nonetheless, the stake of established interest groups in the existing system blocked any major move to free trade. When limited liberalization was attempted, it usually ended up being abandoned a few years later. Why did this suddenly change?

One seemingly obvious answer is the Third World debt crisis of the 1980s, which made the previous system untenable. But economic crises, especially when they involve the balance of payments, traditionally lead to more protectionism, not less. Why was this case different?

Rodrik's answer was that in the 1990s, advocates of free trade in developing countries were able to link free trade to financial and macroeconomic benefits. If trade liberalization is presented as a detailed microeconomic policy, the industries that stand to lose will be well-informed and vociferous in their opposition, while those who stand to gain will be diffuse and ineffective. What reformers in a number of countries were able to do, however, was to present trade liberalization as part of a package that was presumed to yield large gains to the country as a whole. That is, it was not presented as, "Let's open up imports in these 20 industries, and there will be efficiency gains"; that kind of argument does not work very well in ordinary times. Instead it was, "We have to follow the strategy that everyone serious knows works: free markets—including free trade—and sound money, leading to rapid economic growth."

Calling a set of economic measures a package does not mean that they need in fact be undertaken together. One can bring inflation down without liberalizing trade, and vice versa. But voters do not usually en-

---

[5] Dani Rodrik, "The Rush to Free Trade in the Developing World: Why So Late? Why Now? Will It Last?" in *Voting for Reform: The Politics of Adjustment in New Democracies,* ed. Stephan Haggard and Steven B. Webb, New York: Oxford, 1994.

gage in hypothetical line-item vetoes, asking which elements of an economic program are essential and which can be dropped. If a program of economic stabilization-cum-liberalization seems to work, the political process is easily persuaded that all of the package is essential.

And the point was that such packages did work, and in fact initially did so astonishingly well—but not necessarily because of their fundamental economic merits. Rather, the immediate payoff to Washington consensus reforms was in the sudden improvement in investor confidence.

Mexico is particularly noteworthy. Mexico began a major program of trade liberalization in the late 1980s, with no obvious immediate results in terms of faster economic growth. The turning point came when the country negotiated a debt reduction package, which went into effect in 1990. The debt reduction was intelligently handled, but everyone involved realized that it was fairly small, not nearly enough to make much direct difference to Mexico's growth prospects.

And yet what followed the debt reduction was a transformation of the economic picture. With stunning speed, Mexico's problems seemed to melt away. Real interest rates were 30 to 40 percent before the debt deal, with the payments on internal debt a major source of fiscal pressure; they fell between 5 and 10 percent almost immediately. Mexico had been shut out of international financial markets since 1982; soon after the debt deal, capital inflows resumed on an ever-growing scale. And growth resumed in the long-stagnant economy.

Why did a seemingly modest debt reduction spark such a major change in the economic environment? International investors saw the debt deal as part of a package of reforms that they believed would work. Debt reduction went along with free markets and sound money, free markets and sound money mean prosperity, and so capital flowed into a country that was following the right path.

In the 1990s, advocates of the Washington consensus have not had to make abstruse arguments about the benefits of better resource allocation nor plead with the public to accept short-term pain in the interest of long-run gain. Instead, because the financial markets offered an immediate, generous advance on the presumed payoff from free trade and sound money, it was easy to make a case for doing the right thing and brush aside all the usual political objections.

So much for one side of the political-economic cycle. The other side involved the willingness of financial markets to provide lavish rewards for economic reform. In part, of course, the markets believed that such policies would pay off in the long run. But most of the developing countries that suddenly became investor favorites in the 1990s had long histories of disappointed expectations, not just the debt crisis of the 1980s, but track records of abandoned economic reforms reaching back for decades. Why should investors have been so confident that this time the reforms would really stick? Presumably, this time reforms were taking place so extensively, and in so many countries, that investors found it easy to believe that it was a completely new world, that runaway inflation, populist economic policies, exchange controls, and so on were vanishing from the global scene.

But I have just argued, following Rodrik, that the unprecedented depth and breadth of policy reform was largely due to the perception that such reforms brought macroeconomic and financial recovery—a perception driven by the way that financial markets rewarded the reforms! So once again something of a circular logic was at work.

During the first half of the 1990s, a set of mutually reinforcing beliefs and expectations created a mood of euphoria about the prospects for the developing world. Markets poured money into developing countries, encouraged both by the capital gains they had already seen and by the belief that a wave of reform was unstoppable. Governments engaged in unprecedented liberalization, encouraged both by the self-reinforcing conventional wisdom and the undeniable fact that reformers received instant gratification from enthusiastic investors. It was a very happy picture. Why couldn't it continue?

THE REALITY CHECK

FROM A MERE trickle during the 1980s, private capital flows to developing countries soared to about $130 billion in 1993. Relatively little of this money went to those East Asian countries that had already achieved rapid economic growth during the 1980s. Less than 10 percent of the total, for example, went to China, and the four Asian tigers—Singapore, Hong Kong, South Korea, and Taiwan—were all net exporters of capital. Instead, the bulk of the money went to countries that had done poorly in previous years, but whose new commitment to Washington consensus policies was believed to ensure a dramatic turnaround: Latin

American countries, plus a few others such as the Philippines and Hungary. How well were these economies doing?

In one respect, the performance of the main recipients of massive capital inflows did represent a break with the past. The new insistence on sound money had, indeed, led to impressive reductions in inflation rates. Between 1987 and 1991, Mexico's inflation rate had averaged 49 percent; in 1994, it was less than 7 percent. In Argentina the contrast was even more spectacular, from an average inflation rate of 609 percent in 1987-91 to a rate of less than 4 percent last year.

That was the good news. Unfortunately, there was also a substantial amount of disappointing news, on three main fronts. First, while hard currency policies brought down inflation, they did so only gradually. As a result, costs and prices got far out of line with those in the rest of the world. Mexico, for example, allowed the peso to fall only 13 percent between 1990 and the first quarter of 1994, but consumer prices in Mexico nonetheless rose 63 percent over that period, compared with a rise of only 12 percent in the United States. Thus Mexico's real exchange rate—the ratio of Mexican prices in dollars to prices in the United States—rose 28 percent, pricing many Mexican goods out of U.S. markets and fueling an import boom. Argentina's drastic policy, which sought to end a history of extreme inflation by pegging the value of the peso permanently at one dollar, predictably left the country's prices even farther out of line. Between 1990 and early 1991 the Argentine real exchange rate rose 68 percent.

Second, in spite of huge inflows of foreign capital, the real growth in the recipient economies was generally disappointing. Mexico was the biggest disappointment: although capital flows into Mexico reached more than $30 billion in 1993, the country's rate of growth over the 1990-94 period averaged only 2.5 percent, less than population growth. Other countries did better: Argentina, for example, grew at an annual average rate of more than 6 percent after the stabilization of the peso. But even optimists admitted that this growth had much to do with the extremely depressed state of the economy before the reforms. When an economy has been as thoroughly mismanaged as Argentina's was during the 1980s, a return to political and monetary stability can easily produce a large one-shot rise in output. Across Latin America as a whole, real growth in the period 1990-94 averaged only 3.1 percent per year.

Finally, the benefits of growth, which was in any case barely positive in per capita terms, were also very unevenly distributed. Developing country statistics on both unemployment and income distribution are fairly unreliable, but there is not much question that even as Latin American stock markets were booming, unemployment was rising, and the poor were getting poorer.

In sum, the real economic performance of countries that had recently adopted Washington consensus policies, as opposed to the financial returns they were delivering to international investors or the reception their policies received on the conference circuit, was distinctly disappointing. Whatever the conventional wisdom might have said, the underlying basis for the conviction of both investors and governments that these countries were on the right track was becoming increasingly fragile.

Some kind of crisis of confidence was thus inevitable. It could have come in several different ways. For example, there might have been a purely financial crisis: a loss of confidence in emerging markets as investments, leading to capital flight and only then to a loss of political confidence. Or there could have been an essentially intellectual crisis: the growing evidence that the new policies were not delivering in the way or at the speed that conventional wisdom had expected might have led to soul-searching among the policy elite. But given the way that the Washington consensus had originally come to flourish, it should not be surprising that the crisis, when it came, involved the interaction of economics and politics.

Consider the essentials of the Mexican situation as it began to unravel in 1994—the factors that would surely have provoked a crisis even without the uprisings and assassinations. Despite the popularity of the country among foreign investors, growth had slowed in 1993 to a virtual crawl, creating a considerable rise in unemployment. This growth slowdown was in a direct sense due to the rise in Mexico's real exchange rate after 1990, which discouraged any rapid growth in exports and caused growing demand to be spent primarily on imports rather than domestic goods. More fundamentally, the free market policies had not, at least so far, generated the kind of explosion of productivity, new industries, and exports that reformers hoped for.

Given these economic realities, the Mexican government was faced with a dilemma. If it wanted to get even modest growth going again, it would need to do something to make its industries more cost-competitive—that is, devalue the peso. But to do so, given the emphasis that the government had placed on sound money, would be very damaging to its credibility. In the event, the approach of the presidential election seems to have led the Mexicans neither to devalue nor to accept slow growth, but rather to reflate the economy by loosening up government spending. The result was a loss of credibility even worse than that which would have been produced by an early devaluation. And then the usual logic of currency crisis came into play: because investors thought, with some reason, that the currency might be devalued, they became unwilling to hold peso assets unless offered very high interest rates; and the necessity of paying these high rates, together with the depressing effect of high rates on the economy, increased the pressure on the government to abandon the fixed exchange rate—which made investors even less willing to hold pesos, in a rapid downward spiral familiar to scores of former finance ministers around the world.

The point is that while the details could not have been predicted, something like the Mexican crisis was bound to happen. Without the Chiapas uprising or the assassination of presidential candidate Luis Donaldo Colosio, Mexico might not have hit the wall in December 1994, but it probably would not have gone unscathed through 1995. An early, controlled devaluation might have done less damage than the display of confusion that actually took place, but it would still have done considerable harm to the government's credibility. And even if Mexico had somehow avoided getting into trouble, the disparity between the glittering prizes promised by the Washington consensus and the fairly dreary reality was bound to produce a revolution of falling expectations somewhere along the line.

AN AGE OF DEFLATED EXPECTATIONS?

BECAUSE the 1990-95 euphoria about developing countries was so overdrawn, the Mexican crisis is likely to be the trigger that sets the process in reverse. That is, the rest of the decade will probably be a downward cycle of deflating expectations. Markets will no longer pour vast amounts of capital into countries whose leaders espouse free markets and sound money on the assumption that such policies will necessarily produce vigorous growth; they will want to see hard evidence of such growth. This new reluctance will surely be directly self-reinforcing, in that it means that the huge capital gains in emerging market equities will not continue. It will also, more or less directly, lead to a further slowing of growth in those countries, comprising much of Latin America and several outside nations, whose hesitant recovery from the 1980s was driven largely by infusions of foreign capital.

Because reforms will no longer be instantly rewarded by the capital markets, it will be far more difficult to sell such reforms politically. Thus the common assumption that free trade and free market policies will quickly spread around the world is surely wrong. Indeed, there will doubtless be some backsliding, as the perceived failure of Washington consensus policies leads to various attempts either to restore the good old days or to emulate what are perceived as alternative models. Many developing country politicians will surely claim that truly successful development efforts have been based not on free markets and sound money but on clever planning and rationed foreign exchange. At the moment, most developing country governments are still reluctant even to hint at a return to interventionist and nationalist policies because they fear that such hints will be swiftly punished by capital flight. But sooner or later some of them will rediscover the attractions of capital controls. As has happened so many times in the past, some countries will in desperation impose regulations to discourage capital flight. They will discover that while such regulations do raise the cost of doing business, that cost seems minor compared with their newfound ability to contain temporary speculative attacks without imposing punitive interest rates.

And these two trends will surely reinforce each other. As it becomes clear to the markets that reform need not always advance, they will become increasingly reluctant to offer advances on reform. As it becomes clear that such rewards are not available even to the most virtuous of reformers, the willingness to suffer economic pain to placate the markets will erode all the more.

But will the conventional wisdom represented by the Washington consensus be so easily displaced? Before the Mexican crisis, when some warned that the rhetoric about a golden age for global capitalism was excessive, the reply was often that there was no alternative. Communism is dead. The old protectionist development strategies in South Asia and Latin America were unambiguous failures. Even if Victorian virtue does not yield the easy rewards some may have expected, it is still the only plausible course of action left. And such arguments have a point. It is, in fact, probably true that free markets and sound money—if not necessarily fixed exchange rates—are the best policy for developing countries to follow.

But it seems strangely unimaginative to assume that because there are no other popular paradigms for policy currently in circulation, nobody will be able to come up with a rationale for policies that are very much at odds with the Washington consensus. Indeed, there are already audible rumblings about emulating a supposed Asian model. Developing countries should try, some people say, to be like Japan (as they imagine it) rather than America. The intellectual basis for such ideas is far weaker than that for the Washington consensus, but to suppose that bad ideas never flourish is to ignore the lessons of history.⊛

A Response

Emerging Markets Are Here to Stay

BARBARA C. SAMUELS II

PAUL KRUGMAN calls into question the future of emerging markets ("Dutch Tulips and Emerging Markets," July/August 1995). He argues that the efficacy of the "free markets–sound money" model—the so-called "Washington consensus"—was oversold, leading to foreign investments based on hope rather than performance. The recent successes of the emerging markets, he argues, are a "classic speculative bubble," possessing no more substance than the seventeenth-century investment craze in Dutch tulips. The Mexican crisis that began last December is, Krugman concludes, "likely to be the trigger that sets the process in reverse," with "a downward cycle of deflating expectations" in store for the rest of the decade.

The fundamental flaw in Krugman's argument lies in equating the future of emerging markets with the accuracy and longevity of the Washington consensus. Certain recommendations of the consensus, such as

BARBARA C. SAMUELS II is Managing Director of Moody's Emerging Markets Service. The views expressed here are strictly personal and do not necessarily represent those of Moody's Investors Service.

trade liberalization, may not immediately result in growth, but underlying economic, political, and social forces have irreversibly transformed the countries usually referred to as "emerging markets." Despite predictable setbacks in the development process and some experimentation with alternative policies, these broad forces will drive continued reform, growth, and investment in emerging markets.

In his desire to make a sweeping generalization, Krugman fails to differentiate among emerging markets—the very error made by the market optimists he so correctly criticizes. But the problems Krugman trumpets are limited to certain countries recovering from the debt crisis in Latin America. While Mexico's annual real growth in GDP over the last few years has been undeniably low, increasing less than 1 percent in 1993, Thailand's has increased between 8 percent and 13 percent each of the last eight years. Indeed, Asian emerging markets have performed spectacularly over the last 20 years, going back to before the Washington consensus was even thought of; annual increases in real GDP averaged more than 6 percent between 1975 and 1982 and 7.5 percent thereafter, according to the International Monetary Fund. Chile and Colombia have also experienced steady growth over a sustained period. Even the overall long-term growth rate for emerging markets has been much higher on average than rates in the countries Krugman highlights, and the IMF and the World Bank as well as leading private sector economists predict these high rates will continue.

Krugman assumes that all emerging markets are equally dependent on a monolithic "world market" for funds, with equally devastating implications. In reality Mexico was uniquely dependent on external capital flows, which made it extraordinarily vulnerable. The beginning of the decade marked a critical transformation: the cumulative net outflow of approximately $15 billion from 1983 to 1989 became a cumulative net inflow of $102 billion from 1990 to 1994. During the same periods, capital flows into all of Asia went from $117 billion to $261 billion. In 1993 Mexico attracted $31 billion, 20 percent of net capital flows into all emerging markets combined.

Latin America, and Mexico especially, have been more vulnerable than Asia not only because of the sudden reversal in capital flows but also because of the composition of investment. Between 1990 and 1994, 66 percent of net capital flows to western hemisphere countries were concentrated in yield-sensitive and liquid portfolio investments, compared with 24 percent in Asian countries. The greater long-term stability of foreign direct investment, which dominates in Asia, has been proven conclusively, as multinational corporations seek out new markets and low-cost manufacturing. Krugman's scenario of a monolithic market retreating worldwide because of disappointing economic performance in certain countries is simplistic conjecture, not based on hard evidence.

The adoption of free market reforms around the globe is explained not by any Washington or New York group's policy recommendations but by fundamental forces in international economics and politics. The demise of the Soviet Union created an economic crisis, as exports and foreign exchange plummeted overnight in states representing the majority of the world's emerging market population, from the former Soviet republics and East European countries to India and China, Cuba and Vietnam. Worldwide, pragmatic economic priorities rather than East-West political alignments formed the new basis for relations between states. After the Cold War, governments find their policy choices almost without exception confined to a set of options that promote growth and global integration.

Inside the emerging market countries, radically and irreversibly transformed economic policies have in turn given rise to new internal economic forces, new political interest groups, and that tremendously powerful social force, consumerism. The new groups reinforce the new policy choices. Established business leaders have been co-opted as well, as some profit from the policy changes by selling off businesses to new investors, expanding into new export markets, or developing businesses previously prohibited. A fresh dynamic has been established in each country, working to further integrate economic interests across national boundaries. While this still allows for a range of policies, as evidenced most clearly in Asia today, all are variations on the basic principles of the Western free market model.

Changes in the structure of domestic production, with a shift from agriculture to services and industry, along with the trend toward urbanization will continue over the long term. Emerging market cities with populations over five million increased from 11 in 1970 to 20 in 1985 and, the United Nations estimates, will number 34 by the year 2000. Multinationals worldwide have targeted the rapidly growing consumer populations in emerging markets, reaffirming the projections of continued significant growth coming from the World Bank, the IMF, and leading economists.

Social and political indicators, along with the revolution in technology, also point to irreversible and sustained changes in emerging countries. Between 1970 and 1985 enrollment in secondary schools increased from 22 percent to 38 percent among youths aged 12 to 17, and the United Nations predicts a jump to 48 percent by 2000. Leading policymakers in emerging markets now have similar educational backgrounds, many having attended American and European universities. Communications technologies have also altered the economic and social landscape. For example, telephone lines per 1,000 people have increased 242 percent over the last 20 years in emerging countries, and households with television 219 percent over the last 15 years. These technological changes have opened up political systems, heightened awareness of the wider world, created new expectations, and advanced the globalizing creed of consumerism.

While Krugman may be correct in claiming that some free market reforms—trade liberalization, for instance—do not always result directly in growth, many reforms undoubtedly do. Across the emerging markets, productivity as well as domestic and international investment have risen as a consequence of measures enacted to strengthen local financial systems, reduce burdensome regulations, and provide access to foreign exchange. In addition, virtually all emerging markets have adopted policies to augment internal public and private savings. Krugman's argument assumes capital is critical to growth, but in his focus on the international market he neglects to mention the equally important role of domestic savings and investment—key to the growth of the successful Asian countries.

Krugman states, "In sum, the real economic performance of countries that had recently adopted Washington consensus policies, as opposed to the financial returns they were delivering to international investors or the reception their policies received on the conference circuit, was distinctly disappointing." But international investors represent a distinct minority of the total investment in these countries' stock markets, and any profits the foreigners enjoy are presumably enjoyed in spades by local investors. In fact, the principal threats to economic reform lie in the internal dislocations caused by the shifts in economic and political power; witness the widespread debates on the need for social safety nets.

Krugman argues that after Mexico, "markets will no longer pour vast amounts of capital into countries whose leaders espouse free markets and sound money on the assumption that such policies will necessarily produce vigorous growth." Again, the evidence proves him wrong. The Organization for Economic Cooperation and Development reports that developing countries in Europe and Asia continued to raise international capital in the form of bonds and loans at approximately the same rate in the first quarter of 1995—post-Mexico—as during the previous five quarters. Even in Latin America, the drop in capital has not been as conclusive as in Mexico, nor has it had the far-reaching impact Krugman suggests. While the OECD reports a tremendous decline in Latin America's access to the bond and loan markets, a KPMG Peat Marwick study notes $1.9 billion in U.S. direct foreign investment in Latin America in the first quarter of this year, up 50 percent over the first quarter of 1994. Despite volatility due both to developments in specific countries and to cyclical factors such as interest rates, multilateral institutions and international brokers all cite the resurgence of portfolio investment after Mexico, albeit with greater discrimination between countries and with changes in regional allocations.

Studies including the IMF's August 1995 *International Capital Markets* note a gradual but persistent trend toward greater international diversification of the institutional portfolios where savings increasingly are going. The five major industrial countries had close to $13 trillion under management in 1993, but a mere 1 percent is currently invested in emerging markets, significantly below the emerging market's 12 percent share of total world equity market capitalization. Given diversification policies and the consensus forecast that emerging markets will grow approximately twice as fast as the industrial economies between 1995 and 2000, further increases in portfolio investment from the developed world as well as from other emerging countries are considered likely by the World Bank and other experts. In fact, industry surveys suggest that emerging markets have become a respectable asset class, joining real estate and high-yield bonds on the standard menu available to investors. Emerging markets were not created by, nor are they dependent on, decisions made in Washington. They will undoubtedly prove to be much more durable investments than Dutch tulips.

Shadow Play

Paul Krugman

BARBARA SAMUELS and I probably do not disagree as much as her comments might suggest.

Two years ago, anyone who talked to investors about Latin America encountered a sort of unquestioning enthusiasm about the whole region, including Mexico. There is an influential body of opinion that still sees the Mexican crisis as an anomaly. My point is that the same overstatement of the likely impact of reform that led to Mexico's boom-bust cycle has occurred for a number of other important developing countries. Even now, I believe investors have failed to think seriously about the policy dilemmas that major emerging market nations face. How, for example, will Argentina, which has 18 percent unemployment, be able to engineer a recovery while committed to its one peso–one dollar policy? (Alternatively, how could it abandon this policy without a crisis of credibility?) Can Malaysia really continue a growth path based on enormous inflows not only of capital but of labor, and what will happen to its ambitious public investment plans if it cannot?

One institutional investor told me about a presentation by a rating service on Indonesian bonds. Along with others in the audience, the investor was disturbed by the evident unreliability of Indonesia's data. The presenter responded with an analogy to Indonesian puppet shows, in which one looks at the shadows rather than the puppets; in other words, investors were being asked to be optimistic based on the general idea that developing countries have great prospects rather than on a careful examination of this specific country's macroeconomic situation. That kind of sloppy thinking led to Mexico's crisis, and may well lead to comparable crises in other countries.

Does that mean there are no investment opportunities in emerging markets, or that there will be no national success stories? Of course not. Perhaps the best way to put it is to quote a senior Mexican official who remarked in 1993, "You know, four years ago, when we couldn't attract any money, we really weren't that bad. But right now, when everyone wants to give us money, we really aren't that good."☯